International Conference on Computer Graphics, Visualization, Computer Vision and Image Processing (CGVCVIP2021); Connected Smart Cities (CSC2021); and Big Data Analytics, Data Mining and Computational Intelligence (BIGDACI2021)

Held at the 15th Multi-Conference on Computer Science and Information Systems (MCCSIS 2021)

Online
20 - 23 July 2021

ISBN: 978-1-7138-3578-3

Printed from e-media with permission by:

Curran Associates, Inc.
57 Morehouse Lane
Red Hook, NY 12571

Some format issues inherent in the e-media version may also appear in this print version.

Printed with permission by Curran Associates, Inc. (2021)

For permission requests, please contact International Association for Development of the Information Society (IADIS) at the address below.

International Association for Development of the Information Society (IADIS)
Rua Sao Sebastiao Da Pedreira
No. 100, 30, 1050-209
Lisbon, Portugal

Phone: 351 21 3151373
Fax: 351 21 3151244

secretariat@iadis.org

Additional copies of this publication are available from:

Curran Associates, Inc.
57 Morehouse Lane
Red Hook, NY 12571 USA
Phone: 845-758-0400
Fax: 845-758-2633
Email: curran@proceedings.com
Web: www.proceedings.com

TABLE OF CONTENTS

USING FAST MULTIDIMENSIONAL PROJECTIONS TO REVEAL BAND AND CIRCUMPLEX PATTERNS IN REORDERABLE MATRICES 1
Celmar Guimarães da Silva

A 3D SPECTRAL-SPATIAL CLASSIFICATION OF HYPERSPECTRAL REMOTE SENSING IMAGERY USING INCEPTION BASED NETWORK 9
Douglas Omwenga Nyabuga, Guohua Liu

3D FACE RECONSTRUCTION FROM HARD BLENDED EDGES 19
Yueming Ding, P.Y. Mok

CAPSULE NEURAL NETWORKS IN CLASSIFICATION OF SKIN LESIONS 27
Evgin Goceri

A SINGLE RGB IMAGE BASED 3D OBJECT RECONSTRUCTION SYSTEM 35
Damiano Oriti, Andrea Sanna, Francesco De Pace, Federico Manuri, Francesco Tamburello, Fabrizio Ronzino

FACE FEATURES-BASED PERSONALITY ASSESSMENT 43
Krishna Kumar Singh, Sadu Chiranjeevi, Kethavath Sivalal

ANALYSIS OF CAPSULE NETWORKS FOR IMAGE CLASSIFICATION 51
Evgin Goceri

ANALYSIS AND VISUAL EXPLORATION OF PREDICTION ALGORITHMS FOR PUBLIC BICYCLE SHARING SYSTEMS 59
Alexandra Cortez Ordoñez, Pere-Pau Vázquez

HELLO, MY NAME IS SMARTTRAM, HUMAN FACTORS IS ON BOARD, ENJOY THE RIDE! DEVELOPING A HUMAN FACTORS PROGRAM FOR AUTOMATIC TRAMS 69
Hanna Koskinen, Susanna Aromaa, Vladimir Goriachev

A NEW SERVICE MODEL FOR VEHICLE SENSING DATA COLLECTION 76
Christian Prehofer, Preeta Abbasi

DEVELOPMENT OF A SMART CITY SERVICE CATALOGUE FOR SENSOR-BASED DIGITAL SERVICES 85
Yusuf Bozkurt, Jan Fauser, Reiner Braun, Dieter Hertweck, Alexander Rossmann

SMART CITY SOLUTIONS FOR LOCATION TRACKING 95
Neetesh Bhati, Sujala D. Shetty, Aparna Raj

SPELLING BASED RANKED CLUSTERING ALGORITHM TO CLEAN AND NORMALIZE EARLY MODERN EUROPEAN BOOK TITLES 103
Evan Bryer, Theppatorn Rhujittawiwat, John R. Rose, Colin F. Wilder

VISUALIZATION CONCEPTS OF A DIGITAL ECOSYSTEM TO INCREASE UNDERSTANDABILITY 114
Frank Elberzhager, Kathleen Späth, Sven Storck

VISUALIZATION OF THREE-DIMENSIONAL REACHABLE SET FOR THE DUBINS CAR 116
Pavel Vasev, Andrey Fedotov, Valerii Patsko

REAL-TIME OPEN FIELD CATTLE MONITORING BY DRONE: A 3D VISUALIZATION APPROACH 121
Fei Yang, Ningbo Zhu, Shuonan Pei, Irene Cheng

PHYSICALLY BASED MATERIAL SYNTHESIS 126
Tassilo Scharnagl, Dieter Meiller

DATA-ENABLED CRYPTOCURRENCY MARKET ANALYSIS AND VISUALIZATION PLATFORM 130
Ningbo Zhu, Fei Yang, Mingzhi Zhu, Xinyao Sun, Irene Cheng

ON THE ROAD TOWARDS A SMART URBAN DISTRICT SUPPORTED BY A MOCK PLATFORM 135
Frank Elberzhager, Patrick Mennig, Phil Stüpfert

SMART AND SUSTAINABLE URBAN MOBILITY: HOW CONNECTIVITY MAY SUPPORT BIKE-SHARING OPERATORS' BUSINESSES 140
Arash Rezazadeh, Elisabete Sá, Joaquim Silva, Ana Carvalho, Maher Georges Elmashhara, Ricardo Pessoa

M-LEARNING - A MULTI AGENT APPROACH 145
Terje Solsvik Kristensen, Joachim Coetzee Kjærvik

EXTRACTION OF TOURIST ATTENTION POINTS FROM LOW-RATED REVIEWS AND CLASSIFICATION BY VIEWPOINT 151
Junichi Fukumoto, Kazuki Ito

UNMANNED VEHICLES SYSTEM UTILIZING WASTE TRACKING DATA TO TACKLE PLASTIC MARINE LITTERING ON TOURIST ISLANDS 156
George Plakas, Stavros T. Ponis, Eleni Aretoulaki, Theodoros Nikolaos Maroutas

REPORT ON ESTIMATING RICE FIELD QUALITY USING ARTIFICIAL INTELLIGENCE 161
Yahjeb Bouha Khatraty, Nedra Mellouli Nauwynck, Mamadou Tourad Diallo, Mohamedade Farouk Nanne

Author Index

USING FAST MULTIDIMENSIONAL PROJECTIONS TO REVEAL BAND AND CIRCUMPLEX PATTERNS IN REORDERABLE MATRICES

Celmar Guimarães da Silva
School of Technology, University of Campinas, Brazil

ABSTRACT

Matrix reordering techniques are essential to reveal patterns in tabular visualizations (such as heatmaps). Polar Sort is a state-of-the-art, pattern-focused reordering method that uses a multidimensional projection technique – Classical MDS – to reveal Band and Circumplex patterns in reorderable matrices. However, Polar Sort is not scalable due to Classical MDS' asymptotic time complexity (O(n^3)). In this paper, we explore the use of a fast multidimensional projection technique – FastMap (O(n)) – as an alternative to Classical MDS inside Polar Sort. The new reordering algorithm – PSF – reorders rows and columns of a matrix according to bidimensional projections projected by FastMap (instead of Classical MDS), and uses a barycenter-based ordering identical to Polar Sort's approach. The results of an experiment with synthetic matrices point out that PSF maintained the output quality of its predecessor (according to minimal span loss function, Moore stress, and circular correlation) and had lower execution time than other compared methods. We present the results of these experiments and also some examples of real-world matrices that show patterns similar to Band and Circumplex when reordered by PSF.

KEYWORDS

Reorderable Matrices, Patterns, Multidimensional Projection

1. INTRODUCTION

A common concern of many visualization researchers is about where to place visual items on the screen. E.g. graph-layout algorithms put nodes in positions that reveal characteristics such as intrinsic layers and hierarchies, cycles or tree structures; treemap visualizations have many distinct ways to subdivide regions and dispose child nodes of each parent node. In this paper, our concern is about the ordering of rows and columns of a matrix visualization (a.k.a. tabular visualization), such as a heatmap or a Table Lens.

Matrix visualizations are based on the concept of reorderable matrix, i.e. a matrix whose rows and columns can be reordered without information loss. Since it was proposed by Bertin (2010) in 1967 in his first edition of the book "Semiology of Graphics", many researchers have been proposing innovative reordering algorithms that try to reveal patterns that are easy to be visually perceived.

A relevant set of matrix reordering algorithms is called *pattern-focused algorithms* (Silva, 2020). They receive as input a matrix that hides a known pattern due to inappropriate permutations, and reorder the matrix to make that pattern evident. One of these algorithms – Polar Sort – is based on multidimensional projections of rows (and columns) in 2 dimensions (Silva, 2019), and such projections are used as a source for the new row (and column) order. Nevertheless, Polar Sort uses Classical MDS (Torgerson, 1952), a projection method with asymptotic time complexity O(n^3), which makes it harder to scale.

To enhance Polar Sort, we searched for multidimensional projection algorithms that could replace Classical MDS, aiming to reduce Polar Sort's time complexity and to maintain or improve the method's output quality. In this paper, we found that FastMap is an ideal candidate for this replacement. Therefore, our hypothesis was that replacing Classical MDS by FastMap inside Polar Sort would improve Polar Sort's execution time and would not deteriorate the quality of its output. In our experiments, the new ***Polar Sort with FastMap (PSF)*** was able to reveal Band and Circumplex patterns in matrices with quality similar to that of the original Polar Sort, but with improved execution time as expected.

The remainder of this paper is organized as follows. A theoretical background about reorderable matrices is presented at Section 2. Section 3 shows a brief bibliographic review about reordering algorithms; it highlights pattern-focused reordering algorithms, and mainly Polar Sort. It also discusses multidimensional projects in general, and FastMap in details. Section 4 presents PSF and a test methodology of this new proposal. Section 5 discusses the results of our evaluation procedures. Last but not least, Section 6 ends this paper and presents future work.

2. THEORETICAL BACKGROUND

This section presents some core concepts about *matrix reordering*. A *reorderable matrix* is a matrix whose columns (and rows) can be permuted without information loss. The state-of-the-art literature for reorderable matrices points out nine matrix patterns. Half of them are based on adjacency matrices of graphs (Behrisch et al., 2016): Bands, Block-diagonal, Off-diagonal blocks, and Line/star. They represent graph organizations and situations such as meshes, paths, clusters, bipartite graphs, and hubs. The remainder patterns, called *canonical data patterns* (Wilkinson, 2005), are based on multidimensional datasets presented as heatmaps: Equi-correlation (Equi, for short), Simplex, Block, Band and Circumplex.

In this paper, we have a special interest in Band and Circumplex patterns. The *Band pattern* is defined in such a way that its higher values are closer to the main diagonal, and there is a monotonical decreasing of values from this diagonal to the top-right and bottom-left corners of the matrix. More formally, Wilkinson (2005) defines a Band pattern as a matrix $X_{n \times p}$ whose cell values are $x_{i,j} = e^{-t^2} + u_{i,j}$, where $t = (j / p - i / n) / b$, $1 \leq i \leq n$, and $1 \leq j \leq p$. The parameter b defines not only the bandwidth, but also the sharpness of the band. When b is close to 0.2, the pattern presents a thin, well-defined band. On the other hand, when b has values close to 1, the pattern shows a large band whose boundaries are smoothed. Figure 1(a-e) exemplifies these variations. In these matrices, the correlations among near columns (or rows) are high and the correlations among distant columns (or rows) are low; these correlations can be positive or negative. It is worth noting that $u_{i,j}$ is a random error that we implemented as a salt-and-pepper error. Band patterns appear in some similarity matrices, i.e., matrices whose cells indicate a similarity measure between all pairs of elements of a set.

A *Circumplex pattern* is similar to a Band one, but considering its matrix as a torus with an endless band. Its formal definition is almost the same from Band pattern, but using $t = \cos(\Pi\ (j / p - i / n))$. As an example of this pattern, a Circumplex correlation matrix is a symmetric matrix with correlation of pairs of variables, and the set of correlations define a circular correlation structure. Figure 1(f) exemplifies this pattern.

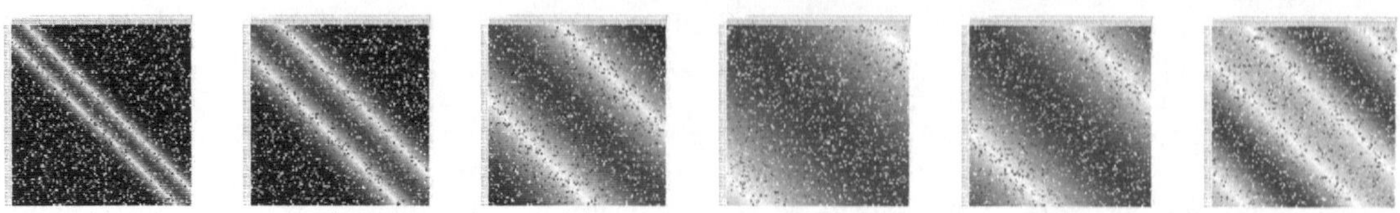

(a) (b) (c) (d) (e) (f)

Figure 1. Patterns in matrices with size 100 × 100 and noise ratio 0.2. The matrices (a) to (e) have Band patterns with the following bandwidth values: (a) 0.1; (b) 0.2; (c) 0.5; (d) 0.7; (e) 1.0. The matrix (f) presents a Circumplex pattern. Red, white and blue stands for high, average and low values, respectively

Regarding matrix nomenclature, a matrix that shows a pattern *"P"* in some permutation of its rows and columns is called a *pre-"P" matrix*. As far as we know, Wilkinson (2005) was the first to use this terminology. In our paper, we focus on pre-Band and pre-Circumplex matrices, given that Polar Sort is able to find a permutation of these matrices such that they reveal their Band and Circumplex patterns.

The current matrix reordering literature presents some *evaluation functions* to assess the quality of a reordered matrix. We highlight Moore stress, minimal span and circular correlation. *Moore stress* (Niermann, 2005) is a measure of local differences of cells. The stress of a cell is defined as the sum of the differences between a cell and each of its 8 neighbors. The stress of a matrix is the sum of all local differences of all matrix's cells. *Minimal span* (Wu et al., 2008) is a measure of how different all pairs of neighbor rows (or columns) of a matrix are. The difference of a pair of neighbor rows (or columns) may be calculated using a distance function such as Euclidean distance. The sum of these differences is the minimal span loss function (MSLF). Correlations between the original order of the rows (or columns) and their order in the reordered matrix can also be used to measure the quality of the reordering (Wilkinson, 2005); however, when comparing a reordered pre-Circumplex matrix and its original circumplex pattern, it is recommended to use *circular correlation* (Rocha et al., 2017) to consider all shifted permutations of this matrix.

3. RELATED WORK

Since the creation of the concept of reorderable matrices by Bertin, a multitude of matrix reordering algorithms was developed (Behrisch et al., 2016; Liiv, 2010). Silva (2020) pointed out a particular class of this type of algorithms, called *pattern-focused matrix reordering methods*. These methods focus on revealing a set of one or more patterns in a reorderable matrix when these patterns are hidden in the input matrix due to inappropriate permutations of its rows or columns. Table 1 summarizes the current set of pattern-focused methods (to the best of our knowledge). In this table, n is the size of a $n \times n$ matrix, and k is a configuration parameter of the Block pattern.

Table 1. Pattern-focused reordering methods

Method	**Expected input matrices**	**Patterns revealed in the output**	**Asymptotic time complexity**
Circumplex Sort (Rocha et al., 2017)	Pre-Circumplex	Circumplex	$O(n^2)$
FVS (Silva et al., 2017)	Pre-Simplex or pre-Equi	Simplex or Equi	$O(n^2)$
Block Reordering (Santos et al., 2016)	Pre-Block	Block	$O(kn^2)$
Polar Sort (Silva, 2019)	Pre-Band or pre-Circumplex	Band or Circumplex	$O(n^3)$
Hybrid Sort (Silva, 2020)	Pre-Band, pre-Simplex, pre-Equi, pre-Circumplex or pre-Block	Band, Simplex, Equi, Circumplex or Block	$O(n^3)$

In this table, we can observe that three algorithms deal with Circumplex pattern (Polar Sort, Hybrid Sort, and Circumplex Sort), and two deal with Band pattern (Polar Sort and Hybrid Sort). Hybrid Sort uses a matrix classifier to classify an input matrix as a pre-Band, pre-Circumplex, pre-Equi, pre-Simplex, or pre-Block matrix. According to this classification, the method uses FVS (Silva et al., 2017) to reorder pre-Simplex or pre-Equi matrices, Polar Sort to reorder pre-Band or pre-Circumplex matrices, and Block Reordering (Santos et al., 2016) to reorder pre-Block matrices. It is worth noting that Polar Sort produced results with better quality than those produced by Circumplex Sort when reordering pre-Circumplex matrices (Silva, 2019); this fact justifies the use of Polar Sort (and not Circumplex Sort) within Hybrid Sort, despite the lower time complexity of Circumplex Sort.

We can classify Polar Sort as a *dimensional reduction* algorithm – one of a set of seven classes of matrix reordering algorithms surveyed by Behrisch et al. (2016). This class of algorithms reorders rows (or columns) of a $m \times n$ matrix according to multidimensional projections of these rows (or columns). (All the following statements about rows are also applied to columns, replacing m by n and vice-versa as needed). A row may be considered a multidimensional point in $\Re^n$. Some dimensional projection methods project these m n-dimensional rows in $\Re^k$, $k<<n$. Usually k=1 or k=2. When k=1, the rows are projected into a line, and their relative order may be replicated as the order of the rows in the matrix. Wilkinson (2005) used k=1 with interactive MDS and SVD. When k=2, the rows are projected into a plane. In the particular case of Band and Circumplex matrices, this projection has the format of an arc or a circle, respectively, when they are projected by Classical MDS (Silva, 2019).

Polar Sort uses k=2 and Classical MDS (Torgerson, 1952) to create such arcs or circles. After that, it calculates the barycenter of the arc or circle, and uses it as the center of a polar coordinate system. The rows are ordered according to the angle of their respective points in this coordinate system, starting close to the biggest gap between neighbor points.

Polar Sort's main concern is its $O(n^3)$ asymptotic time complexity, derived from the time complexity $O(n^3)$ of the Classical MDS method for projecting a set of n input objects. The lack of scalability of this projection method motivated the search for a suitable and scalable multidimensional projection method to replace Classical MDS inside Polar Sort. A recent survey about multidimensional projection methods from Nonato and Aupetit (2019) pointed out the existence of 27 "core methods" and a variety of variants of them. Classical MDS has one of the worst time complexities according to this survey. The fastest dimensional projection method presented by Nonato and Aupetit is FastMap (Faloutsos & Lin, 1995). Its asymptotic time complexity is $O(nk)$, where n is the number of d-dimensional objects considered for the projection, and k is the dimensionality of the "target space", i. e., the projection space. Nonato and Aupetit (2019) indicate that this time complexity is $O(n)$, considering k as a constant.

In a given iteration r, $1 \leq r \leq k$, FastMap calculates the rth coordinate of the n objects in the projection space. Consider that the input of this iteration has α-dimensional objects, where $\alpha = k + 1 - r$. At the start of an iteration, the algorithm heuristically selects two objects (called "pivot objects", O_a and O_b) whose distance is maximal in the dataset, and considers the line p that intersects them. Each of the n objects is projected on p. Given an object O_i and its projection O_i', the distance between O_a and O_i' defines the coordinate of this object in the rth dimension of the projected space. All the objects are projected on a hyperplane H that is perpendicular to p. Given that H is a hyperplane inside an α-dimensional space, H has α-1 dimensions. The next iteration of the method starts using the (α-1)-dimensional objects projected on H as the input objects to be projected on a (k-1)-dimensional space. After the k iterations, all n objects have k coordinates, one for each dimension of the projection space. Figure 2 exemplifies one iteration of FastMap for four 3D points (O_a, O_b, O_1, and O_2). O_a and O_b are the pivot objects in this case. O_1' and O_2' are projections of O_1 and O_2 on the line p, respectively. P_1 and P_2 are the projections of O_1 and O_2 on H, respectively. In this case, the projections of O_b and O_a on H coincide at O_a.

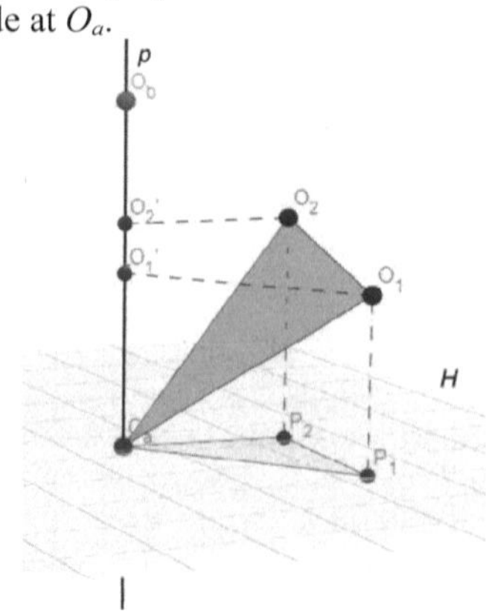

Figure 2. Example of one iteration of FastMap whose input was a set of four 3D objects (Oa, Ob, O1, and O2). The blue dashed line segments are perpendicular to the line p. The red dashed line segments and p are perpendicular to the hyperplane H (which, in this case, is a plane). (We painted the red and green triangles only as a visual aid for readers)

4. METHODOLOGY

Aiming to reduce Polar Sort's asymptotic time complexity, we proposed the following methodology:

1) Search for a multidimensional projection method with low time complexity.
2) Find an implementation of the selected method.
3) Create a new version of the Polar Sort method, replacing Classical MDS by the method found in Step 1.
4) Test the ability of the new version of Polar Sort to reveal Band and Circumplex patterns in pre-Band and pre-Circumplex input matrices, respectively, and compare this method with the original Polar Sort and other related reordering methods.

According to the literature review, we chose FastMap (Faloutsos & Lin, 1995) as the fastest multidimensional projection algorithm among the ones reported by Nonato and Aupetit (2019). It has the lowest asymptotic time complexity among the surveyed algorithms: $O(kn)$. In our case, we want to project points (which represent rows or columns) on a plane, therefore k=2. In other words, we can consider this complexity as $O(n)$.

The Projection Explorer tool (Paulovich et al., 2007) provides a Java implementation of FastMap. We adopted it, and inserted Projection Explorer as a library of the Java-based tool Matrix Reordering Analyzer (MRA) (Silva et al., 2014), which was used to run our evaluation procedures.

The new version of the Polar Sort method with FastMap (**PSF** for short) was created based on the original Polar Sort, in with we replaced Classical MDS by FastMap. Therefore, the PSF method does the following steps to reorder an $n \times n$ input matrix M:

- *Step 1.* Project the rows of M in $\Re^2$, using FastMap ($O(n)$).
- *Step 2.* Convert the Cartesian coordinate system into a new polar coordinate system whose center is the barycenter of the projected points ($O(n)$).
- *Step 3.* Sort the points by their angular coordinates ($O(n \log n)$). Find the pair of adjacent points with maximum angular distance between them ($O(n)$). The ordered list of points must start with one point of this pair.
- *Step 4.* Replicate this order for the matrix rows ($O(n)$).
- *Step 5.* Repeat steps 1 to 4 for columns instead of rows. ($O(n \log n)$).

Therefore, the asymptotic time complexity of PSF is $O(n \log n)$, which is a good improvement when compared to the $O(n^3)$ from its predecessor.

We executed an evaluation experiment through MRA to discover how PSF performance can be compared to other similar algorithms when reordering pre-Band and pre-Circumplex synthetic matrices. Our experiment compared four algorithms to PSF: Classical MDS (with k=1), SVD (with k =1), FastMap (with k =1), and Polar Sort; in this case, k is the dimensionality of the target space of the multidimensional projections. The first three algorithms are multidimensional projection algorithms used to reorder rows and columns of the input matrices. We defined k=1 for both Classical MDS and SVD as used by Wilkinson (2005). We inserted FastMap as a direct concurrent of Classical MDS and SVD, in equal projection configurations (i.e., k=1). Polar Sort and PSF, by definition, use k=2 for their multidimensional projection algorithms – Classical MDS and FastMap, respectively. The experiment settings are as follows:

- Patterns to be tested: Band (with bandwidth b=0.1, 0.2, 0.5, and 1.0), and Circumplex;
- Matrix sizes: 250 × 250, 500 × 500, 750 × 750, and 1000 × 1000;
- Noise levels (i.e., the proportion of cells whose content is replaced by random values): 0.01, 0.05, 0.1, 0.3, and 0.5;
- Functions for assessing the output matrices: minimal span loss function and Moore stress, for pre-Band matrices; circular correlation for pre-Circumplex matrices.

For each combination of pattern, matrix size and noise level, we created 50 matrices, which were randomly permuted. After permutation, they were reordered by the selected reordering algorithms and assessed by evaluation functions.

We also selected real-world examples of matrices to be reordered with PSF, aiming to illustrate its utility. The next section shows these examples and the results of our experiments.

5. RESULTS AND DISCUSSION

Figure 3 summarizes the main results related to our experiment about synthetic data. We selected 6 charts (related to the matrices with size 1000 x 1000**)** that represent the overall dataset of results, due to space limitations. We also omitted results related to column reordering due to their similarity to the results of row reordering. In the figure, "Cl.MDS" stands for Classical MDS.

Regarding the results about pre-Band matrices (Figure 3(a-d)), we did the following observations:

a) The Moore stress chart at Figure 3(a) shows that the average stress tends to be lower for Polar Sort and PSF results for b=0.1 (we also noted the same for b=0.2). For b=0.5 (Figure 3(b)), the average stresses of each tested algorithm are very similar each other when considering the same noise level. These results are independent of the matrix size.

b) It is possible to perceive the same pattern from (a) in the minimum span charts (whose representative chart is the Figure 3(c)). Besides, we noted in the overall results that SVD, Polar Sort and PSF have very similar minimum span measures.

c) The execution time chart (Figure 3(d)) highlights the performance of FastMap and PSF, which was an expected result due to the low time complexity discussed before. For matrices with size

1000 × 1000, FastMap and PSF spent approximately 3 seconds, while their competitors spent hundreds of seconds. For matrices with size 250 × 250 (not shown in Figure 3), the execution time of FastMap and PSF is in the order of hundredths of a second, while the time spent by their competitors is in the order of seconds.

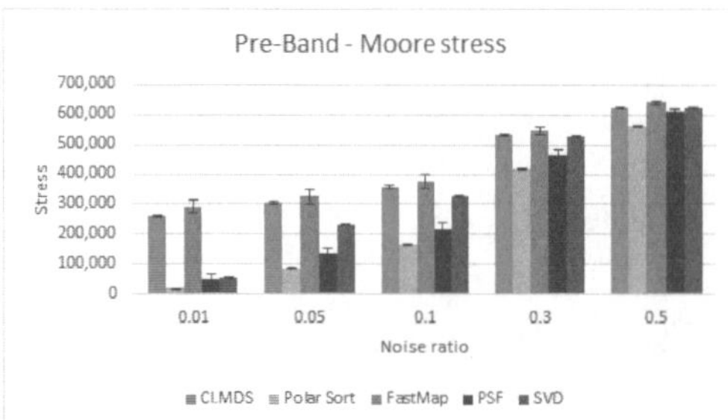

(a) b=0.1

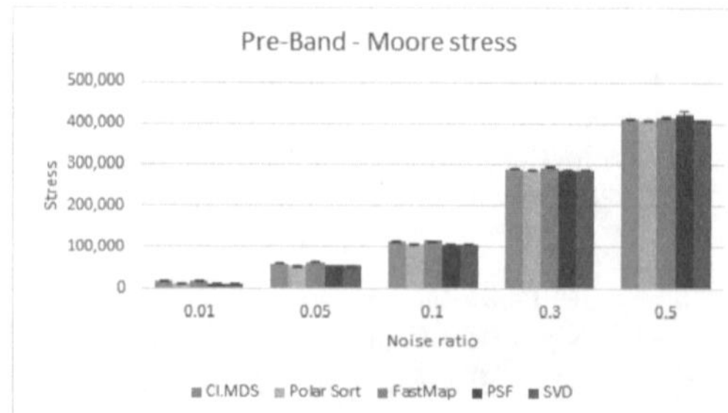

(b) b=0.5

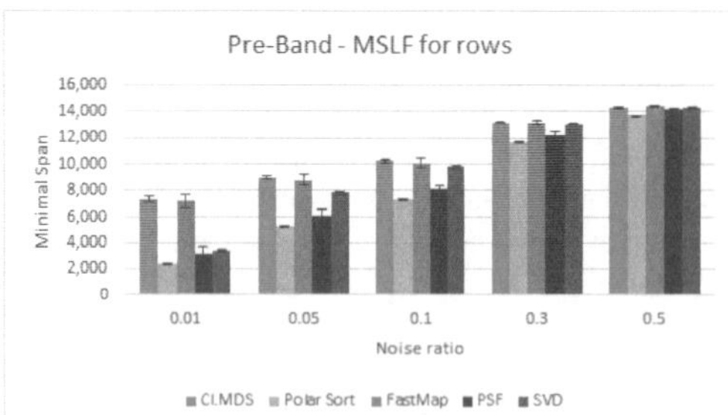

(c) b=0.1

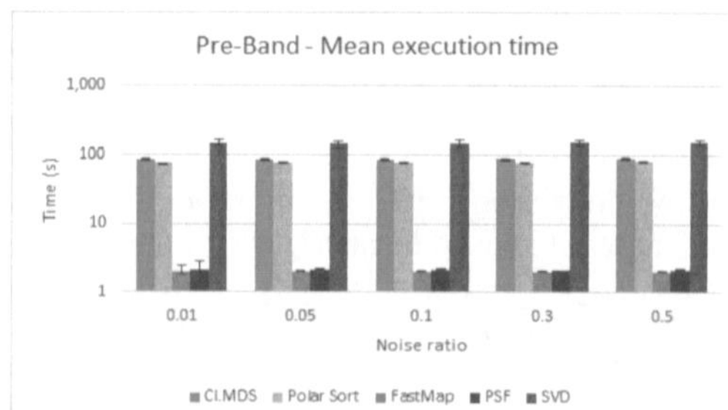

(d) b=0.5

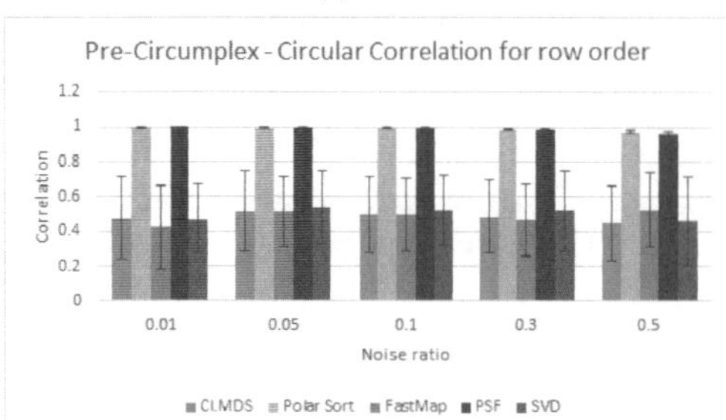

(e)

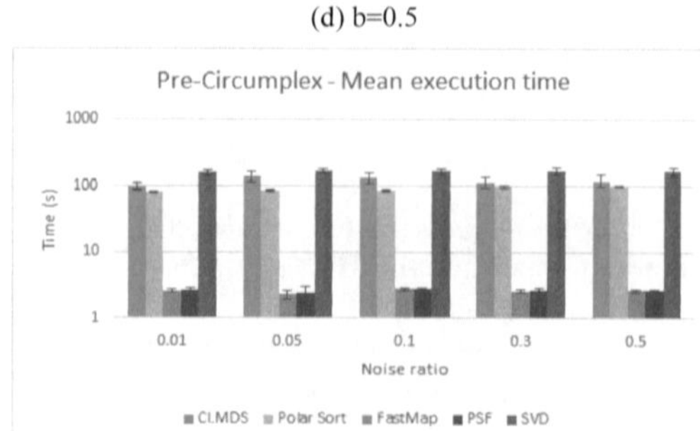

(f)

Figure 3. Charts with some experiment results. (a) to (d): charts related to pre-Band matrices; (e) and (f): charts related to pre-Circumplex matrices

The previous comments enable us to state that PSF tends to be the best choice that combines the criteria of quality and better execution time to unveil a Band pattern in a pre-Band matrix, when compared to the other tested algorithms.

We also highlight the following results related to pre-Circumplex matrices (Figure 3(e,f)):

a) In the circular correlation charts (represented by Figure 3(e)), Polar Sort and PSF have average correlations close to 1 (which is the desired value). The average values of the concurrent algorithms are near 0.5, and they also have a big standard deviation. This entire situation happens regardless the noise level and the matrix size.
b) The execution time charts for pre-Circumplex matrices (Figure 3(f)), similarly to those from pre-Band matrices, indicate that FastMap and PSF were the fastest algorithms among the tested ones. As an example, their execution times were in the order of seconds or hundredths of seconds, respectively, for matrices with size 1000 × 1000 (Figure 3(f)) and 250 × 250. These times are two orders of magnitude lower than the times of their competitors.

We concluded from the experiment results that the best choice to reorder pre-Circumplex matrices, among the tested algorithms, is also PSF, given its execution time and output quality.

For the sake of completeness, we note that our experiment run into a high-performance cluster that has 160 cores Power 755 3.3 GHz, 8 cores Power 720 3.0 GHz, and 24 cores Intel X5650 2.6 GHz. However, we cannot define exactly which processor executed the jobs.

This experiment revealed that PSF can produce fast and good quality results when reordering pre-Band and pre-Circumplex matrices with the tested sizes. Due to its O($n \log n$) asymptotic time complexity, PSF tends to be faster than the remainder tested algorithms even for matrices with size greater than 1000 × 1000; however, we have no proof that the output quality will remain so good for these untested situations as it was in our tests. It is worth to consider that PSF could replace Polar Sort inside Hybrid Sort, which will also reduce Hybrid Sort's time complexity to O($n \log n$).

We selected two real-world datasets to exemplify the utility of PSF. The first example presents how PSF can unveil a pattern that is similar to a Circumplex pattern. Figure 4 shows a matrix of the correlation between pairs of 12 mood-related adjectives (Browne, 1992), in three distinct permutations: (a) the matrix in its original order; (b) a scrambled version of it; and (c) the results of using PSF to order the scrambled matrix. The color scheme is such that reddish and bluish cells stands for high and low correlations, respectively. Note that (a) and (c) have the same circular list of adjectives in their rows (and columns), but in reverse order and starting at a distinct adjective.

The second example (Figure 5) is related to distances between cities. It is based on a table of travel distances between cities in Portugal (https://portugal.com/portugal/travel-tips/distances, accessed in April 1, 2021). We converted this table into a table of how close these cities are to each other. Each distance measure $d(x,y)$ was converted to a proximity measure $p(x,y)=1 - d(x,y) / maxd$, where $maxd$ is the greatest distance between any pair of cities in the dataset. Figure 5(a) presents a heatmap whose cities follow the same order provided in the original matrix. Figure 5(b) shows how PSF sorted this heatmap, which is close to a Band pattern. Note that the order provided by PSF follows approximately the latitudinal coordinates of the cities, from north to south.

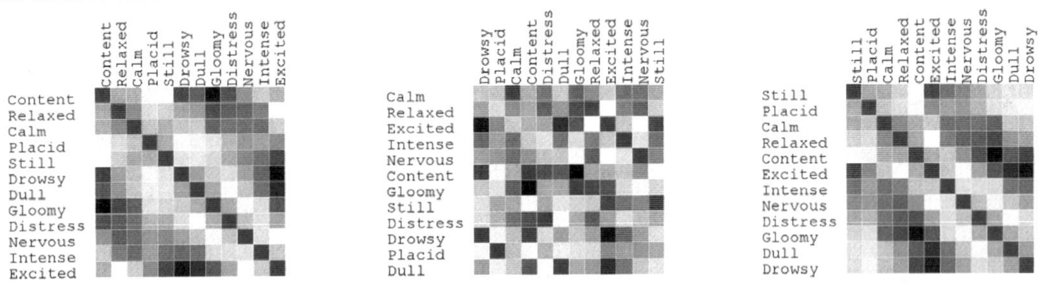

(a) Original matrix (b) Scrambled matrix (c) Reordered by PSF

Figure 4. Using PSF to reorder a pre-Circumplex matrix

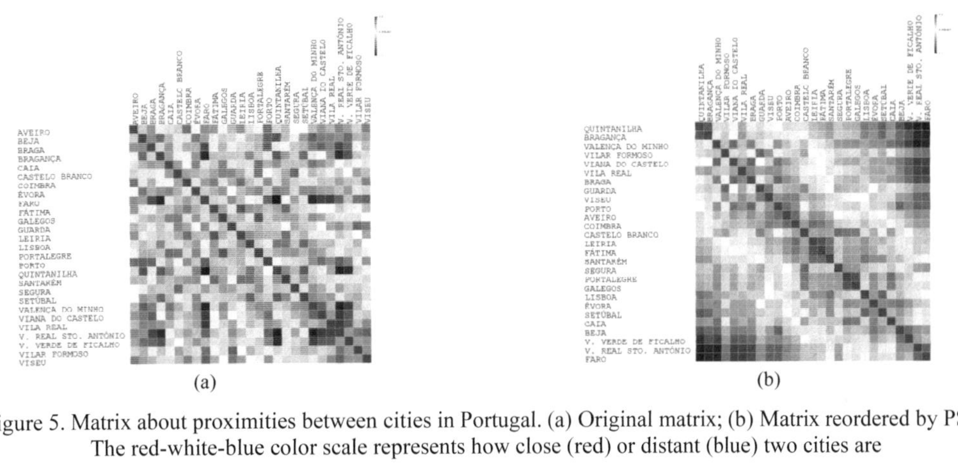

(a) (b)

Figure 5. Matrix about proximities between cities in Portugal. (a) Original matrix; (b) Matrix reordered by PSF. The red-white-blue color scale represents how close (red) or distant (blue) two cities are

6. CONCLUSION AND FUTURE WORK

In this paper, we proposed PSF, a new version of the matrix reordering algorithm Polar Sort that uses the multidimensional projection algorithm FastMap. In the same way as Polar Sort, the goal of PSF is to reveal Band and Circumplex patterns by reordering appropriately rows and columns of pre-Band and pre-Circumplex matrices. PSF's time complexity ($O(n \log n)$) surpasses the $O(n^3)$ time complexity of its antecessor without reducing the quality reordered matrices, as we noted in the results of experiments with synthetic data. We also presented the potential of this method for revealing information in real-world data. Future work includes studying other matrix patterns, such as the ones defined by Behrisch et al. (2016), and discovering or proposing fast reordering algorithms that are able to reveal these patterns.

ACKNOWLEDGEMENT

This study was financed in part by the Coordenação de Aperfeiçoamento de Pessoal de Nível Superior – Brasil (CAPES) – Finance Code 001. We also thank the grant #2396/21 from FAEPEX/PRP/Unicamp.

REFERENCES

Bertin, J., 2010. Semiology of Graphics: Diagrams, Networks, Maps. USA: Esri Press.

Behrisch, M. et al., 2016. Matrix reordering methods for table and network visualization. *Computer Graphics Forum* 35(3), pp. 693–716.

Browne, M. W. 1992. Circumplex models for correlation matrices. *Psychometrika, 57*(4), pp. 469–497.

Faloutsos, C. and Lin, K., 1995. FastMap: A Fast Algorithm for Indexing, Data-Mining and Visualization of Traditional and Multimedia Datasets. *SIGMOD Conference*, pp. 163-174.

Liiv, I., 2010. Seriation and matrix reordering methods: An historical overview, *Statistical Analysis and Data Mining*, *3*(2), pp. 70–91.

Niermann, S., 2005. Optimizing the ordering of tables with evolutionary computation. *The American Statistician*, Vol. 59, No. 1, pp. 41-46.

Nonato, L. G. and Aupetit, M., 2019. Multidimensional Projection for Visual Analytics: Linking Techniques with Distortions, Tasks, and Layout Enrichment. *IEEE Transactions on Visualization and Computer Graphics* 25, pp. 2650-2673.

Paulovich, F. et al., 2007. The Projection Explorer: A Flexible Tool for Projection-based Multidimensional Visualization. *Proc. of SIBGRAPI 2007 - 20th Brazilian Symposium on Computer Graphics and Image Processing*, pp. 27-36.

Rocha, M. M. N. et al., 2017. Circumplex Sort: a two-phase method for revealing circumplex data patterns in reorderable matrices. *Proc. Int. Conf. Computer Graphics, Visualization, Computer Vision and Image Processing 2017 and Big Data Analytics, Data Mining and Computational Intelligence 2017*. Lisbon, Portugal, pp. 181–188.

Santos, A. M. et al., 2016, Block Reordering: Um algoritmo para evidenciar padrão Block em matrizes reordenáveis. *Workshop of Undergraduate Works (WUW) in the 29th Conference on Graphics, Patterns and Images* (SIBGRAPI'16), São José dos Campos, Brazil.

Silva, C. G. et al., 2014. PQR sort: using PQR trees for binary matrix reorganization. *Journal of the Brazilian Computer Society*, Vol. *20*, Issue 1, Article 3.

Silva, C. G., 2019. Polar Sort: combining multidimensional scaling and polar coordinates for matrix reordering. *Proc. Int. Conf. Interfaces and Human Computer Interaction 2019; Game and Entertainment Technologies 2019; and Computer Graphics, Visualization, Computer Vision and Image Processing 2019*, Porto, Portugal, pp. 239–243.

Silva, C. G., 2020. Hybrid Sort - a pattern-focused matrix reordering approach based on classification. *Proc. Int. Conf. on Computer Graphics, Visualization, Computer Vision and Image Processing 2020, Big Data Analytics, Data Mining and Computational Intelligence 2020, and Theory and Practice in Modern Computing 2020*, online, pp. 35–43.

Silva, C. G. et al., 2017. A fast feature vector approach for revealing simplex and equi-correlation data patterns in reorderable matrices. *Information Visualization*, *16*(4), pp. 261–274.

Torgerson, W. S., 1952. Multidimensional scaling: I. theory and method. *Psychometrika*, Vol. 17, No. 4, pp. 401–419.

Wilkinson, L., 2005. *The Grammar of Graphics*. Springer Science & Business Media. New York, USA.

Wu, H.-M. et al., 2008. *Matrix Visualization*. Handbook of Data Visualization. Springer, pp. 681–708.

A 3D SPECTRAL-SPATIAL CLASSIFICATION OF HYPERSPECTRAL REMOTE SENSING IMAGERY USING INCEPTION BASED NETWORK

Douglas Omwenga Nyabuga and Guohua Liu
School of Computer Science and Technology, Donghua University
Shanghai City 201620, China

ABSTRACT

Hyperspectral remote sensing images (HSRSI) comprise hundreds of adjacent channels with rich spectral-spatial signatures, making it possible to discriminate earth objects. Thus, it has contributed to its wide use in urban mapping, environmental management, and crop analysis. To completely take advantage of the abovementioned uses, it often requires the identification of the class of each pixel, which at times faces scarcity or limited availability of labeled training samples. Hence, it is an open challenge to achieve higher interpretation accuracies when processing such increased spectral-spatial resolution imagery. To this end, we, therefore, propose a 3D inception spectral-spatial network model (3D-ISSN). First, we adopt the principal component analysis (PCA) for dimensional reduction of spectral channels that are very much correlated while preserving the desirable information, second, we fuse the hierarchical spectral-spatial related features extracted for CNN1-D and CNN2-D, with our model for learning and achieving the correct classification with a softmax regression classifier. We verified our model through experiments carried out on two HSRSI data sets, namely Botswana (BT) and Kennedy Space Center (KSC), and compared our classification accuracies with the state-of-the-art (SOTA) methods.

KEYWORDS

Remote Sensing, Hyperspectral, Spectral-Spatial, Inception

1. INTRODUCTION

Hyperspectral remote sensing image (HSRSI) holds very vital information about the land objects, i.e., the spatial and spectral information (Tang et al., 2020), which contributes toward efficient and accurate image processing. Also, HSRSI classification (Tong et al., 2014) is vital for its interpretation and processing. Hyperspectral sensors acquire hundreds of information from consecutive land material segments, with a supply of rich spectral information and improved capability to discriminate unevenly distributed land-use materials (Bing, 2011). To classify and distinguish these images, some traditional HSRSI classification approaches have been used but nearly all are founded both on the handcraft features (Yanshan Li et al., 2019; Wang et al., 2019), and traditional classifiers (Melgani & Bruzzone, 2004).

In recent years, deep learning (DL) methods have experienced tremendous advancement for the study of HSRSI data. The extracted features through the convolutional neural network (CNN) possess more excellent semantic representation and stronger robustness compared with the handcraft features. CNN has also been deployed to the categorization of HSRSI. For example, (Hu et al., 2015) presented a 1-D-CNN-based method for the extraction of in-depth feature vectors of HSRSI in spectral measurement.

In past years, scholars mined spatial features from raw HSRSI data cube by cropping the spectral resolution through the deployment of some dimension reduction (DR) techniques, for instance, principal component analysis (PCA), and reducing spatial regions of $k \times k$ pixel-based regions. The authors such as (Haut et al., 2019) trained a CNN2-D with a single principal component (PC), at the same time (C. Li et al., 2015) applied three PCs in the training of the CNN2-D in addition to post-processing of the unearthed spatial information with sparse coding (SC) (Song et al., 2014) to produce more typical spatial representations of a sparse dictionaries for categorization. For instance, the simple and straightforward process involves providing an approach having 3-D contiguous domains of $k \times k \times n_{channels}$ where $n_{channels}$ can represent a definite count of PCs. Hereof, some techniques make an initial DR crop the redundancy and correlation of spectral channels.

The reduction of spectral dimensions has received a lot of attention. Because neighbor intensities are closely correlated at such a high spatial resolution, a spectral signature involves a wealth of redundant data. Often, problems such as the curse of dimensionality and class imbalance occur in the HSRSI data set. Dimensionality reduction (DR) is a fundamental pre-processing step to complement an HSRSI data set classification process. Several studies, for example, (Datta et al., 2018; Koumoutsou et al., 2021; Rodarmel & Shan, 2002) deployed the well-known technique, i.e., the PCA to fix the aforementioned problems. Motivated by the stated advantage in our proposed model we applied PCA to surmount the problems caused by the high dimensionality covered in the HSIRS images.

To classify the HSI images (Zhang et al., 2019), presented a method known as a multi-scale dense Network (MSDN). The authors applied various dimension information in the proposed framework design and fused dimensional features throughout the framework. In the process of obtaining the necessary feature vectors, the framework implemented the discriminating and imbalanced of two dimensions. The framework deployed the rebuilding of extraction of abstract features and multi-scale fusion for the classifying of HSI data. It had better performance concerning the representation of HSI images. Also, it improved the speed of the training of the framework and its accuracy, which specifically enhanced the convergence speed. Even though there was an added feature network layer on the dimension, which condensed the deep framework in the process of feature extraction, which is attributable to the threshold response of complexity, the precision improvement was not any longer robust after the complexity got to a particular level. (Roy et al., 2019) combined a CNN3-D with a CNN2-D, where they applied CNN3-D basically to extract spatial-spectral features and subsequently distinguished by the CNN2-D.

The HSRSIs contains hundreds of adjacent channels with rich spectral-spatial signatures, making it possible to discriminate earth objects. Thus, it has contributed to its wide use in crop analysis, urban administration, and environmental management. To completely take advantage of the abovementioned uses, it often requires the identification of the class of each pixel, which at times faces scarcity or limited availability of labeled training samples. Hence, it is an open challenge to achieve higher interpretation accuracies when processing such increased spectral-spatial measurement imagery. To this end, we, therefore, propose a 3D inception spectral-spatial network model which contributes to the correct classification of two publicly available HSRSI dataset, i.e., BT and KSC. The inclusion of the 3D-inception network immediately after the 3D convolutional filters for discriminative spatial feature learning is the key difference between our proposed model and spatial-spectral approaches. Furthermore, the following are the key advantages of our 3D-ISSN model:

1) First, we adopt the principal component analysis (PCA) for dimensional reduction of spectral channels that are very much correlated while preserving the desirable information

2) We fused the ordered spectral-spatial related features extracted for CNN1-D and CNN2-D with our 3D-ISSN model for the exploitation of spatial features. To train the CNN1-D and CNN2-D, the input data for the CNN-1D and CNN-2D were convolved with 1D kernels and 2D kernels, respectively.

3) We further introduced a softmax regression classifier for the correct classification of HSRSI images.

The study demonstrates that this model can improve the classification accuracy of HSRSI, and offer new scientific ideas and reference for the related research.

The remaining part of the paper takes the following structure, the related works are reviewed in part 2, our proposed methodology is discussed in part 3, the experimental setup, dataset, compared SOTA methods and parameter setting takes part 4, in part 5 we discuss the experimental results. Finally, we give a conclusion of the study in part 6.

2. RELATED WORK

Lately, HSRSI classification technology based on DL has become a hot research area (Zhu et al., 2017). Likened with artificially constructed features, DL methods spontaneously extract deep feature vectors of small details to those of important facts and translates imageries into feature vectors that are simple to identify and classify. For instance, the deep brief network (DBN) (Chen et al., 2015) method apply unsupervised approaches to mine extensive feature vectors in a layer-based training mode. In achieving the objective, flattening of the 1-D training sample set must be performed to fit the required standard size in as the model inputs, which often suffer a loss of the spatial details of the raw image. The CNN2D introduced by (Zhao & Du, 2016) for the extraction of spatial contents from the representation of the reduced dimensions via PCA and mines spectral information deploying their proposed method. Lastly, fused with spatial/spectral information to enhance the HSI classification precision. Nevertheless, the 2-D CNN method by (Makantasis et al., 2015) mines spatial/spectral feature vectors solely but needs convoluted pre-processing.

The discriminating spatial dimension of HSRSIs facilitates in supplying a diversity of features of low-levels indicating detailed spatial information. On the other hand, the spectral contents offer essential and distinct details to exhibit the characteristics of land-use materials (Du et al., 2016). Making excellent use of rich spectral-spatial contents, therefore, facilitates the improvement of the HSRSI classification accuracy. (Ying Li et al., 2017) proposed 3-D CNN's approach to obtaining a complete blending of spectral-spatial features concurrently from the raw 3-D data cube. Though, their proposed method could not efficiently extract extensive information attributable to the stacked CNN layer and its simplicity. Besides, the limitation of an active feature combination approach increases the depth of the network, which enables it to transmit information. The CNN potentiality feature expression grows as the layers increase the depth. As a result, the current DL techniques have enhanced the classification of HSRSI images, for instance, stacking 2D-CNN and 3D-CNN with a dense layer network. Nevertheless, the best learning process can have a steady and length improvement, but discriminate and meaningful features mostly get lost or even dissipate in the course of depth transfer.

Spatial-spectral learning can be accomplished by 2D-CNN frameworks presenting spectral-spatial handcrafted information. For example, (He et al., 2019) trained the 2D-CNN method under the concept covariance matrices (CM), which encodes the spatial-spectral features of various measurements, i.e., regions of twenty principal components (PCs), attaining multi-scale of covariance maps. (Yue et al., 2015) designed a 2D-CNN framework to study the spectral-spatial contents by blending the spectral contextual as maps of three distinct features and combining them to the spatial patches (downsized three PCs through PCA). Additionally, a manifold of approaches combines the 2D-CNN with other different methods to achieve the extraction of the spatial-spectral features in a sole manner. Although, the aforementioned methods were used in the image classification task, they have limitations in their application due to the use of only 2D-CNN approaches.

Besides, for the 1D CNN and 2D CNN methods, there is a frequent implementation of the 3-D-CNN method in classifying spatial-spectral feature vectors, whereby the 3-D filters with a size of $f^{(k)} \times f^{(k)} \times f^{(k)} \times z^{(k)}$ can automatically perform the extraction of complex spatial-spectral features, where the extracting f represents an output feature dimensions. For example, (Ying Li et al., 2017) accomplished a fascinating evaluation among the spectral-spatial 3-D-CNN architecture two spectral-based models, i.e., the SAE, spatial 2-D-CNN, and DBN for the classification of hyperspectral imagery, showing that the CNN3D-based model was able to excel this SOTA methods. As with CNN1-D and CNN2-D approaches, the scientific works presents more multifaceted and advanced strategies for the study of hyperspectral images, which includes CNN3D frameworks. However, the process of analyzing and classifying HSI is complicated and involves diverse representations, these CNN3D frameworks have specific limitations. Therefore, it's important to engage both CNN2-D and CNN3-D architectures for the study of HSI images from the perspective of structural features. In addition, we fused the inception network in our model to decrease the complexity of the model compared to training CNN-2D and CNN-1D separately. The inception network has not been utilized in the study of HSRSI images for the previous works.

3. METHOD

In this part, we describe our proposed model, which we illustrate in Figure 1. We subjected the deep extracted 3D spectral-spatial features to the principal component analysis (PCA) technique for dimensionality reduction and removal of redundant features. Next, the 3D-ISSN model jointly employed the spectral/spatial HSRSI information. The hyperspectral tensor, which takes three-dimensional cubes, i.e., $S \times S \times L$, where $S \times S$ is the width and height of the spatial dimensions and L is the spectral dimension represents our HSRSI input image, which expressed as

$$I \in \mathbf{R}^{W \times H \times C} \tag{1}$$

where I denotes the raw HSRS input image, the W and H is the width and height of the spatial features and C denotes the spectral channels in the image.

Due to the redundancy and the intra/inter-class similarities, we adopted the PCA as classic dimensionality reduction technique which we directly applied to the extracted feature vectors of the HSRSI input image and it takes the form of equation (2).

$$P \in \mathbf{R}^{W \times H \times T} \tag{2}$$

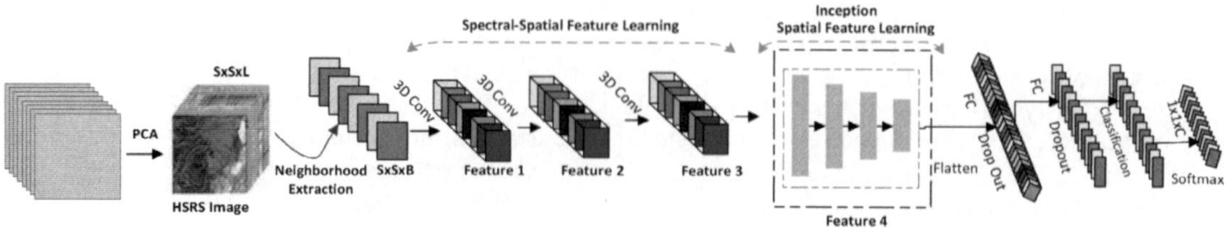

Figure 1. The 3D-ISSN proposed Architecture

To learn the spatial-spectral features, we convoluted a 3-D kernel with the 3-D-data. In our 3D-ISSN architecture for HSRSI data, through employing the 3-D kernel over a manifold of neighborhood channels in the input layer, the feature maps of the convolution layer are produced; this apprehends the spectral features. The expression in the 3-D convolution, the activation value at the spatial domain (x, y, z) in the jth feature map of the ith layer represented as $v_{(i,j)}^{(x,y,z)}$ we define it as

$$v_{i,j}^{x,y,z} = \phi\left(b_{i,j} + \sum_{r-1}^{d_{l-1}} \sum_{\lambda=-\eta}^{\eta} \sum_{\rho=-\gamma}^{\gamma} \sum_{\sigma=-\delta}^{\delta} w_{i,j,\tau}^{\sigma,\rho,\lambda} \times v_{i-1,\tau}^{x+\sigma,y+\rho,z+\lambda} \right) \tag{3}$$

where ϕ is the activation function, $b_{i,j}$ is the bias parameter for the jth feature map of the ith layer, d_{l-1} is the number of feature map in $l-1^{th}$ layer, $2\gamma+1$ is the width of kernel, $2\delta+1$ is the height of kernel, $2\eta+1$ is the depth of kernel along spectral resolution, and $w_{i,j}$ is the value of weight parameter for the jth feature map of the ith layer.

We trained the bias b and the kernel weight w parameters using supervised strategies with the aid of a gradient descent optimization technique. The 3-D-CNN kernel finally derives the feature vector depictions of spectral-spatial contents concurrently from HSRSI data, but at the cost of increased computational complexity. To further learn more abstract level spatial representation, we apply CNN2-D on top of the CNN3-D.

By convolving the input image from the CNN3-D with the 2D kernels, we were able to learn the spatial feature. We achieved the convolutions by calculating the sum of the dot product between input data and kernel filter of the spatial resolutions, which only present all the feature maps of earlier network layers resulting in 2-D discriminative feature maps. The kernel filter is stride over the input data to cover the full spatial region. The convolved features are passed through the activation function to insert the non-linearity in the model. In 2-D convolution, the activation value at spatial position (x, y) in the jth feature map of the ith layer, is denoted as $v_{(i,j)}^{(x,y)}$ and can be generated using equation (4).

$$v_{i,j}^{x,y,z} = \phi\left(b_{i,j} + \sum_{r-1}^{d_{l-1}} \sum_{\rho=-\gamma}^{\gamma} \sum_{\sigma=-\delta}^{\delta} w_{i,j}^{\sigma,\rho} \times v_{i-1,\tau}^{x+\sigma,y+\rho} \right) \tag{4}$$

where ϕ denotes the activation function, $b_{i,j}$ denotes the bias parameter for the jth feature map of the ith layer. The d_{l-1} represents the value of feature map in the $l-1^{th}$ network layer, and $w_{i,j}$ represents the depth of kernel filter for the jth feature map of the ith network layer. $2\gamma + 1$ represents the width of kernel filter, $2\delta+1$ is the height of kernel filter, and $w_{i,j}$ represents the value of weight parameter for the jth feature map of the ith network layer.

To avoid the overfitting problem and fast-track the model's convergence speed and enhance the accuracy, we selected a rectified linear unit (ReLU) (Maas et al., 2013) as the nonlinear activation function. Hence, defined as

$$f(x) = \max(0, x) \tag{5}$$

We randomly initialized all the model's weights and trained it through Back-propagation (BP) algorithm with the gradient drop algorithm, i.e., the adaptive moment estimation (Adam) optimizer, by applying the softmax loss. We trained our proposed framework for 100 epochs without data augmentation and batch normalization (BN). The softmax regression layer, which is used to predict the conditional probability distribution of each class for correctly classification of the dataset was expressed as

$$P(y = \frac{i}{x} W, b) = \frac{e^{(W_{ix}+b_i)}}{\sum_{i=1}^{k} e^{(W_{jx}+b_j)}} \tag{6}$$

where W and b denotes the weights and bias of the softmax regression layer classifier, respectively.

4. EXPERIMENTS

4.1 Dataset

In evaluating the performance of our proposed model, this study analyzes two classic HSRSI data set, namely the Botswana (BT) and Kennedy Space Center (KSC) data set (*Hyperspectral Remote Sensing Scenes - Grupo de Inteligencia Computacional (GIC)*, n.d.). We divided all sampled data into two set sizes, i.e., the train/test size sets. We adopted a ratio of 3:7, i.e., 30% for training set size and 70% for testing set size.

During the validation process, we selected the network with the highest classification accuracy and retained the corresponding weight parameters—this attributed to the use of the early stopping generalization technique that we applied in our model. Finally, we employed the test set to evaluate the classification capability of the trained model. We quantitatively carried a random of ten trains and determined the average and standard deviation of the multiple sets of overall accuracy (OA), mean accuracy (AA), and kappa coefficient (k), which we picked as overall accuracy. The classification accuracy of the best performance for the validation set was thus, saved during the training process. Moreover, we compared our proposed 3D-ISSN with the SOTA) methods, namely the HybridSN (Roy et al., 2019), MSDN (Zhang et al., 2019), respectively, to show the performance of our model on the two HSRSI data sets. Table 1 and Table 2 report per class accuracy classification result of the three methods with their respective OA, k, and AA. The classification maps of our model are as shown in Figure 2 and Figure 3.

4.1.1 The Botswana (BT) Data Set

NASA in the year 2001-2004, through EO-1 satellite, gathered a BS data in sequence structure. The BS data set has 242 bands, covering a wavelength/spectrum range of 400-2500 nm and 30 m—spatial resolution over a 7.7 km strip. The personnel discarded the lousy inter-detector miscalibration effects, detectors, and recurrent abnormalities from the data set after preprocessing of the BT data. They also removed noisy, disordered, and imperfect bands that cover water absorption features that are (10-55, 82-97, 102-119, 134-164, & 187-220) and thus remained with 145 bands. The data set consists of 14 classes considered for our experiments. The total number of classification samples is 3248.

4.1.2 The Kennedy Space Center (KSC) Data Set

The dataset was captured by NASA scientists using the Airborne Visible/Infrared Imaging Spectrometer (AVIRIS) instrument in the year 1996. AVIRIS captures data with 400-2500 nm center wavelengths in—224 bands of 10nm width and 18 m-spatial resolution. Discarding the low SNR bands and water absorption from the dataset, the KSC personnel used 176 bands and 13 classes for their study. We used all the 13 classes for classification, which represent diverse land cover types that happen in nature settings. The selection of our training data solely depends on the land cover. The total number of classification samples is 5211.

4.2 Parameter Setting

The proposed 3D-ISSN via the gradient of the back-propagation (BP) loss function updated the parameters of the 3-D convolution in the architecture. We adopted Adam optimizer as the gradient descent algorithm in our model to optimize the loss function. For both KSC and BT data set, we trained 100 epochs. The learning rate (lr) was 0.001. We simulated our experiments on a MacBook Pro laptop computer with the CPU of Intel Core i5, 2.3 GHz, the Intel Iris Plus Graphics 640 1536 MB, and the memory of 8 GB 2133 MHz LPDDR3 as the hardware, and all experiments executed on GPU-Google Colab ltd platform.

5. EXPERIMENTAL RESULTS AND DISCUSSIONS

5.1 BT Data Set Performance Results

Further, we used the BT data set to demonstrate the performance of the MSDN, HybridSN, and our proposed model. It comprises 14 classes with a total of 3248 samples. We applied a dropout rate of 55% to prevent the method's overfitting due to the limitation of labeled samplings, which produced a high performance. Table 1 lists the accuracy classification performance. On individual classes, we can see that our proposed model significantly improved on classification of classes such as Floodplain Grasses 1 = 99.94%, Reeds 1 = 98.40%, Riparian =100%, and Water =100% compared to the baseline methods. The overall accuracy (OA) of our model outperformed the other SOTA methods, i.e., MSDN and HybridSN. The apparent predicted reference in Figure 2 illustrates the BT data set.

Table 1. Per class performance of our proposed method comparing to other SOTA methods, i.e., MSDN, and HybridSN methods on 30% training set size of BT data set

Class. No	Class label	MSDN	HybridSN	Proposed
C1	Acacia grasslands	100	100	100
C2	Acacia shrublands	100	100	100
C3	Acacia woodlands	99.45	100	100
C4	Exposed soils	100	96.97	100
C5	Floodplain Grasses 1	99.45	99.86	**99.94**
C6	Firescar 2	100	100	100
C7	Floodplain Grasses 2	100	100	100
C8	Hippo grass	100	100	100
C9	Island interior	100	100	100
C10	Mixed mopane	100	100	100
C11	Reeds 1	96.76	94.68	**98.40**
C12	Riparian	92.89	99.47	**100**
C13	Short mopane	100	100	100
C14	Water	97.35	98.90	**100**

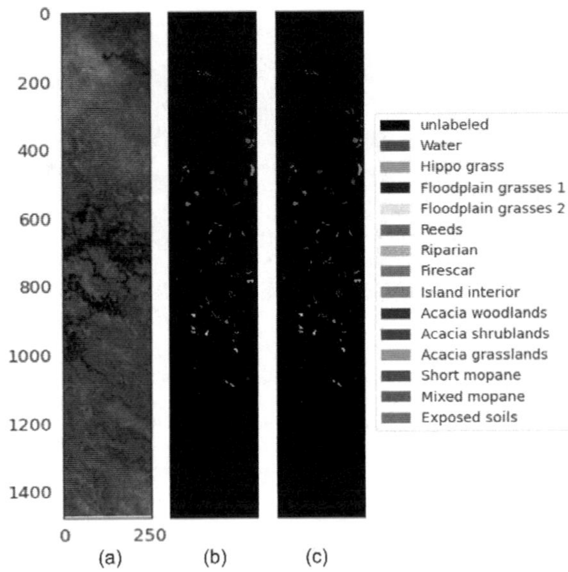

Figure 2. The Botswana (BT) hyperspectral remote sensing data set, a) the false-color composite, b) the ground truth label and c) the predicted reference

5.2 KSC Data Set Performance Results

The KSC dataset had a smaller number of classes (i.e., 13 classes) but comparatively broad feature sampling resolutions. From Table 2, we can observe that its overall accuracy performance excels compared to HybridSN and the MSDN models. We can also see that our model was superior in individual classes with higher accuracy, such as Cabbage-palm/oak-hammock (98.89%), Spartina-marsh (98.98%), Willow-swamp (100%), Hardwood-swamp (100%), and Oak/broadleaf-hammock (100%). Figure 3 represents the false-color composite, ground-truth label, and the predicted reference of our proposed model, respectively.

Table 2. Per class performance of our proposed method comparing to other SOTA methods, i.e., MSDN, and HybridSN methods on 30% training set size of KSC data set

Class. No	Class label	MSDN	HybridSN	Proposed
C1	Cabbage-palm/oak-hammock	100	95.46	97.73
C2	Cabbage-palm-hammock	98.41	97.21	**98.89**
C3	Slash-pine	99.10	100	100
C4	Spartina-marsh	96.67	98.35	**98.98**
C5	Water	100	100	100
C6	Willow-swamp	99.89	98.82	**100**
C7	Cattail-marsh	100	96.11	100
C8	Graminoid-marsh	100	99.34	100
C9	Hardwood-swamp	99.75	94.6	**100**
C10	Mud-flats	99.71	95.17	**100**
C11	Oak/broadleaf-hammock	96.99	95.63	**100**
C12	Salt-marsh	100	100	100
C13	Scurb	100	99.44	99.62

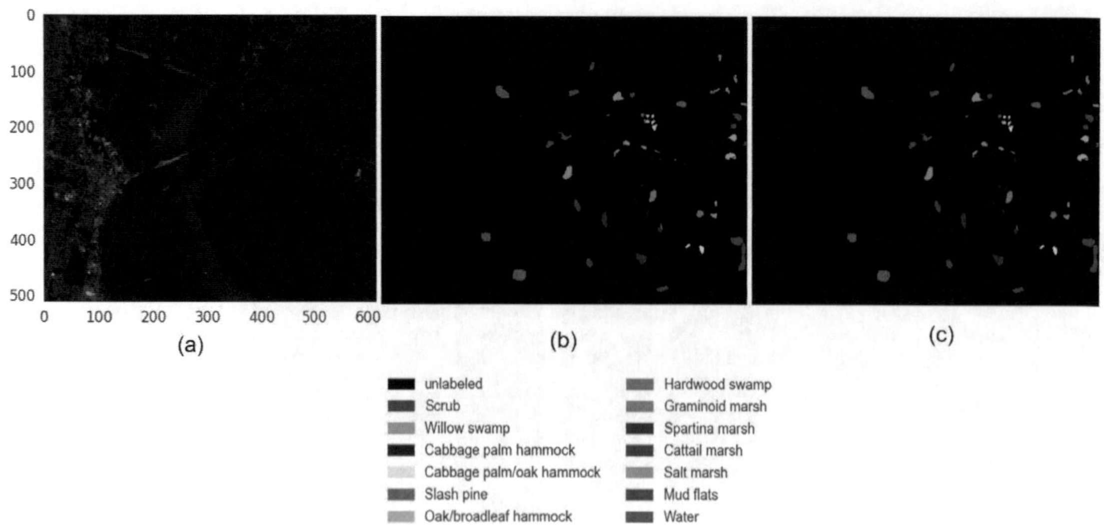

Figure 3. The Kennedy Space Center (KSC) hyperspectral remote sensing data set, a) the false-color composite, b) the ground truth label and c) the predicted reference

Table 3 and Table 4 lists the classification results of both BT and KSC data sets, respectively. The achieved classification results demonstrate that our proposed approach outperforms the MSDN and HybridSN models.

Table 3. The BT data set classification results

	MSDN	HybridSN	Proposed
OA (%)	98.77	99.43	99.87
AA (%)	98.96	99.36	99.89
$\kappa \times 100$	98.66	99.38	99.86

Table 4. The KSC data set classification results

	MSDN	HybridSN	Proposed
OA (%)	99.45	98.22	99.48
AA (%)	99.42	97.71	99.48
$\kappa \times 100$	99.39	98.02	99.42

Figure 4 and Figure 5 depicts our model's accuracy and loss convergence graphs on 100 epochs for the two datasets we analyzed. With the accuracy convergence of our model in Figure 4, we can see that the model converges quickly at approximately 55 epochs of the BT dataset. Also, we can see that the accuracy convergence in Figure 5, i.e., the KSC dataset, our model converged faster at approximately 60 epochs.

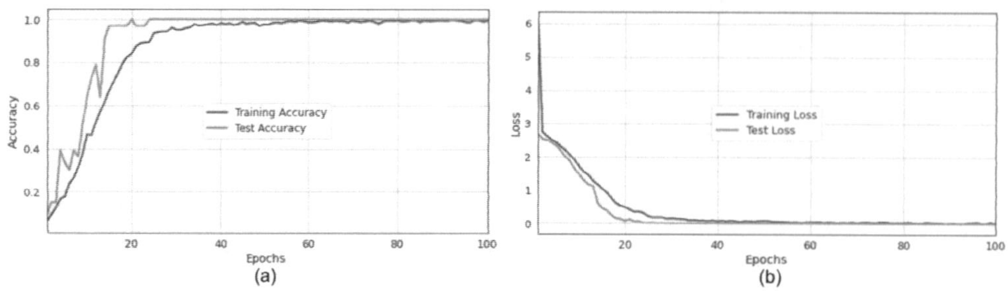

Figure 4. The convergence graphs for model accuracy and loss for 100 epochs on BT hyperspectral remote sensing data set

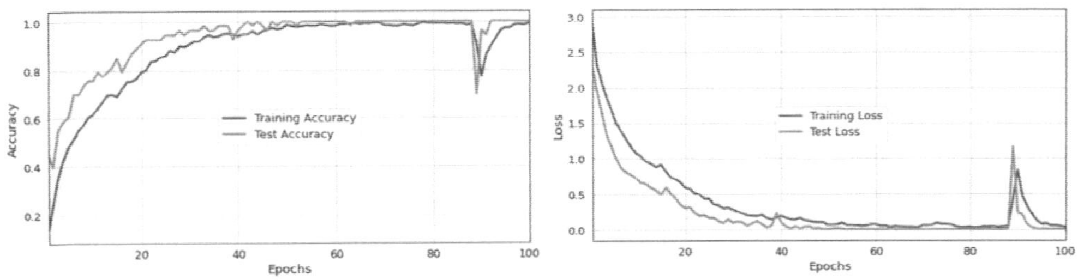

(a) (b)

Figure 5. The convergence graphs for model accuracy and loss for 100 epochs on KSC hyperspectral remote sensing data set

Table 5 lists the computation time in seconds for our proposed model with other SOTA methods. Regarding computational complexity of our proposed model to the baseline methods, ours significantly. This is attributed to the use of inception network in our model decreased the complexity of the model compared to training CNN-2D and CNN-1D separately.

Table 5. The comparison of computation time (s) results

	BS Data Set		KSC Data Set	
Methods	Training Time (s)	Testing time (S)	Training Time (s)	Testing time (S)
MSDN	5595.2	25.49	11111.42	51.4
HybridSN	4213.8	22.36	10521.4	46.5
Ours	4020.23	18.73	908.69	38.7

6. CONCLUSION

Hyperspectral remote sensing images (HSRSI) comprises hundreds of adjacent channels with rich spectral-spatial signatures, making it possible to discriminate earth objects. Thus, it has contributed to its wide use in urban mapping, environmental management, and crop analysis. These applications often require the identification of the class of each pixel, usually face scarcity or a small number (limited availability) of labeled training samples. Hence, it is an open challenge to achieve higher interpretation accuracies when dealing with such increased spectral-spatial resolution imagery. To this end, we, therefore, propose a 3D-inception spectral-spatial network model. First, we adopted principal component analysis (PCA) for dimensional reduction of spectral channels that are very much correlated while preserving the desirable information, second, we fused the hierarchical spectral-spatial related features extracted for CNN1-D and CNN2-D, with our model for learning and achieving the correct classification with a softmax regression classifier. Our proposed model achieved an excellent result on the two HSRSI data sets, namely Botswana (BT) and Kennedy Space Center (KSC), which confirms the significant superiority of our model over the other SOTA methods. For future work, we suggest to include more training set size for further analysis.

ACKNOWLEDGEMENT

This work was supported in part by the Development of Shanghai Industrial Internet (Grant No. 2019-GYHLW-01004).

REFERENCES

Bing, Z., 2011. Intelligent remote sensing satellite system. *Journal of Remote Sensing*.

Chen, Y., Zhao, X., & Jia, X., 2015. Spectral-Spatial Classification of Hyperspectral Data Based on Deep Belief Network. *IEEE Journal of Selected Topics in Applied Earth Observations and Remote Sensing*, *8*(6), pp 2381–2392.

Datta, A., Ghosh, S., & Ghosh, A., 2018. *PCA, Kernel PCA and Dimensionality Reduction in Hyperspectral Images*. Advances in Principal Component Analysis.

Du, P., Xia, J., Xue, Z., Tan, K., Su, H., & Bao, R., 2016. Review of hyperspectral remote sensing image classification. *Yaogan Xuebao/J. Remote Sensing*, *20*(2), pp 236–256.

Haut, J. M., Paoletti, M. E., Plaza, J., Plaza, A., & Li, J., 2019. Hyperspectral Image Classification Using Random Occlusion Data Augmentation. *IEEE Geoscience and Remote Sensing Letters*, *16*(11), pp 1751–1755.

He, N., Paoletti, M. E., Haut, J. M., Fang, L., Li, S., Plaza, A., & Plaza, J., 2019. Feature extraction with multiscale covariance maps for hyperspectral image classification. *IEEE Transactions on Geoscience and Remote Sensing*, *57*(2), pp 755–769.

Hu, W., Huang, Y., Wei, L., Zhang, F., & Li, H., 2015. Deep convolutional neural networks for hyperspectral image classification. *Journal of Sensors*, *2015*.

Hyperspectral Remote Sensing Scenes - Grupo de Inteligencia Computacional (GIC). (n.d.). Retrieved January 6, 2020, from http://www.ehu.eus/ccwintco/index.php?title=Hyperspectral_Remote_Sensing_Scenes

Koumoutsou, D., Charou, E., Siolas, G., & Stamou, G., 2021. *Class-Wise Principal Component Analysis for hyperspectral image feature extraction*.

Li, C., Chen, C., Carlson, D., & Carin, L., 2015. Preconditioned Stochastic Gradient Langevin Dynamics for Deep Neural Networks. *30th AAAI Conference on Artificial Intelligence, AAAI 2016*, pp. 1788–1794.

Li, Yanshan, Li, Q., Liu, Y., & Xie, W., 2019. A spatial-spectral SIFT for hyperspectral image matching and classification. *Pattern Recognition Letters*, *127*, pp 18–26.

Li, Ying, Zhang, H., & Shen, Q., 2017. Spectral-spatial classification of hyperspectral imagery with 3D convolutional neural network. *Remote Sensing*, *9*(1).

Maas, A. L., Hannun, A. Y., & Ng, A. Y., 2013. Rectifier nonlinearities improve neural network acoustic models. *In ICML Workshop on Deep Learning for Audio, Speech and Language Processing*.

Makantasis, K., Karantzalos, K., Doulamis, A., & Doulamis, N., 2015. Deep supervised learning for hyperspectral data classification through convolutional neural networks. *2015 IEEE International Geoscience and Remote Sensing Symposium (IGARSS)*, *2015-Novem*, pp. 4959–4962.

Melgani, F., & Bruzzone, L., 2004. Classification of hyperspectral remote sensing images with support vector machines. *IEEE Transactions on Geoscience and Remote Sensing*, *42*(8), pp 1778–1790.

Rodarmel, C., & Shan, J., 2002. Principal Component Analysis for Hyperspectral Image Classification. *Surv Land Inf Syst*, *62*.

Roy, S. K., Krishna, G., Dubey, S. R., & Chaudhuri, B. B., 2019. HybridSN: Exploring 3-D-2-D CNN Feature Hierarchy for Hyperspectral Image Classification. *IEEE Geoscience and Remote Sensing Letters*, pp 1–5.

Song, B., Li, J., Dalla Mura, M., Li, P., Plaza, A., Bioucas-Dias, J. M., Benediktsson, J. A., & Chanussot, J., 2014. Remotely sensed image classification using sparse representations of morphological attribute profiles. *IEEE Transactions on Geoscience and Remote Sensing*, *52*(8), pp 5122–5136.

Tang, H., Li, Y., Han, X., Xie, W., & Huang, Q., 2020. A Spatial-Spectral Prototypical Network for Hyperspectral Remote Sensing Image. *IEEE Geoscience and Remote Sensing Letters*, *17*(1).

Tong, Q., Xue, Y., & Zhang, L., 2014. Progress in hyperspectral remote sensing science and technology in China over the past three decades. *IEEE Journal of Selected Topics in Applied Earth Observations and Remote Sensing*, *7*(1), pp 70–91.

Wang, Q., He, X., & Li, X., 2019. Locality and structure regularized low rank representation for hyperspectral image classification. *IEEE Transactions on Geoscience and Remote Sensing*, *57*(2), pp 911–923.

Yue, J., Zhao, W., Mao, S., & Liu, H., 2015. Spectral-spatial classification of hyperspectral images using deep convolutional neural networks. *Remote Sensing Letters*, *6*(6), pp 468–477.

Zhang, C., Li, G., & Du, S., 2019. Multi-Scale Dense Networks for Hyperspectral Remote Sensing Image Classification. *IEEE Transactions on Geoscience and Remote Sensing*, *57*(11), pp 9201–9222.

Zhao, W., & Du, S., 2016. Spectral-Spatial Feature Extraction for Hyperspectral Image Classification: A Dimension Reduction and Deep Learning Approach. *IEEE Transactions on Geoscience and Remote Sensing*, *54*(8), pp 4544–4554.

Zhu, X. X., Tuia, D., Mou, L., Xia, G.-S., Zhang, L., Xu, F., & Fraundorfer, F., 2017. Deep Learning in Remote Sensing: A Comprehensive Review and List of Resources. *IEEE Geoscience and Remote Sensing Magazine*, *5*(4), pp 8–36.

3D FACE RECONSTRUCTION FROM HARD BLENDED EDGES

Yueming Ding[1] and P.Y. Mok[1,2]
[1] *The Hong Kong Polytechnic University, Inst. Textiles & Clothing, Hong Kong*
[2] *Laboratory for Artificial Intelligence in Design, Hong Kong*

ABSTRACT

3D face reconstruction from 2D images is an important research topic because it supports a wide range of applications, such as face recognition, animations, games, and AR/VR systems. 3D face reconstruction from contour features is a challenging task, because traditional edge detection algorithms produce a lot of noises, which are prone to making the reconstruction model trapped in a local optimum or even being degraded. With the development of deep learning, a lot of researcher introduce neural network into contour detection, which can extract relatively clear contours compared with previous methods. In this article, we employ a hard blended face contour feature from neural network and canny edge extractor for face reconstruction. Our method not only improves the 3D face model reconstruction accuracy on synthesis images, but performs more accurately and robustly on in-the-wild images under blurriness, makeup, occlusion and ill-illumination conditions.

KEYWORDS

3D Face Reconstruction, Feature Extraction, Deformable Model

1. INTRODUCTION

3D face reconstruction based on 2D images is a well-explored subject in computer vision, which has been widely applied in animation, virtual try-on systems as well as in face identification (Pavlakos *et al.*, 2019). Traditional face reconstruction approach is pixel-wise analysis-by-synthesis (Blanz & Vetter, 1999), in which the distance between real image and synthetic image from face model is minimized pixel-by-pixel directly. A less direct approach is feature-based reconstruction (Huber *et al.*, 2015), in which the similarity between features extracted from the input and estimated face model is minimized instead of computing pixel-wise difference. In contrast, the feature-based reconstruction is comparatively more robust and computational efficient (Egger *et al.*, 2020).

In the feature-based reconstruction, landmark feature is widely used in initialization stage and important in a lot of state-of-art works. However, there are several deficiencies on landmark features. One of disadvantages is that the locations of landmarks are easily drifted or occluded in large pose conditions. Another disadvantage is that different annotation strategies employ different number of landmarks, which make it hard to unify different dataset in reconstruction. In contrast, edge features represent more detailed geometric information about the face shape and with less limitation. However, the traditional edge detectors, such as canny, are sensitive to illumination, makeup and occlusion. As a result, their generated edge features contain a lot of noises, which are prone to making face reconstruction trapped at local optimum.

Instead of using traditional edge detectors, we employ a neural network to help us extract facial contours for face reconstruction. The key contributions of this paper are as follows:

- We introduce facial contour heatmap features extracted from deep neural networks into the edge-based 3D face reconstruction.
- We propose the hard blended edges which combine edges generated from the features from neural network and from canny edge detector.
- Our 3D face reconstruction method achieve great accuracy and robust on the synthetic facial image dataset and in-the-wild image dataset.

2. RELATED WORK

Landmark and contour are two most common sparse facial features being used for the task of face reconstruction. Landmark features represent the sparse facial geometric information, which have been widely used in face alignment, face recognition as well as in face reconstruction (Blanz & Vetter, 1999; Schönborn *et al.*, 2013). In recent years, the deep neural network achieves significant performance in landmark prediction. For instance, Chen *et al.* (2014) proposed a cascaded neural network to detect landmarks. Zhu and Ramanan (2012) used a multi-task network to detect landmarks and classify facial attributes. In contrast with deterministic landmarks, heatmap landmarks provide a likelihood representation for landmark locations. The heatmap landmark representation is first used by Newell *et al.* (2016) in human pose landmark detection, who proposed an hourglass network to extract both local and global features for human pose estimation. Yang *et al.* (2017) extended hourglass network into face landmark detection.

However, as mentioned before, there exist several limitations on landmark features. Thus, a lot of researches introduce contour or edge information into face reconstruction. Blanz and Vetter (1999) used boundary features in face model fitting, and establish an active shape model. Moghaddam *et al.* (2003) used multi-view silhouettes to fit the 3DMM model (Paysan et al., 2009). Romdhani and Vetter (2005) formulated edge distance cost as a mixed energy function in optimization. Keller *et al.* (2007) showed that the cost function of face reconstruction based on contour and edge is not differentiable or continuous because of the occlusion and noise on those features. Fitzgibbon (2003) use the soft boundary on face reconstruction, which is robust but with relatively less accuracy. Thus, because of the challenge of obtaining clean edges or contours, edge or contour based face reconstruction is still an open question (Egger *et al.*, 2020). In one of the state-of-arts, Bas *et al.* (2016) found that reconstructing face from hard edges performance better than from soft edges.

Based on previous researches, face reconstruction based on edge or contour features is limited by traditional edge detectors. A lot of researchers focus on extracting object contours from images using deep neural networks for segmentation and object detection purposes (Shen *et al.*, 2015; Yu *et al.*, 2017). The LAB model (Wu *et al.*, 2018) focus on extracting face contour heatmaps to assist landmark location on in-the-wild images, which can extract relatively clean face contour heatmaps from in-the-wild images on different conditions. We will introduce this framework to extract facial contour features on the face model reconstruction.

Except landmark and contour features, there are other features used in face reconstruction. Huber *et al.* (2015) reconstruct face models from images based on scale-invariant feature transform (SIFT) local features. Zhu *et al.* (2016) proposed a 3D reconstruction solution based on dense features. Shang *et al.* (2020) used the multi-view dense features on 3D face reconstruction. Other researchers reconstruct the 3D face model from the face shading (Zhu *et al.*, 2015), because shadow and illumination provide clues to the human face shape. However, those dense features will spend more computing source and lead optimization less prone to convergence.

3. METHOD

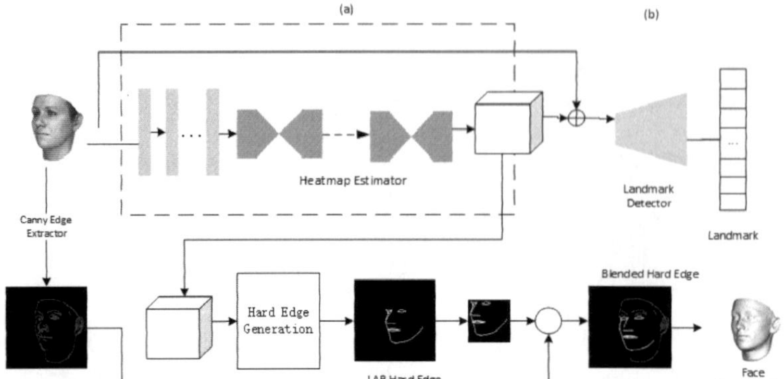

Figure 1. 3D Face Reconstruction from Blended Contour

Figure 1 shows an overview of our method, which includes four stages. In the first stage, we extract the facial contour heatmaps from the LAB neural network which predicts landmark location with the assist of contour information (Wu *et al.*, 2018). In the second stage, we convert the LAB heatmap features, representing the likelihood of facial contours, into the LAB hard edges. In the third stage, we fuse the LAB hard edges with the hard edges detected from canny edge detector to generate the blended hard edges. In the final stage, the parameters of 3D Morphable Model (Paysan *et al.*, 2009) will be predicted based on the blended hard edges.

3.1 Boundary

There are two types of boundary defined in the literature: occluding contours and texture edges (Keller *et al.*, 2007). The occluding contour represents the information related to face shape, which separates the face from background. The texture edges are segmented edges related to the texture information, which are sensitive to make up and illumination. In Figure 2, the red lines represent the occluding contours, and the blue edges represent the texture edges. In this article, we use the term 'boundaries' to represent edges extracted from 2D images. The boundaries, including both occluding contours and texture edges, are usually segmented.

Figure 2. Texture Edges and Occluding Contours

The occluding contour from a 3D model is generated through determining of the variation of the mean vertex normal from adjacent faces as well as the visibility of those vertices. On a 3D face model, if the normals of the adjacent faces are more than 90 degree, the vertices along the connecting edges are on the occluding contours. Then, we use z-buffer, also known as depth buffer, to filter the visibility of the vertices on the occluding contours. Finally, the 2D coordinates of vertices on the occluding contours will be obtained through orthographic projection.

3.2 Blended Hard Edges

In our 3D face reconstruction method, we make use of the LAB framework (Wu *et al.*, 2018) to assist the contour extraction. The LAB framework predicts facial landmark coordinates from input face images. The LAB framework consists of two parts. The first part, shown as part (a) in Figure 1, includes several hourglass networks for generating facial contour heatmaps. Hourglass network structure is good at extracting both local and global information. The second part, shown as part (b) in Figure 1, is for landmark detection, which consists of several convolutional layers and fully connected layers. The inputs to part (b) include the extracted facial heatmaps from part (a) as well as the original input image. In the training process, the differences between ground truth landmarks and the predicted landmarks are back propagated to update the entire network framework. Since Gaussian heatmaps are fuzzy and of high variance, Wu *et al.* (2018) thus introduced the generative adversarial training strategy to generate relatively clear heatmaps by putting more focuses on boundary areas.

We use face heatmaps generated from the part (a) from the LAB framework (Wu *et al.*, 2018) to generate facial contour features, which are of size $13 \times 64 \times 64$, representing the Gaussian distribution of face contours. According to Bas *et al.* (2016), soft edges (i.e. Gaussian contours heatmaps) are not as effective as hard edges for 3DMM reconstruction. Thus, we transform the soft contours into hard edges. To do so, we first upsample the features be of the same size as the input images by bilinear interpolation, i.e. a size of $13 \times 384 \times 384$. Next, since the face contour heatmap are non-convex, we segment those contour to convex subsets. Another challenge is that the Gaussian contours heatmaps are anisotropic in the horizontal (row) and vertical (column) directions. For example, the contours of the chin shows larger variances in the horizontal direction compared with those in the vertical direction. To address this, we conduct the same processes in both the row and the column directions. For example, in the row direction, we calculate the gradient for each pixel in each column and record coordinates from those pixels with continuous non-zero gradients in convex subset in row. Because each segment is convex in the row subset, we can select coordinates with top 3 pixel value easily to generate the coordinate set. Then, we combine coordinate sets from convex subsets both in the row and the column directions to generate a hard LAB edges, as detailed in Figure 3.

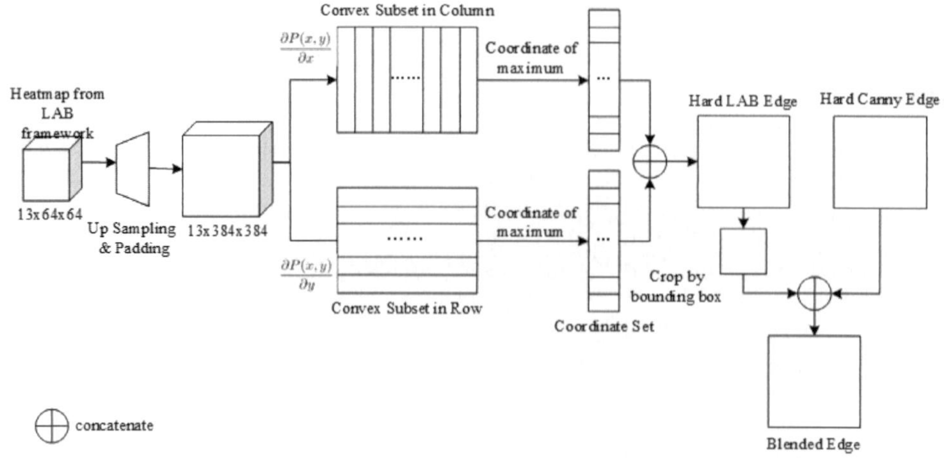

Figure 3. Generate hard blended edges from LAB features and canny edges

Moreover, since the LAB framework only considers the face part without other information, such as the shape of ears and neck, we therefore blend texture edges obtained from canny edge detector with the LAB hard edges in our face reconstruction task. After detecting the bounding box of the LAB hard edges, we use it to splice the canny edge map and combine hard canny edges with the LAB facial edges to obtain the blended edges. The details of the hard edges transformation and the blended edge generation are shown in Figure 3.

3.3 Optimization

An iterative edge-points optimization is employed to predict the 3DMM shape parameters. In the first step, the pose and shape parameters are initialized through landmark alignment. After initiation, we generate the 2D coordinates of vertices on the occluding contours from the 3D face model by the method described in Section 3.1. Then, the K-Nearest Neighbor algorithm is used to find the corresponding points on the detected edges of the 2D image for each vertex on the occluding contours. Next, the pose and shape parameters are iteratively updated by minimizing the distance between points on edges of the 2D image and on occluding contour from the predicted 3D model. In the final stage of the optimization, the pose parameters is fixed, the shape parameters are optimized until the error is less than the threshold. A hybrid loss function will be employed combined the weighted landmark and edge loss function, and the penalty of shape parameters.

Landmark Loss function The landmark loss is used both in the initialization and in the formal training stage. We calculate the squared distance between landmarks predicted from 2D image and the corresponding projected pre-defined vertices on 3D face model.

$$E^{lmk} = \frac{1}{N}\sum_{n=i}^{N}\left\|v_i^{lmk} - P\left(v'^{lmk}_i\right)\right\|^2 \quad (1)$$

where $P(\cdot)$ represents orthographic projection operation; v'^{lmk} denotes N landmark points predicted from input image; v^{lmk} are the corresponding predefined points on 3D mesh.

Contour loss function The contour loss employs square distance to calculate the distance between the points on the detected facial edges of the 2D image and the points on the projected occluding contours from a 3D face model.

$$E^{edge} = \frac{1}{N_C}\sum_{j\in C}\left\|v_j^{cont} - P\left(v'^{edge}_j\right)\right\|^2 \quad (2)$$

where v_j^{cont} represent vertex on the occluding contour of the predicted mesh model, $j \in C$ and C is the number of vertices on the contour; v'^{edge}_j denotes the point on the input image, which corresponds to the vertex j on the occluding contours.

Penalty loss function The shape parameters of the 3DMM model is expected to follow a normal distribution (Egger *et al.*, 2020). To prevent the face shape from diverging, a regularization term is utilized to normalize the face shape model.

$$E^p = \sum_{k=1}^{N} \alpha^2 \tag{3}$$

where α is vector of shape parameters, which correspond to N principal components about the shape of the face model.

Hybrid loss function A hybrid loss function is used in the final optimization stage, which combines the weighted landmark loss function, the contour loss function, and the penalty function.

$$\mathrm{E} = \omega_1 E^{lmk} + \omega_2 E^{edge} + \omega_p E^p \tag{4}$$

where ω_1 represents the weight of landmark cost function E^{lmk}, ω_2 represents the weight of edge cost function E^{edge}, and ω_p represents the weight of penalty function E^p.

4. EXPERIMENTS

4.1 Database and Evaluation Metric

Synthetic image dataset The synthetic image dataset is generated from the Basel Face Model. As the method in (Bas *et al.*, 2016), we randomly generate 10 groups of shape and texture parameters to obtain 10 ground true face shape and appearance models, which represent 10 identities. Then, synthetic images are rendered from each mesh under 17 degrees $(0^\circ, \pm 10^\circ, \pm 20^\circ, \pm 30^\circ, \pm 40^\circ, \pm 50^\circ, \pm 60^\circ, \pm 70^\circ, \pm 80^\circ)$ through orthographic projection. Experiments are evaluated on the synthetic image dataset.

In-the-wild image dataset WFLW dataset (Wu *et al.*, 2018) named wider facial dataset in-the-wild is employed as the in-the-wild image dataset in our experiment. This database has ground true landmarks with 98 points. Because the dataset contains rich attribute annotations, such as occlusion, illumination, blurriness and makeup, we can evaluate the robustness of our method under different image conditions. However, there is no ground true 3D data in this dataset, so an indirect evaluating metric is used when experiments are conducted on this dataset.

Evaluation metrics The performances of different methods on synthetic dataset are evaluated through calculating the mean vertex Euclidean distance between ground true models and predicted models after Procrustes analysis. We employ the ground true landmarks in WFLW as our ground true values. For each estimated face model, we use K Nearest Neighbor search algorithm to find the k closet corresponding points among the vertices on the occluding contour.

4.2 Comparison with Existing Methods

4.2.1 Evaluation on Synthetic Images

Our proposed method is compared with hard canny edges based method of Bas *et al.* (2016) on synthetic images. Three experiments were conducted under the synthetic image dataset. In the first experiment, we conducted experiment on soft LAB features which were generated from face contour heatmap features extracted from LAB framework. In the second experiment, we transferred those soft LAB features into hard LAB edges by the method described in Section 3.2, then fit the 3D morphable model to those hard LAB edges. In the third experiment, we obtained 3D model from blended edges, by blending the global canny edges with our hard LAB features.

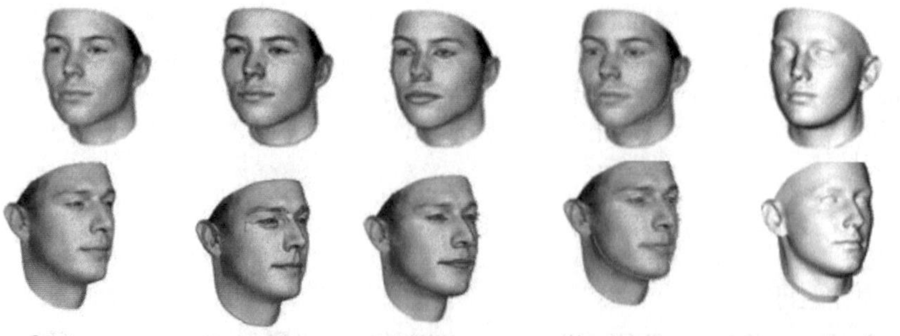

Figure 4. The edge features and 3D face reconstructions on synthetic dataset. From the left to right: inputs, hard canny edges, hard LAB edges, hard blended edges and face reconstructions

The qualitative examples from synthetic image dataset are shown in Figure 4. As images in the second column shown, even though there exists few ill-illumination and blurriness condition in those synthetic images, canny edge detector still generate a lot of noise. Compared with canny edges, LAB edges contain less noise. Our proposed hard blended edges not only contain relatively less noise but provide more geometric information. The quantitative results are reported in Table 1. We show our results in synthetic dataset over all pose angles of the evaluation metrics. Our blended edges method performs well in most of the pose angles and achieves 1.60 mean distance (mm). This shows that using the blended edges improve the performance of face reconstructions from contour images.

Table 1. Average Euclidean vertex distance (mm) on synthetic dataset

Method	Rotation angle									Mean
	0°	±10°	±20°	±30°	±40°	±50°	±60°	±70°	±80°	
Hard canny edges	2.36	2.29	2.01	2.06	2.04	2.24	1.80	1.91	2.10	2.09
Proposed (soft LAB features)	2.21	2.13	2.19	2.56	3.10	3.63	3.11	3.57	3.07	2.84
Proposed (hard LAB edges)	2.15	1.98	2.05	2.02	2.44	2.83	2.60	2.40	2.34	2.31
Proposed (hard blended edges)	**1.59**	**1.64**	**1.60**	**1.46**	**1.50**	**1.45**	**1.43**	**1.68**	**2.08**	**1.60**

4.2.2 Evaluation on In-the-Wild Images

We extend our experiments and evaluations using in-the-wild images. We compare our reconstruction method based on hard blended edges with the methods based on hard canny edges (Bas *et al.*, 2016) using in-the-wild images from WFLW dataset (Wu *et al.*, 2018). The results are shown in Table 2. We use Normalized Mean Error (NME) as metric, which measure the distance between ground true landmarks and their corresponding vertices from the predicted 3D model. We conducted our experiments on images from WFLW dataset with attributes of blurriness, illumination, makeup and occlusion, respectively. The results show that our blended edges method perform more robustly in these conditions.

Table 2. Normalized Mean Error (NME) on in-the-wild dataset

Method	Blurriness	Illumination	Makeup	Occlusion	Mean
Hard canny edges	22.29	22.57	27.37	27.31	24.88
Proposed (hard LAB edges)	21.89	21.96	21.96	27.02	24.80
Proposed (hard blended edges)	**21.72**	21.26	**21.16**	**26.74**	**24.28**

The qualitative results are shown in Figure 5. We select images with makeup, blurriness, occlusion and ill-illumination annotations, respectively. The canny edges detected from in-the-wild images are shown in the second row in Figure 5. Under the makeup and occlusion conditions, a lot of noises are generated. The fourth row shows the reconstructed face models from Canny edges. Our proposed hard blended edges are shown in the third row, which show less noises and more clear contours. The corresponding 3D face reconstruction using blended edges are shown in the last row, and it can be shown the predicted models have better fitting to the faces in the inputs.

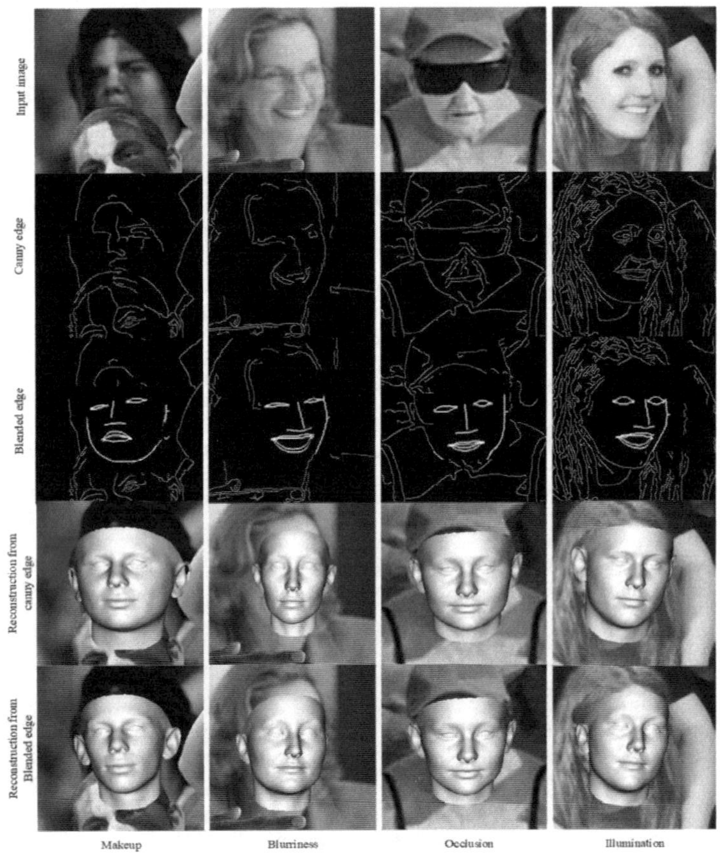

Figure 5. Qualitative Results on in-the-wild Dataset: From the left to right: makeup, blurriness, occlusion and illumination. From the top to bottom: input images, hard canny edges, hard blended edges, reconstructions from canny edges, reconstructions from blended edges

5. CONCLUSION

We present a 3D face reconstruction method based on hard blended edges in this paper. The experiments show that the hard LAB edges represent relatively clean facial boundary information. In the contrast, the canny edges provide global information, such as the shape of head and neck, but contain a lot of noise. The combination of the two kinds of feature improve the reconstruction accuracy on synthesis image dataset significantly. According to the experiment on the in-the-wild images, the canny edges are more sensitive to illumination, makeup and blurriness, which cause the reconstruction easily to be affected. Our proposed hard blended edges can improve the accuracy and robustness of the 3D face reconstruction. In the future, we will explore the integration of other contour detection neural networks, and extend our method to multi-view contours reconstruction.

ACKNOWLEDGEMENT

The work described in this paper was supported by grants from the Research Grants Council of the Hong Kong Special Administrative Region, China (Grant Numbers 152161/17E & 152112/19E). This work was also partially funded by the Laboratory for Artificial Intelligence in Design (Project Code: RP1-1), Hong Kong Special Administrative Region.

REFERENCES

Bas, A., Smith, W. A., Bolkart, T., & Wuhrer, S., 2016. Fitting a 3D morphable model to edges: A comparison between hard and soft correspondences. *In Proceedings of the Asian Conference on Computer Vision*, Taipei, Taiwan, pp. 377-391.

Blanz, V., & Vetter, T., 1999. A morphable model for the synthesis of 3D faces. *In Proceedings of the 26th annual conference on Computer graphics and interactive techniques,* New York, United States, pp. 187-194.

Chen, D., Ren, S., Wei, Y., Cao, X., & Sun, J., 2014. Joint cascade face detection and alignment. *In European conference on computer vision*, Zurich, Switzerland, pp. 109-122.

Egger, B., Smith, W. A., Tewari, A., Wuhrer, S., Zollhoefer, M., Beeler, T., Bernard, F., Bolkart, T., Kortylewski, A., Romdhani, S., Theobalt, C., Blanz, V., & Vetter, T., 2020. 3d morphable face models - past, present, and future. *ACM Transactions on Graphics (TOG)*, 39(5), Vol. 39, No. 157, pp:1-38.

Fitzgibbon, A. W., 2003. Robust registration of 2D and 3D point sets. *Image and vision computing*, Vol. 21, No. 13-14, pp:1145-1153.

Huber, P., Feng, Z. H., Christmas, W., Kittler, J., & Rätsch, M., 2015. Fitting 3d morphable face models using local features. *In 2015 IEEE international conference on image processing.* Québec, Canada, pp. 1195-1199.

Keller, M., Knothe, R., & Vetter, T., 2007. 3D reconstruction of human faces from occluding contours. *In International Conference on Computer Vision/Computer Graphics Collaboration Techniques and Applications*, Berlin, Heidelberg, pp. 261-273.

Moghaddam, B., Lee, J., Pfister, H., & Machiraju, R., 2003. Model-based 3D face capture with shape-from-silhouettes. In *2003 IEEE International SOI Conference. Proceedings* (Cat. No. 03CH37443), Newport Beach, United States, pp. 20-27.

Newell, A., Yang, K., & Deng, J., 2016. Stacked hourglass networks for human pose estimation. *In European conference on computer vision*, Amsterdam, Netherlands, pp. 483-499.

Paysan, P., Knothe, R., Amberg, B., Romdhani, S., & Vetter, T., 2009. A 3D face model for pose and illumination invariant face recognition. *In Proceedings of the IEEE international conference on advanced video and signal based surveillance*, Genova, Italy, pp. 296-301.

Pavlakos, G., Choutas, V., Ghorbani, N., Bolkart, T., Osman, A. A., Tzionas, D., & Black, M. J., 2019. Expressive body capture: 3d hands, face, and body from a single image. *In Proceedings of the IEEE Conference on Computer Vision and Pattern Recognition*, Long Beach, United States, pp. 10975-10985.

Romdhani, S., & Vetter, T., 2005. Estimating 3D shape and texture using pixel intensity, edges, specular highlights, texture constraints and a prior. *In Proceedings of the IEEE Computer Society Conference on Computer Vision and Pattern Recognitio*n, San Diego, United States, pp. 986-993.

Schönborn, S., Forster, A., Egger, B., & Vetter, T., 2013. A monte carlo strategy to integrate detection and model-based face analysis. *In German Conference on Pattern Recognition*, Berlin, Heidelberg, pp. 101-110.

Shen, W., Wang, X., Wang, Y., Bai, X., & Zhang, Z., 2015. Deepcontour: A deep convolutional feature learned by positive-sharing loss for contour detection. *In Proceedings of the IEEE conference on computer vision and pattern recognition*, Boston, United States, pp. 3982-3991.

Shang, J., Shen, T., Li, S., Zhou, L., Zhen, M., Fang, T., & Quan, L., 2020. Self-supervised monocular 3d face reconstruction by occlusion-aware multi-view geometry consistency. arXiv preprint arXiv:2007.12494.

Wu, W., Qian, C., Yang, S., Wang, Q., Cai, Y., & Zhou, Q., 2018. Look at boundary: A boundary-aware face alignment algorithm. *In Proceedings of the IEEE conference on computer vision and pattern recognition*, Salt Lake City, United States, pp. 2129-2138.

Yang, J., Liu, Q., & Zhang, K., 2017. Stacked hourglass network for robust facial landmark localisation. *In Proceedings of the IEEE Conference on Computer Vision and Pattern Recognition Workshops,* Honolulu, United States, pp. 79-87.

Yu, Z., Feng, C., Liu, M. Y., & Ramalingam, S., 2017. Casenet: Deep category-aware semantic edge detection. *In Proceedings of the IEEE conference on computer vision and pattern recognition*, Honolulu, United States, pp. 5964-5973.

Zhu, X., Lei, Z., Yan, J., Yi, D., & Li, S. Z., 2015. High-fidelity pose and expression normalization for face recognition in the wild. In *Proceedings of the IEEE conference on computer vision and pattern recognition*, Boston, United States, pp. 787-796.

Zhu, X., & Ramanan, D., 2012. Face detection, pose estimation, and landmark localization in the wild. In *Proceedings of the IEEE conference on computer vision and pattern recognition*, Rhode Island, United States, pp. 2879-2886.

CAPSULE NEURAL NETWORKS IN CLASSIFICATION OF SKIN LESIONS

Evgin Goceri
Biomedical Engineering Department, Engineering Faculty, Akdeniz University
Dumlupinar Boulevard, 07058, Antalya, Turkey

ABSTRACT

Classification of skin lesions is a difficult issue even for highly experienced dermatologists and pathologists because of several reasons such as low contrast between lesions and surrounding skin tissue, high noise, fuddled lesion boundaries, visual similarities of skin lesions. On the other hand, early and accurate classification of lesions is crucial for timely and accurate treatment of skin diseases. Therefore, automated methods have been developed to perform objective, quantitative and re-producible results. Recent methods in pattern recognition and image classification is based on deep networks, particularly convolutional neural networks. However, pooling layers providing down-sampling in these networks lead to data loss and cause low performance in generalization. Also, convolutional neural networks cannot transfer spatial information and instantiation parameters (e.g., pose of low-level features to each other, deformation and texture information). To overcome these problems with dynamic routing, capsule neural networks have been proposed. Capsules can transfer pose parameters and part-whole relationship using likelihood and spatial information between low-level features. In this work, capsule networks applied for skin lesion classification have been explored and their performances have been evaluated. It has been observed that although capsule networks can overcome deficiencies of convolutional neural networks, there are only four techniques based on capsule networks in the literature to achieve automated classifications of skin lesions. Motivated by the lack of articles on this topic, a comprehensive assessment of the capsule networks proposed for skin lesion classification is presented in this paper. Also, strengths and weakness of those four techniques have been presented to help the researchers interested in this area.

KEYWORDS

Capsule Network, CapsNet, Skin Disease, Lesion Classification, Deep Neural Networks, Pattern Recognition

1. INTRODUCTION

Skin diseases can occur due to various reasons (e.g., environmental factors, aging, depression, trauma, etc). They are serious widespread disorders affecting about 1.9 million people worldwide (Liu et al. 2020) and have an important effect on the quality of life. Existence of more than three thousand kinds of them identified with different severity and symptoms is known (Fritsch et al. 2006; Tizek et al., 2019). For example, malignant melanoma, which may cause death, is a kind of skin cancer grown from pigments containing cells (melanocytes). Those affected cells are generally located in the skin. They can also be found in the eye, mouth, on women's legs or men's backs. Also, they may arise from a mole with several changes (e.g., color change, un-even edges, irritation, an escalation in size, and skin break-down). Another example is psoriasis that is a chronic and also relapsing disorder (Marks et al., 2012). It is very challenging to distinguish psoriasis and erythemato-squamous disorders, such as eczema lichen planus, seborrheic dermatitis, tinea corporis, leprosy, pityriasis, etc. (Pal et al., 2016, Pal et al., 2018, Roy et al.,2017). Psoriasis occurs when the immune-system causes over-production of novel skin cells by sending faulty signals mistakenly. Then, nucleated cells and neutrophils can infiltrate in stratum corneum. The diagnostic marker of psoriasis in clinical pathology is Munro's microbes (Marks et al., 2012). Challenge in detecting Munro's microbes lies in the fact that because of variations in staining, neutrophils in stratum corneum are generally mis-classified due to their dark staining as nucleated-keratinocytes. In addition, various artefacts caused by imaging process increase the difficulties. Therefore, accurate diagnosis of lesions by naked-eye according to visual cues is a challenging issue, even for vastly experienced clinicans and pathologists.

Deep Neural Networks (DNNs), particularly Convolutional Neural Networks (CNNs) as special types of DNNs, are effective architectures for image classification and accelerate decision making in clinical environments (Litjens et al., 2017). However, they can classify only when a certain feature does exist in the image from the testing dataset by ignoring spatial relations. This causes false negatives. Also, the same lesions viewed from different angles can be assigned to different classes. This causes false positives. Capsule Networks (CapsNets) have been designed to overcome these problems.

A CapsNet structure is constructed using one capsule layer as the final layer and many convolution layers. It uses capsules (which are vectors representing an element with size and direction) other than pooling. A CapsNet includes dynamic routing and layer-based squashing. By this way, CapsNets can help in avoiding false negatives and false positives.

A basic CapsNet including 2 convolutional layers and a capsule layer is shown in Figure 1 (Sabour et al., 2017). In this architecture, the 1st convolution layer is used to obtain low-level features from the image with size 28x28x1. There are 256 channels and each of them uses a 9x9 convolution kernel. The 2nd layer is constructed as a convolutional capsule layer including a total of 6x6x32 capsules which are called as primary capsules. Every capsule produces an eight-dimensional vector. Every group of those capsules in the 2nd layer is convolved by eight convolution units. The 3rd layer, which is called as digital capsule layer, is a fully connected layer including 10 capsules. Each capsule in this layer is 16-dimensional vector and performs the classification process. The output of these digital capsules is sent to three fully connected layers (i.e., decoder) to minimize the summation of the squared difference of the corresponding pixels between the input and the reconstructed image. The length for each capsule (i.e., the classification possibility) is calculated in the final layer and a loss function is used at the end of the network. In the training stage, if correct digital capsule cannot be predicted by a vector, then zero value is assigned to the vector. Input image is constructed only by the digital capsules providing correct predictions.

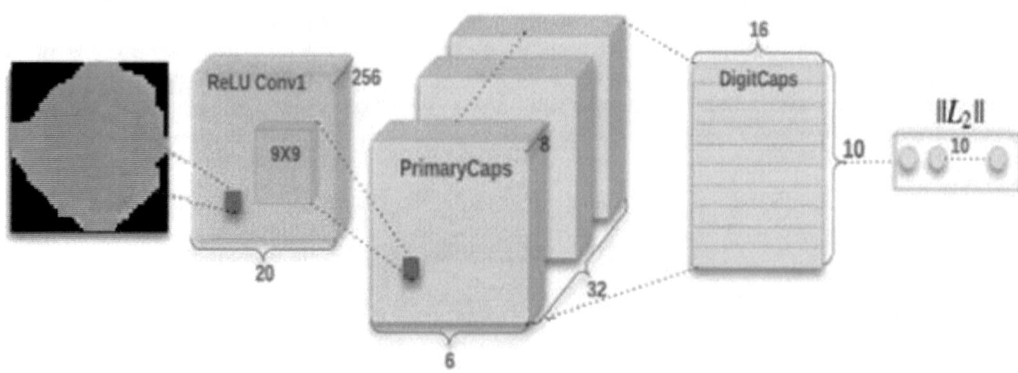

Figure 1. A basic CapsNet architecture

Although several advantages of CapsNets such as fast convergence speed without reduction in accuracy, there are only four techniques based on CapsNets in the literature to achieve automated classifications of skin lesions. According to the best of our knowledge, in the literature, there is no any work focused on assessment of capsule networks proposed for skin lesion classification. Therefore, we believe that this work will fill this gap in the literature and be helpful for the researchers who are working or interested in this area and want to improve those approaches by aware of their strengths, weaknesses and potential challenges to solve the classification problem.

2. RELATED METHODS AND MATERIALS

In the literature, only four techniques based on CapsNets have been proposed to solve lesion classification problem and their authors have handled different types of skin diseases. They have also used different types of images. These techniques and the image data sets used by them have been examined in detailed in this section.

2.1 Classification of benign nevus and malignant melanoma (Tiwari et al., 2021)

The data sets used for classification of benign nervus and malignant melanoma have been constructed with non-dermoscopic images which have been provided from the Groningen Medical Center University. The number of images including nevus (100) and melanoma (70) samples is 170. Example images are shown in Figure 2. To increase the size of image data sets to provide efficiency in the training stage, original images have been rotated and 2040 images have been obtained.

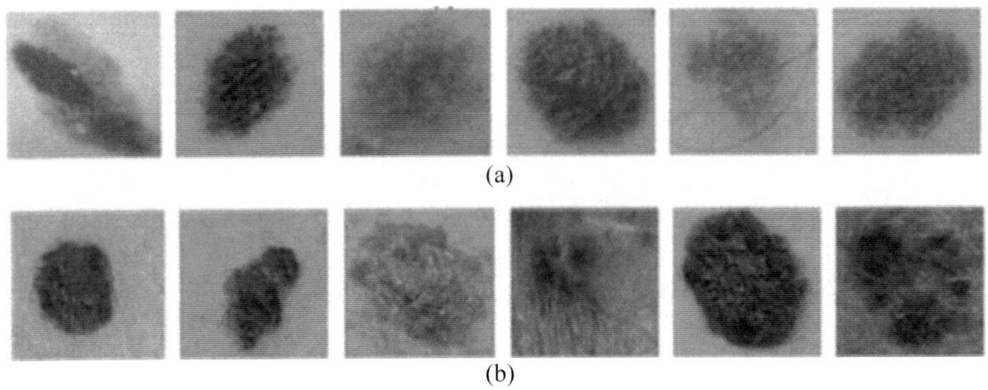

Figure 2. Example images for nervus (a) and melanoma (b) (Tiwari et al., 2021)

Three classification models, which are Multi-Layer Perceptron (MLP), CNN and CapsNet, have been applied. Default functions (such as, maximum pooling, adaptive moment estimation (adam), rectified linear unit (ReLU) and cross-entropy loss function) have been used in these models. (More details can be read from (Tiwari et al., 2021).

100 epochs have been enough to train these three models. 70% of the data has been used for training whereas 30% of the data has been used for validation. According to the reported results, the graphs of validation accuracies (Figure 3) indicate that the CapsNet outperforms than MLP and CNN.

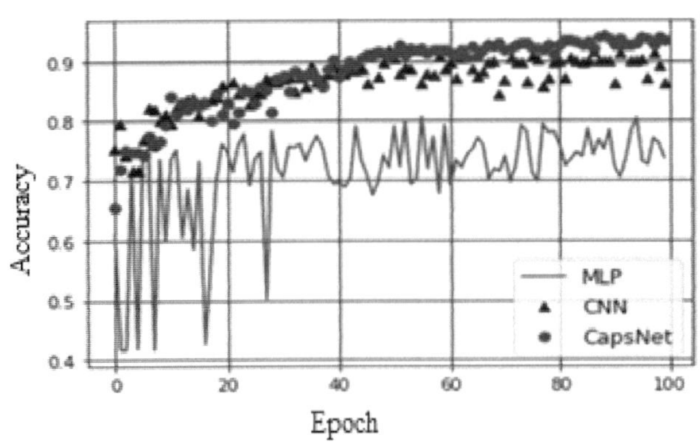

Figure 3. Validation accuracies obtained from MLP, CNN and CapsNet (Tiwari et al., 2021)

The results in terms of average accuracy, average precision, F1 scores and recall values have been presented in Table 1 (Tiwari et al., 2021). These quantitative values indicate better performance of CapsNet than MLP and CNN architectures.

Table 1. Accuracies, precisions, F1 scores and recall values

Models	Average accuracy	Average precision	F1 scores	Recall values
MLP	0.76	0.78	0.78	0.76
CNN	0.95	0.95	0.95	0.95
CapsNet	0.99	0.98	0.98	0.98

2.2 Classification of Stratum Corneum to Diagnose Psoriasis (Pal et al., 2018)

Stratum corneum classification has been performed using skin biopsy images (Figure 4), which have been taken from 120 patients. If stratum corneum layer has been lost during tissue processing, then the image has been ignored. 2 experts have labelled these images.

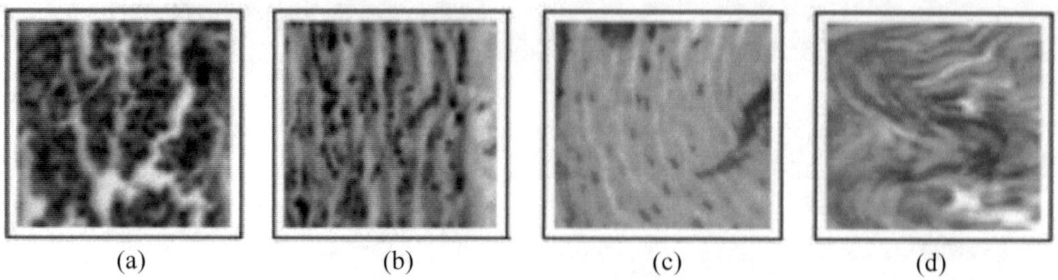

Figure 4. Example image patches showing neutrophils, which are dark blue colored and circular shaped cells, and nucleus which are light blue colored and oval shaped cells (a,b); Image shows only nucleus (c); Image shows neither neutrophils nor nucleus (d) (Pal et al., 2018)

Affected tissues have been obtained in 10% formalin by experienced dermatologists after clinical confirmation of psoriasis. Thin sections (5μM) have been selected to prepare slides and stained by using biomarkers (i.e., hematoxylin and eosin). These slides have been saved under a microscope with the highest magnification (i.e., 10X magnification) to fit whole-biopsy samples efficiently and the images (1936x2584 pixels) have been obtained by the microscope.

The CapsNet architecture designed in this work includes 2 sections called as primary and secondary capsule. The architecture has been constructed so that the receptive fields can avoid crowding. Here, the term crowding corresponds to existence of multiple-samples of the same entity in the receptive fields in a capsule.

In a region of interest of the image patch I, the probability (K) of neutrophils is denoted by the length of the output vector that is obtained from secondary capsule. Several neutrophils can be found in the image patch. Therefore, the probability of neutrophils has been obtained by taking average of the K probabilities. If the probability of neutrophil in a patch I is represented by p_I and the default loss function (binary cross-entropy) L is used in the training stage, the function to be minimized is written by y_I, which has zero value when the patch does not include a neutrophil and one otherwise, as;

$$L = - y_I * log(p_I) - (1 - y_I) * log(1 - p_I) \quad (1)$$

The results of patch classifiers with ResNet-50 and the proposed method have been presented with several metrics. They are given in Table 2 for comparative evaluations.

Table 2. Accuracies, precisions, F1 scores, numbers of the parameters, load time and prediction time

Architecture	Accuracy	Precision	F1 score	Recall	Parameters (Million)	Load Time (in second)	Prediction Time (second/image)
ResNet-50	0.94 ±0.02	0.95 ±0.015	0.91 ±0.036	0.87 ±0.078	23.5	2.15	0.021
The network in (Pal et al., 2018)	0.92 ±0.013	0.94 ±0.027	0.88 ±0.027	0.84 ±0.064	0.1	0.26	0.087

2.3 Classification of Skin Cancer Lesions (Cruz et al., 2020)

Automated classification of lesions to diagnose skin cancer using a CapsNet architecture has been performed with publicly available image sets (Figure 5). These data sets have been provided from BioGPS (Web_1, 2021) and the HAM-10000 dataset (Tschandl et al., 2018), which contains 10015 dermatoscopic images of 7 pigmented lesions, (benign keratosis-like lesions, melanocytic nevi, basal cell carcinoma, dermatofibroma melanoma, vascular skin lesions, and actinic keratoses)

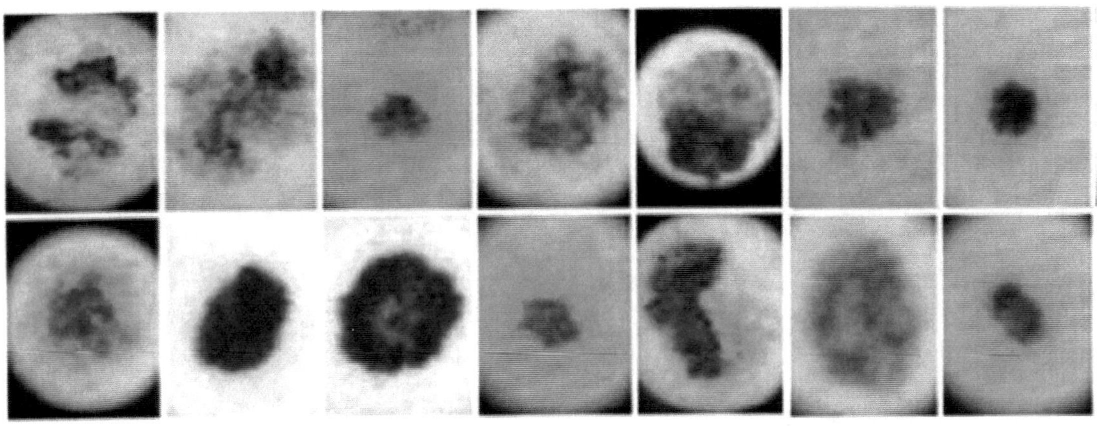

Figure 5. Example cancer images showing skin lesions (Cruz et al., 2020)

Transfer learning has been used to train the network architecture to identify cancerous cells from images. The network has been trained and tested by using 7010 and 3005 images respectively. In the CapsNet architecture (Figure 1), ReLU, softmax adam and cross-entropy functions have been used. The number of epochs, batch sizes and learning rate have been determined as 50, 10 and 0.001 respectively.

Epochs and the accuracies obtained from validation and training steps are shown in Figure 6a. The validation and training loss are presented with red and blue color respectively in Figure 6b.

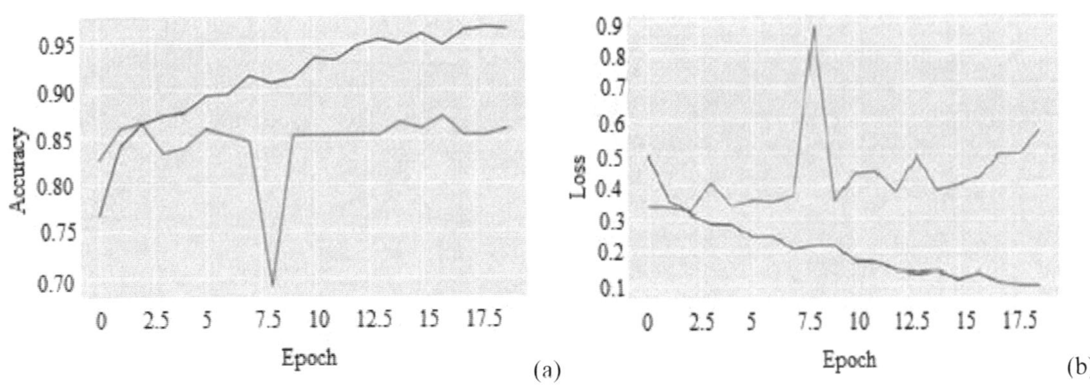

Figure 6. Testing and training accuracy are presented with red and blue respectively (a); Validation and training loss are presented with red and blue color respectively (b) (Cruz et al., 2020)

2.4 Classification of Melanoma Type of Skin Cancer (Boaro et al., 2020)

Skin cancers can be grouped as non-melanoma and melanoma. For this classification, image data sets including 4018 images (1084 melanoma cases and 2934 non-melanoma cases) have been provided from ISIC database (Web_2, 2021). Mirroring and rotations have been applied to increase the number of images. After these operations, 5509 images have been obtained totally and they have been re-sized to 600x408.

Binary masks obtained from ISIC have been used to achieve high classification performance by highlighting only the lesion areas and excluding ir-relevant regions. Figure 7 shows an example image (Figure 7a), a binary mask (Figure 7b) and the lesion region (Figure 7c) generated by using the mask image.

(a) (b) (c)

Figure 7. Example image showing a lesion (a), binary mask (b), the lesion region (c) (Boaro et al., 2020)

The network architecture consists of VGG16 network (which has been pre-trained using commonly known ImageNet (Russakovsky et al., 2015)), and the original CapsNet (Figure 1). In the combined architecture, image features have been obtained by the VGG16 and relationships in these feature sets have been obtained by the CapsNet.

The results obtained from the original CapsNet and the combined architecture are given in Table 3 as average accuracies, recalls, specificities and also areas under the Receiving Operating Characteristic (ROC) curves (Boaro et al., 2020).

Table 3. Accuracies, recalls, specificities and areas under the ROC curves

Architecture	Accuracies	Recalls	Specificities	Area under the ROC
CapsNet	0.86	0.85	0.86	0.86
VGG16 and CapsNet	0.92	0.91	0.93	0.90

Validation loss and validation accuracy graphics have also been shown in Figure 8 to indicate performance of the combined network structure.

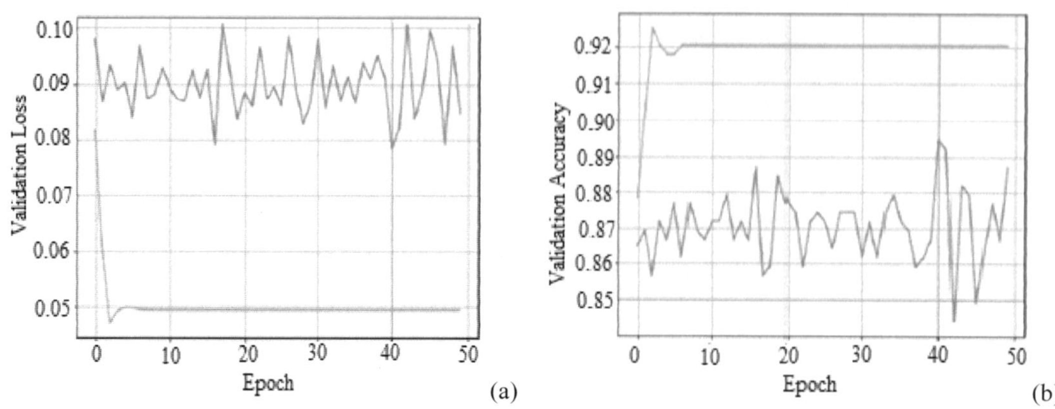

Figure 8. Validation loss (a) and accuracy (b) of CapsNet (blue) and the combined model (yellow) (Boaro et al., 2020)

3. CONCLUSION AND DISCUSSION

In this work, the role of CapsNets in classification of skin lesions has been examined by addressing those related works proposed in the literature.

Skin lesion classifications with CapsNets provide quite promising results when they are compared to the results obtained from related works.

Experimental works to determine presence or absence of neutrophils in an image patch to diagnose psoriasis showed that the CapsNet based model, although it has with less parameters, achieves comparable performance to ResNet-50.

Experiments for melanoma detection indicated that the performance of classification with CapsNet can be improved when high-level features are extracted using a pre-trained VGG16. Also, studies on the application of multi-layer perceptron, CNN and CapsNet to classify benign nevus and malignant melanoma showed that the CapsNet is the most appropriate classification architecture for these images.

Therefore, in the literature, although different skin diseases and image data sets having different characteristics have been handled, it has been observed that CapsNet based architectures provide efficiency in terms of accuracy and parameters required for lesion classification from skin images. However, further researches with increased number of images are still needed in this area.

Also, datasets are usually unbalanced which can compromise the learning step of the network. Therefore, balanced number of images should be used in the data sets to avoid biasing. To increase the number of images, operations such as rotation and mirroring should not be used since they only lead to repeat the same image in the data set. More efficient image augmentation algorithms should be applied to generate new synthetic images.

REFERENCES

Boaro J.M.C., Cutrim dos Santos P.T., et al., 2020. Hybrid Capsule Network Architecture Estimation for Melanoma Detection. *Int. Conf. on Systems, Signals and Image Processing (IWSSIP)*, Niteroi, Brazil, pp. 93-98.

Cruz M.V., Namburu A., Chakkaravarthy S., Pittendreigh M., Satapathy S.C. 2020. Skin Cancer Classification using Convolutional Capsule Network (CapsNet), *Journal of Scientific and Industrial Research*, Vol. 79, No. 11, pp. 994-1001.

Fritsch P., Burgdorf W. 2006. The Skin and Its Diseases: An Overview. European Journal of Dermatology, Vol.16, No.1, pp.209-212

Litjens G., Kooi T., Bejnordi B.E., Setio A.A.A., Ciompi F., Ghafoorian M. et al. 2017. A Survey on Deep Learning in Medical Image Analysis, *Medical Image Analysis,* Vol. 2017, No. 42, pp. 60–88.

Liu Y., Jain A., Eng C. et al., 2020. A Deep Learning System for Differential Diagnosis of Skin Diseases. *Nat. Med.*, Vol. 26, No. 1, pp. 900–908

Marks R.M., Knight A.G., Laidler P. 2012. *Atlas of Skin Pathology*. Springer, Netherlands

Pal A., Chaturvedi A., Garain U., Chandra A., Chatterjee R. 2016. Severity Grading of Psoriatic Plaques Using Deep Cnn Based Multi-task Learning. *In 23rd Int. Conf. on Pattern Recognition (ICPR 2016)*, Cancun, Mexico, pp. 1478-1483

Pal A., Chaturvedi A., Garain U., Chandra A., Chatterjee R., Senapati S. 2018. CapsDeMM: Capsule Network for Detection of Munro's Microabscess in Skin Biopsy Images. *International Conference on Medical Image Computing and Computer-Assisted Intervention (MICCAI 2018),* Granada, Spain, pp. 389-397

Pal A., Garain U., Chandra A., Chatterjee R., Senapati S. 2018. Psoriasis Skin Biopsy Image Segmentation Using Deep Convolutional Neural Network. *Computer Methods and Programs in Biomedicine*, Vol. 159, No.1, pp.59 – 69.

Roy A., Pal A., Garain U. 2017. Jclmm: A finite mixture model for clustering of circular-linear data and its application to psoriatic plaque segmentation. *Pattern Recognition*, Vol. 66, No.1, pp.160-173

Russakovsky O., Deng J., Su H., Krause J., Satheesh S., Ma S., Huang Z. et al. 2015. Imagenet Large Scale Visual Recognition Challenge, *International Journal of Computer Vision*, Vol. 115, No. 3, pp. 211–252.

Sabour S., Frosst N., Hinton G.E. 2017. Dynamic Routing Between Capsules. *Int. Conf. On Advances in Neural Information Processing Systems*, Long Beach, USA, pp. 3856–3866.

Tiwari S. 2021. Dermatoscopy Using Multi-Layer Perceptron, Convolution Neural Network, and Capsule Network to Differentiate Malignant Melanoma from Benign Nevus. *International Journal of Healthcare Information Systems and Informatics*, Vol. 16, No.3, pp.58-73

Tizek L., Schielein M.C., Seifert F. et al. 2019. Skin Diseases Are More Common Than We Think: Screening Results of An Unreferred Population at The Munich Oktoberfest. *European Academy of Dermatology and Venereology*, vol. 33, No.1, pp. 1421-1428.

Tschandl P., Rosendahl C., Kittler H. 2018. The HAM10000 Dataset, A Large Collection of Multi-source Dermatoscopic Images of Common Pigmented Skin Lesions. *Sci Data*, Vol.5, No.1, pp.1–9

Web_1, 2021. BioGPS, http://biogps.org (Access date: February 20, 2021)

Web_2, 2021. ISIC, https://www.isic-archive.com (Access date: February 20, 2021)

A SINGLE RGB IMAGE BASED 3D OBJECT RECONSTRUCTION SYSTEM

Damiano Oriti, Andrea Sanna, Francesco De Pace, Federico Manuri, Francesco Tamburello and Fabrizio Ronzino
Dipartimento di Automatica e Informatica, Politecnico di Torino
Corso Duca degli Abruzzi, 24, Torino, I-10129, Italy

ABSTRACT

Easy and fast digitalization of real objects is especially useful when considering augmented reality (AR) and virtual reality (VR), as reconstructed objects allow a better interaction between the real and virtual worlds than using pre-made 3D CAD models. Thanks to the ubiquity of smartphones and to the spread of immersive VR devices, the AR and VR technologies are rapidly becoming popular. However, an affordable, robust and easy to use solution for object digitalization is still missing. This paper presents a reconstruction system that allows users to convert a single photo of a real object into a digital 3D asset. A smartphone is used to capture a snapshot of the object, whereas a secondary computing device performs the reconstruction process by exploiting a pipeline of three Deep Learning methods. Several experiments have been conducted in order to assess the accuracy and robustness of the system by using a standard metric for measuring the reconstruction accuracy (chamfer distance). The main outcomes show that the proposed system has a comparable accuracy with respect to the state-of-the-art methods for 3D object reconstruction.

KEYWORDS

Machine Learning, Object Reconstruction, Object Pose Estimation, Augmented Reality, Virtual Reality

1. INTRODUCTION

In computer graphics and computer vision, 3D object reconstruction tackles the problem of generating a digital three-dimensional representation of an object given some observations (e.g., multiple images from different points of view) of it. Nowadays, digital 3D objects are extensively used in architecture, gaming, augmented reality (AR) and virtual reality (VR), filmmaking, product design, advertisement, manufacturing, cultural heritage, and in many other fields. Common techniques used to generate digital 3D objects are photogrammetry and digital sculpting; the former is the process of extracting three-dimensional information from two-dimensional data by identifying common points in two or more photos taken from different positions (stereo photogrammetry), whereas the latter can be seen as an *artistic approach* that allows specialized artists to use software and hardware tools to manually make the digital models of objects.

The digitalization of many human activities in recent decades, connected to the explosion in popularity of computers and smartphones, AR and VR, Internet of Things, and robotics, have entailed a rising demand for less expensive and better 3D object reconstruction systems.

The most common representations of 3D objects are polygonal meshes, voxels and point clouds (Figure 1 shows different 3D representations of the Stanford bunny[1]). A polygonal mesh is a collection of vertices connected through edges and faces, whereas the point clouds are sets of points with no topological information. The voxels are elements of a regular grid similar to a pixel matrix but in 3D space. Besides the positional information, vertices and points can also have normals and colors.

[1] https://graphics.stanford.edu/software/scanview/models/bunny.html

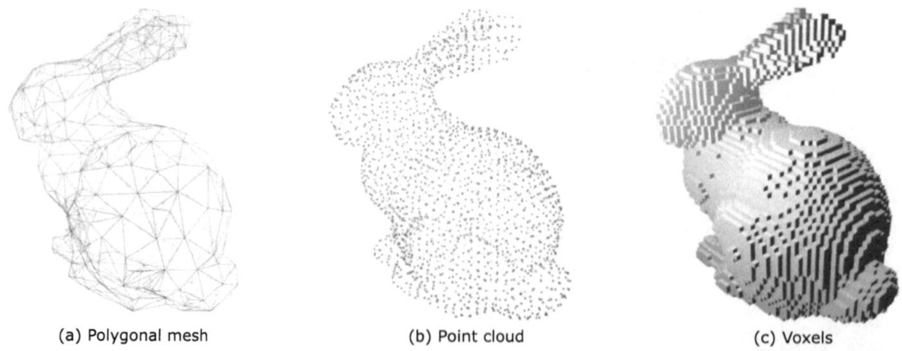

Figure 1. The Stanford bunny represented as (a) polygonal mesh, (b) point cloud and (c) voxels

Recently, some researchers have considered implicit representations for 3D objects such as implicit occupancy functions (Mescheder et al., 2019; Saito et al., 2020) and signed distance functions (Lin et al., 2020).

Following the success of Machine Learning (ML), and specifically Deep Learning (DL) and neural networks (NNs), in solving several image-related tasks (e.g., classification, segmentation, super sampling, deblurring, edge detection, keypoint detection, etc.), many researchers (Guo et al., 2015; Izadinia et al., 2016; Mescheder et al., 2019; Avetisyan et al., 2019; Han et al., 2019; Chen et al., 2020; Lin et al., 2020; Li et al., 2020; Popov et al., 2020) have been trying to apply the same basic principle of learning from data to the 3D object reconstruction problem. Since three-dimensional data can have various representations, different approaches have been proposed that have specific advantages and disadvantages in different applications (Xiao et al., 2020; Fahim et al., 2021).

This work proposes a 3D object reconstruction system designed for indoor scenes that only requires a computer and a smartphone supporting the Google ARCore framework. The smartphone is used (a) to acquire a single RGB image of each real object that the user intends to reconstruct, (b) to visualize the digital object after it has been reconstructed and, if necessary, (c) to adjust its position, rotation and scale relative to the real environment. The computer is used to compute the 3D object geometry as the smartphone is not powerful enough to support the reconstruction task, which is organized as a pipeline whose major steps are the following: (a) image masking aimed at isolating the object of interest by removing the background, (b) watertight mesh construction and (c) rotation estimation. The core of the reconstruction system is a DL solution called BSP-Net (Chen et al., 2020) capable of producing a mesh representation of an object given a single picture of it. The contribution of this paper is twofold: (a) a reconstruction pipeline based on state-of-the-art DL methods for reconstructing a 3D model of a real object given a single RGB image and (b) a smartphone-based system to generate the whole scene that can be used, for example, for AR and VR single or multi-user applications.

This paper is organized as follows: the most relevant works on object reconstruction are presented in Section 2, whereas the proposed reconstruction system is presented in Section 3. The experiments are discussed in Section 4 along with the related results; finally, some possible future work is proposed in Section 5.

2. RELATED WORK

2.1 Single RGB Image 3D Object Reconstruction Methods

Several methods for 3D object reconstruction from a single RGB image have been proposed in the last decade. Mescheder et al. (2019) use a NN classifier to represent an implicit 3D surface, whereas Chen et al. (2020) combine planes whose parameters are inferred using a NN to produce concave shapes.

SDF-SRN (Lin et al., 2020) learns signed distance functions from 2D images and it only requires a single view of objects at training time. Popov et al. (2020) can reconstruct multiple objects at the same time from a single image computing them in a common coordinate frame.

2.2 Smartphone-based 3D Object Reconstruction Systems

In this Section the most relevant object reconstruction systems that use a smartphone (or a tablet) as a capturing device are presented. Some reconstruction approaches (Tanskanen et al., 2013; Ondrúška et al., 2015) are based on creating a dense representation of the desired object by capturing several observations from different points of view. Tanskanen et al. (2013) use the integrated inertial sensors on the device to make the tracking and mapping process more robust; an efficient stereo matching algorithm is used to compute the depth values from which a dense 3D model with absolute scale is created. Ondrúška et al. (2015) propose an interactive system similar to the KinectFusion (Newcombe et al., 2011) where depth maps obtained through stereo-matching of RGB images are fused volumetrically; an implicit surface representation of the object is extracted, thus allowing the system to estimate a 6 degrees of freedom (DoF) pose for each frame. Muratov et al. (2016) can reconstruct an object with a 2-stage process: in the first stage they scan (i.e., capture multiple pictures) the real object by using the monocular camera of a smartphone while simultaneously acquiring IMU sensors data; then, in the second stage, depth maps are calculated by a bundle adjustment technique (Triggs et al., 2000) and used to construct a textured polygonal mesh. Donlic et al. (2017) exploit the Digital Light Processing (DLP) projector available on some tablets and pair it to the commonly available RGB camera to make a depth sensor, which works similarly to the Microsoft Kinect; they also take advantage of the built-in IMU sensors to get a robust and accurate point registration that is used to fuse multiple depth maps in a single voxel representation of the object.

The work presented in this paper differs from those approaches by requiring only one picture of the real object, thus making the proposed system much simpler to use.

3. THE 3D OBJECT RECONSTRUCTION SYSTEM

The proposed system is composed of an Android smartphone, which runs an application based on Unity3D[2] and Google ARCore[3], and a computer running an application written in Python. The system is designed as a client-server architecture; the client (i.e., a smartphone) is used (a) for capturing pictures of an indoor scene with embedded camera pose information and (b) for 3D object visualization in an AR visualization mode (Section 3.1), whereas the server (i.e., a computer) is used to process the captured photos of objects in order to transform them into 3D models (Section 3.2).

3.1 The Client

The smartphone application has two modes: (a) *photo mode* and (b) *AR object visualization mode* (Figure 2 illustrates the two modes). The photo mode allows users to take photos of the environment; similar to the photo application available on Android or iOS phones, this mode provides a gallery where users can visualize all the pictures they have taken and eventually delete some of them. After taking a picture, the users can save it in the gallery or discard it to take another image.

The application converts a new photo from the YUV-420-888 encoding format, that ARCore returns when using the function *GoogleARCore.CameraImageBytes()*, to the RGB format that is required for the correct visualization of the pictures in the Unity3D application and for the reconstruction software running on the server.

Besides using ARCore to take pictures, the smartphone application takes advantage of the Google AR framework to map the environment; in this way, it is possible to keep track of the smartphone position and rotation relative to a coordinate frame that is constructed at the start of the application.

[2] https://unity.com
[3] https://arvr.google.com/arcore

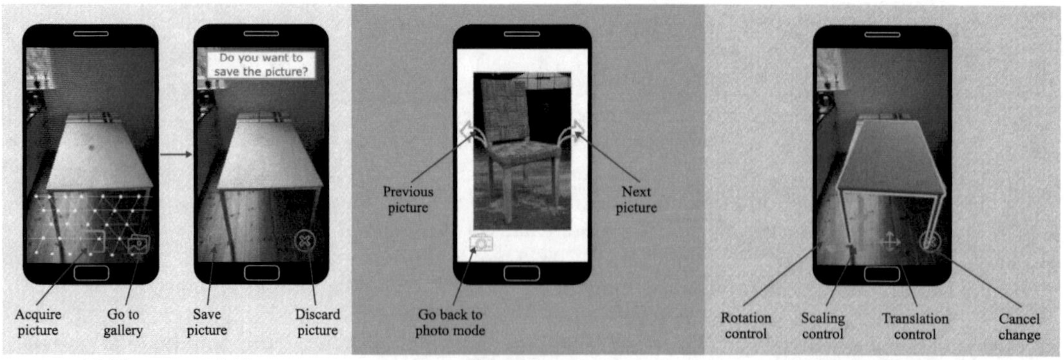

(a) Picture acquisition (b) Gallery (c) Pose adjustment

Figure 2. The smartphone application has two modes: (a-b) *photo mode* and (c) *AR object visualization mode*. The user can capture new photos of the environment in the photo mode (a), whereas images can be displayed in the gallery (b). The transformation controls can be used to move, rotate or scale virtual objects in the scene in the AR visualization mode (c). The scale is uniform across all dimensions, whereas rotation is limited to the vertical axis. When translated, virtual objects are constrained to stay within the room boundaries

In order to place the digital objects within the boundaries of the real environment, the ARCore plane detection functionality is used to detect floors and walls, which are shown as virtual grids overlapping the actual scene. The user can place one anchor for each object, which is used as a placeholder to position the digital object, on the planes detected by ARCore. On the contrary, the rotation is automatically estimated by the server during the reconstruction process by using a DL solution, as explained in Section 3.2.

When at least one object has been reconstructed by the server and sent to the client, users can switch to the AR object visualization mode in order to visualize the reconstructed virtual objects. By selecting an object, the user can apply three different transformation operations: translation, rotation and scaling. When an object is selected, the transformation controls appear at the bottom of the screen, as shown in Figure 2 (c). Since the real objects are supposed to lie upright on the ground, the rotation control is limited to the vertical axis, allowing the user to correct the rotation in case the estimation fails. Since the reconstruction process preserves the relative dimensions of the actual object, the scaling control is uniform across all the three dimensions. Translation is constrained to be on the floor and within the room walls that ARCore detects, as the virtual objects should overlap the real objects.

3.2 The Server

The server executes the reconstruction pipeline which is illustrated in Figure 3. The first step segments the image in foreground (i.e., the region of the image containing all the pixels of the object) and background (i.e., all pixels not belonging to the object), inasmuch it is not guaranteed that the user can take pictures with a perfectly uniform background, which is necessary for BSP-Net to output a clean mesh.

In order to determine which pixels belong to the foreground object, Mseg (Lambert et al., 2020) has been used. Mseg is a neural network model based on HRNet (Sun et al., 2019) designed for high resolution semantic segmentation of images; semantic segmentation is the task of assigning a class or category label (i.e., determining which class the object belongs to) to every pixel in the image. Given the original color picture, Mseg provides a new image with gray-coded segmentation regions, where each tone of gray represents a specific object class.

Assuming that the central image pixel includes the object of interest, a flood fill operation can be executed in order to convert the semantic segmentation image to a binary mask that can be later used to separate the foreground object from the background. At the current stage, if the photo contains multiple instances of the same object category, the segmentation works correctly only if the instances are clearly separated. Before executing BSP-Net, the new image with the removed background is first converted to a grayscale image, then it is cropped, resized and padded in order to have a fixed-sized image with constant padding, which helps to have consistent results, as shown in Section 4.

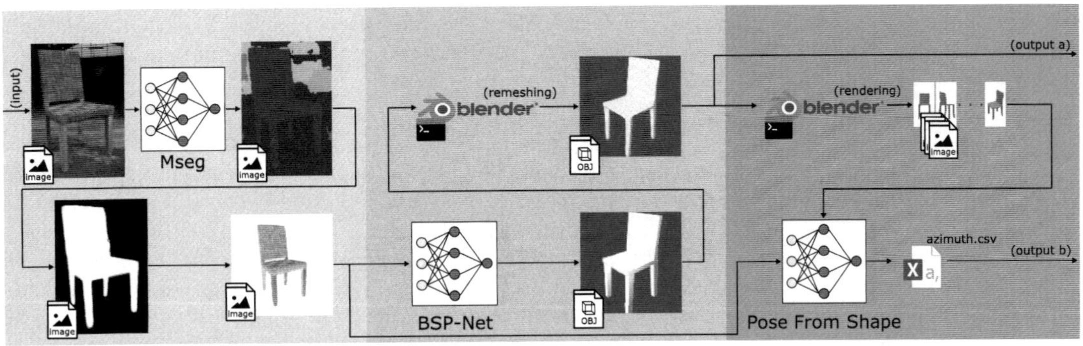

(a) Image segmentation (b) Reconstruction (c) Rotation estimation

Figure 3. The reconstruction pipeline consists of three steps: (a) isolation of the object of interest in the image by removing the background, (b) construction of a watertight mesh and (c) estimation of the object rotation about the vertical axis. The three major steps are in turn divided into seven sub-steps

The second step is the construction of a mesh given the grayscale picture of the object without the background. A grayscale image is required for BSP-Net because the neural network is designed to process grayscale images, although it could technically be modified to accept color images as input. Secondly, BSP-Net has been trained on $128{\times}128px$ images, thus the grayscale image is also downscaled to the required pixel resolution. After converting the input to the appropriate format, BSP-Net is executed and the constructed mesh is saved on the disk.

The constructed mesh is watertight, that is, it consists of one closed surface without holes. BSP-Net has been designed to exploit the binary space partitioning idea: a 3D shape is constructed as a union of convex parts, which are in turn obtained by combining multiple planes. Since BSP-Net constructs the 3D shape as a union of convex parts, it can produce concave shapes. However, the output tends to be very messy with a lot of intersections among the convex parts. In order to get a topologically cleaner mesh, a remeshing algorithm provided by Blender[4] is employed (Figure 4 shows a comparison between the output of BSP-Net and the remeshed object).

The final step of the reconstruction pipeline is the estimation of the object rotation about the vertical axis, since it is assumed that the objects lie upright on a horizontal plane (usually the floor). The Pose From Shape (Xiao et al., 2019) neural network is employed in order to estimate the object rotation. As its name suggests, Pose From Shape is capable of estimating the pose of a real object given several views of it, or even of a simplified 3D model approximating the real object. The proposed solution exploits the reconstructed mesh in order to produce, through rendering, twelve views of the object with an azimuth in the range [0, 360°] with a delta angle of 60° and a roll in the range [0, 30°] with a delta angle of 30°.

(a) BSP-Net output (b) Blender remesh

Figure 4. Comparison between the polygonal mesh model produced by BSP-Net and the remeshed model. Blender is used in command-line mode in order to remesh the output of BSP-Net. The typical mesh constructed by BSP-Net has an irregular topology (a); the new mesh has a cleaner topology after remeshing (b)

[4] https://www.blender.org

The rendered model is the remeshed object and Blender is used in command-line mode to automatically render the required views (Figure 3 (c) illustrates the described process from rendering to object pose estimation).

3.2.1 Server Configuration and Interprocess Communication

The computer used as server is equipped with a Nvidia GPU supporting CUDA in order to speed up the DL code that handles the semantic segmentation, the proper reconstruction and the rotation estimation steps of the pipeline.

The reconstruction program and the program handling the data transfer between the server and the client are two separate processes and they are executed independently of each other. Communication and synchronization between the two processes are handled through file writing and reading. When the server receives an image and its identifier from a client through the data transfer process, it reconstructs the corresponding object mesh through the reconstruction process and it sends the result with its corresponding identifier back to the client.

4. EXPERIMENTS

The proposed reconstruction pipeline has been tested by using samples from the Pix3D dataset (Sun et al., 2018), which contains images of real objects and associated ground-truth (GT) 3D models. Three object categories have been tested on which both BSP-Net and Mseg had been trained: chairs, sofas and tables.

In order to quantitatively evaluate the reconstruction accuracy, the chamfer distance (CD) (Chen et al., 2020) metric has been used for each pair of reconstructed model and GT CAD model. The meshes obtained by using the described reconstruction pipeline have been initially converted to a voxel grid with resolution 32^3, then the voxels have been converted to a point cloud by taking the center point of each voxel. The same procedure has been used to convert the GT meshes provided by Pix3D to point clouds. Before computing the CD, the point clouds have been translated in order to have the bounding box centered in the world origin, then they have been scaled in order to have the same size along the longest dimension.

Table 1 shows the average CD for the original BSP-Net when operating on synthetic images and the proposed pipeline operating on real photos. The results show that the proposed pipeline produces reasonably accurate reconstructions starting from a single real photo, despite the fact that BSP-Net had been trained only on synthetic images and Mseg does not produce an accurate segmentation (Figure 5 shows some reconstructed objects from real photos).

Table 1. Reconstruction accuracy of BSP-Net (synthetic data) and the proposed pipeline (real photos) for three different object classes. The evaluation metric is the chamfer distance (lower is better)

Class	BSP-Net (synthetic data)	Ours (real photos)
Chair	0.067	0.073
Sofa	0.090	0.071
Table	0.129	0.174
Mean	0.092	0.093

The pipeline has been designed to be as modular as possible, allowing to easily swap existing modules. As an example, the semantic segmentation module can be replaced with an improved version or with an alternative solution. The modular architecture of the reconstruction pipeline allows, for example, to use an occupancy network in place of BSP-Net, as long as it accepts an image as input and it outputs a 3D object representation that can be converted to a mesh. Experiments in this regard were conducted in order to find a suitable reconstruction method, which ended with the choice of BSP-Net as it performed better (Chen et al., 2020) that the tested occupancy network proposed by Mescheder et al. (2019) for the categories of interest, such as chairs, sofas and tables.

Figure 5. Some reconstructed models obtained by applying the proposed pipeline on Pix3D image samples

5. CONCLUSION

This paper presents a new 3D object reconstruction system intended for AR and VR applications, especially those where users can share the same environment. The system exploits three different state-of-the-art DL methods in order to construct a three-dimensional model of a real object given a single RGB photo captured using a smartphone and processed using a computer.

One limitation of the proposed system is that it requires a smartphone, even when the user is using a VR or AR head-mounted display device that is equipped with a camera and that, therefore, could be used in place of the smartphone for image acquisition and object pose adjustment. Another limitation is that overlapping objects of the same class in the image are not properly handled because the segmentation network cannot distinguish among instances. Moreover, the segmentation tends to include not negligible parts of the background in the object image region.

Some possible future developments will investigate the possibility of running the DL program on the same device used to acquire the pictures of the scene (e.g., a Microsoft HoloLens 2), enhancing BSP-Net in order to take into account the object color and retraining it with real or photorealistic images.

REFERENCES

Avetisyan et al., 2019. Scan2CAD: Learning CAD Model Alignment in RGB-D Scans. *Proceedings of IEEE/CVF Conference on Computer Vision and Pattern Recognition (CVPR)*. Long Beach, CA, USA, pp. 2609-2618.

Chen et al., 2020. BSP-Net: Generating Compact Meshes via Binary Space Partitioning. *Proceedings of IEEE/CVF Conference on Computer Vision and Pattern Recognition (CVPR)*. Seattle, WA, USA, pp. 42-51.

Donlic et al., 2017. On Tablet 3D Structured Light Reconstruction and Registration. *Proceedings of IEEE International Conference on Computer Vision Workshops (ICCVW)*. Venice, Italy, pp. 2462-2471.

Fahim et al., 2021. Single-View 3D reconstruction: A Survey of deep learning methods. *Journal Computers & Graphics*, Vol. 94, pp. 164-190.

Guo et al., 2015. Predicting Complete 3D Models of Indoor Scenes. *Journal CoRR*, Vol. abs/1504.02437.

Han et al., 2019. Image-Based 3D Object Reconstruction: State-of-the-Art and Trends in the Deep Learning Era. *Journal IEEE Transactions on Pattern Analysis and Machine Intelligence*, Vol. 43, No. 5, pp. 1578-1604.

Izadinia et al., 2017. IM2CAD. *Proceedings of IEEE Conference on Computer Vision and Pattern Recognition (CVPR)*. Honolulu, HI, USA, pp. 2422-2431.

Lambert et al., 2020. MSeg: A Composite Dataset for Multi-Domain Semantic Segmentation. *Proceedings of IEEE/CVF Conference on Computer Vision and Pattern Recognition (CVPR)*. Seattle, WA, USA, pp. 2876-2885.

Li, K., Rünz, M., et al., 2020. FroDO: From Detections to 3D Objects. *Proceedings of IEEE/CVF Conference on Computer Vision and Pattern Recognition (CVPR)*. Seattle, WA, US, pp. 14708-14717.

Lin et al., 2020. SDF-SRN: Learning Signed Distance 3D Object Reconstruction from Static Images. *Proceedings of Advances in Neural Information Processing Systems 33 (NeurIPS 2020)*. USA, pp. 11453-11464.

Mescheder et al., 2019. Occupancy Networks: Learning 3D Reconstruction in Function Space. *Proceedings of IEEE/CVF Conference on Computer Vision and Pattern Recognition (CVPR)*. Long Beach, CA, USA, pp. 4455-4465.

Muratov et al., 2016. 3DCapture: 3D Reconstruction for a Smartphone. *Proceedings of IEEE Conference on Computer Vision and Pattern Recognition Workshops (CVPRW)*. Las Vegas, NV, USA, pp. 893-900.

Newcombe et al., 2011. KinectFusion: Real-time dense surface mapping and tracking. *Proceedings of 10th IEEE International Symposium on Mixed and Augmented Reality*. Basel, Switzerland, pp. 127-136.

Ondrúška et al., 2015. MobileFusion: Real-Time Volumetric Surface Reconstruction and Dense Tracking on Mobile Phones. *Journal IEEE Transactions on Visualization and Computer Graphics*, Vol. 21, No. 11, pp. 1251-1258.

Popov et al., 2020. CoReNet: Coherent 3D Scene Reconstruction from a Single RGB Image. *Proceedings of European Conference on Computer Vision (ECCV)*. Glasgow, UK, pp. 366-383.

Saito et al., 2020. PIFuHD: Multi-Level Pixel-Aligned Implicit Function for High-Resolution 3D Human Digitization. *Proceedings of IEEE/CVF Conference on Computer Vision and Pattern Recognition (CVPR)*. Seattle, WA, USA, pp. 81-90.

Sun et al., 2019. High-Resolution Representations for Labeling Pixels and Regions. *Journal CoRR*, Vol. abs/1904.04514.

Sun et al., 2018. Pix3D: Dataset and Methods for Single-Image 3D Shape Modeling. *Proceedings of IEEE/CVF Conference on Computer Vision and Pattern Recognition*. Salt Lake City, UT, USA, pp. 2974-2983.

Tanskanen et al., 2013. Live Metric 3D Reconstruction on Mobile Phones. *Proceedings of IEEE International Conference on Computer Vision*. Sydney, NSW, Australia, pp. 65-72.

Triggs et al., 1999. Bundle Adjustment - A Modern Synthesis. *Proceedings of the International Workshop on Vision Algorithms: Theory and Practice*. Corfu, Greece, pp. 298-372.

Xiao et al., 2020. A survey on deep geometry learning: From a representation perspective. *Journal Computational Visual Media*, Vol. 6, pp. 113-133.

Xiao et al., 2019. Pose from Shape: Deep Pose Estimation for Arbitrary 3D Objects. *Proceedings of 30th British Machine Vision Conference (BMVC)*. Cardiff, UK.

FACE FEATURES-BASED PERSONALITY ASSESSMENT

Krishna Kumar Singh[1], Sadu Chiranjeevi[1] and Kethavath Sivalal[2]
[1]*Dept. of Computer Science and Engineering*
[2]*Dept. of Electronics and Communication Engineering*
RGUKT Nuzvid, Nuzvid, India-521 202, India

ABSTRACT

Personality assessment has been widely used in the professional psychology and signal processing fields. Recently, it has been a great interest from the computer vision research community in assessing personality from visual data. Many state-of-the-art models are assigned the Big-Five personality indicators using either external judges or personal interviews. We propose Face Features-based Personality Assessment (FFPA) that assesses the personality of a person based on one's facial features. It maps facial appearance into the Big-Five personality indicators, namely Extraversion, Agreeableness Conscientiousness, Neuroticism and Openness. The geometry-based and appearance-based approaches are used to extract features from the face and mapped to the personality indicators using Partial Least Square Regression (PLSR). The corresponding personality indicator values are collected by filling the online form of the Big-Five personality assessor. The computational experiments are performed on a synthetic dataset, consisting of the face images of 200 students. The experimental results show that the proposed model predicts the personality indicators with 0.95 coefficient of determination (approx.) and Mean Squared Error (MSE) is 0.001 (approx.).

KEYWORDS

Personality Assessment, Face/Facial Features, Big-Five Personality Indicators

1. INTRODUCTION

Personality is the combination of one's emotion, motivation, behavior and characteristics of their thought patterns. It has a great impact in representing one's life, well-being, health along with desires and preferences. Thus, the ability to detect one's personality traits has numerous applications in the fields of psychology, neuropsychology and signal processing.

Face appearance has a high influence on social interactions, which in turn could potentially influence personality (Rublee et al., 2011). Face or facial features may speak a lot about a person. There is a popular saying; Face is the index of mind (John & Srivastava, 1999). These have various applications in the field of computer vision. Its applications include face recognition, security, crime investigation and healthcare. However, facial features change when emotion changes.

Personality assessment is widely used in professional psychology for the administration and interpretation of experimentally supported personality traits. Physiognomy (Aparna & Ravi Kumar, 2014) deals with inferring the person using the facial features. It assesses the personality of a person based on outer appearance, especially the face. That is, it extracts the facial features and enables one for judging the personality of a person based on extracted facial features. The experiments were done on a small dataset, consisting of 25 people and the results show that their personality matched the output obtained by approximately 72%. Numerous computer vision approaches are proposed to analyze body postures, faces, and behaviors and infer apparent personality traits (Rammstedt & O. John, 2007; Sharat Chandra et al., 2015; Shu Liao et al., 2006; Noura Al Moubayed et al., 2014; Julio C. S. Jacques Junior, et al., 2019).

1.1 Big-Five Indicators

The Big-Five personality indicators are derived from examinations of the natural language terms, individuals use to portray themselves as well as other people. Its taxonomy serves an integrative function and provides a starting place for various researches in the descriptive taxonomy. The Big-Five dimensions Facet (John & Srivastava, 1999; Rammstedt & O. John, 2007) are enlisted in Table 1.

Table 1. Big Five Dimensions Facet

1. **Extraversion vs. introversion Gregariousness (sociable)**
Assertiveness (forceful)
Activity (energetic)
Excitement-seeking (adventurous)
Positive emotions (enthusiastic)
Warmth (outgoing)
2. **Agreeableness vs. antagonism Trust (forgiving)**
Straightforwardness (not demanding)
Compliance (not stubborn)
Modesty (not show-off)
Tender-mindedness (sympathetic)
3. **Conscientiousness vs. lack of direction Competence (efficient)**
Order (organized)
Dutifulness (not careless)
Achievement striving (thorough)
Self-discipline (not lazy)
4. **Neuroticism vs. emotional stability Anxiety (tense)**
Angry hostility (irritable)
Depression (not contented)
Self-consciousness (shy)
Impulsiveness (moody)
Vulnerability (not self-confident)
5. **Openness vs. closeness' to experience Ideas (curious)**
Fantasy (imaginative)
Aesthetics (artistic)
Actions (wide interests)

We propose FFPA to assess the personality of a person based on facial features. There are basically three parts of the work; first extracting facial features from the face images, second is to get the values of the corresponding Big-Five personality indicators, and the third is to map the extracted features to the corresponding personality indicators. Although facial features change on emotion, we have captured static features of the faces with the normal state in order to capture static personality aspects.

2. RELATED WORKS

In this section, the major category of approaches, which have been proposed to extract the facial features from the images and to assess one's personality are discussed. In a nutshell, as follows:

2.1 Face Features Extraction

2.1.1 Geometric-based Approaches

To extract facial features, these approaches use the size and the relative position of important components of the face. First, edges of important components of the face and the direction are detected. Then, feature vectors are built from the detected edges and direction (Urvashi Bakshi & Rohit Singhal, 2014). Gradient analysis and Canny filter are usually used for this purpose. In order to avoid lighting effects, Local Binary Patterns (LBP) (Sharat Chandra et al., 2015) is applied. LBP builds a histogram to create a feature vector for the face image.

2.1.2 Appearance-based Approaches

In these approaches, the image is processed as two-dimensional patterns (Urvashi Bakshi & Rohit Singhal, 2014). These achieved the best performance to extract face features because these maintain the important information of the image and reject the less important information. The Independent Component Analysis (ICA) and Principal Component Analysis (PCA) are widely used approaches to extract the feature vector (Sharat Chandra et al., 2015). It is observed that the ICA achieved better performance than PCA in the presence of noise such as expressions of face and variations in lighting.

2.1.3 Color-based Approaches

To detect the skin region, these approaches use different color models such as RGB (Urvashi Bakshi & Rohit Singhal, 2014). First, the gray-scale image is transformed into the Hue Saturation Value (HSV). The color and saturation values are eliminated to consider only the luminance part. The luminance part is transformed into a binary image by using a certain threshold. After thresholding, certain opening and closing operations are applied to remove noise. Then facial features are extracted from the binary image.

2.2 Personality Assessment

The Vedic Personality Inventory (Dasa, D.G., 1999) is based on the Vedic concept of the three gunas, or modes of nature. It is an instrument that assesses the validity of the three guna constructs. A sample of 619 persons of varying ages and occupations from the Southeastern United States is studied. In (Beatrice Rammstedt, & Oliver P. John b, 2007), the authors proposed Automatic Personality Perception (APP) that automatically predicts the personality indicators of the people that they attribute to others. They mapped facial appearance into the Big-Five personality indicators to assess the personality of individuals. The experiments are performed on the Facial Recognition Technology (FERET) corpus, consisting of a total of 829 face images. The results show that it predicts with an accuracy of around 65%. In (Rublee et al., 2011), the authors give more importance to the first impression of the faces generated artificially and visualize the characteristics having an effect on first impressions for several personality traits. The shape variations and texture of the faces are extracted by Principal Component Analysis (PCA). They established the relationship between first impressions, facial characteristics and self-reported personality traits. The experimental results reveal that the model fails to reliably infer personality indicators from either first impressions or facial features.

An approach is proposed based on physiognomy in (Aparna & Ravi Kumar, 2014). It first extracts facial features and enables one for assessing the personality of a person based on the extracted facial features. The authors also considered various measurements of facial features such as ear length, nose length, forehead length, lip axis, eye axis, the distance between the eyes and forehead width. A personal interview with the individual is conducted to get the Big-Five personal indicators. The experiment is conducted on a small dataset, consisting of 25 individuals. It is found that their personalities are matched with the output obtained by approximately 72%.

A new approach is proposed to automatic personality recognition based on Facebook profile pictures in (Cristina Segalin et al., 2017). The authors extracted visual features such as hue, valence and saturation and also content features from the Instagram profile pictures to predict the personality in (Bruce Ferwerda & Marko Tkalcic, 2018). In (Guntuku et al., 2019), the authors extracted interpretable features of profile and posted pictures to uncover the associations with users' depression and anxiety. A Deep Neural Networks based is proposed for estimating the personality traits from portrait pictures in (Moreno-Armendáriz et al., 2020).

The proposed FFPA is different from the state-of-the-art approaches in terms of region of face features and the way of assigning Big-Five indicators. The state-of-the-art approaches are mainly assigned the Big-Five indicators either with the help of external judges or personal interviews. In our method, the Big-Five indicators are collected from the participants by filling the online standard questionnaire. Further, many existing approaches have considered the rectangular face image that includes ears and neck also. Whereas, the proposed approach considers the face features that reside inside the convex hull of the first 27-facial landmarks (V. Kazemi & J. Sullivan, 2014). Then, PLSR (Ng, K.S., 2013) used for mapping the extracted facial features with the personality indicators.

3. THE PROPOSED WORK

The steps involved in the proposed FFPA are as follows:

1. The face is cropped from the face image. Haar Cascade (P Viola and M J. Jones, 2001) method is used to detect the faces.
2. The facial features are extracted using Oriented FAST and Rotated BRIEF (ORB) method (Rublee et al., 2011).
3. The landmark points of the face are identified using the dlib[1] python library.
4. A convex hull considering the first 27 landmarks of the step-3 is drawn.
5. The face features falling inside the convex hull are considered as facial features for mapping. These features are the response part of the ORB features.
6. Finally, the extracted face features are mapped to personality indicators using PLSR.

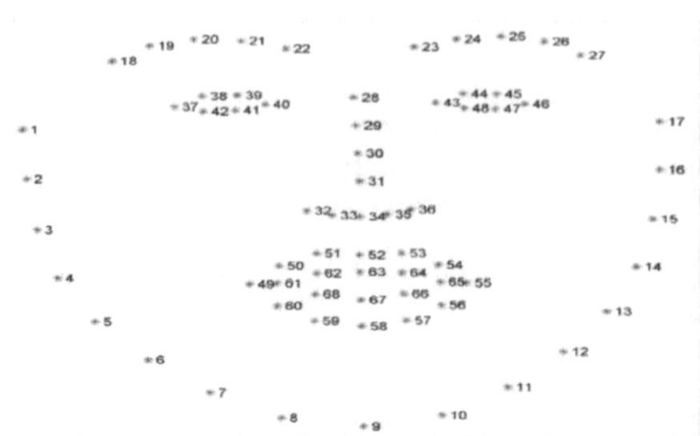

Figure 1. The 68 Facial Landmark Points extracted based on (V. Kazemi & J. Sullivan, 2014)

[1] http://dlib.net/

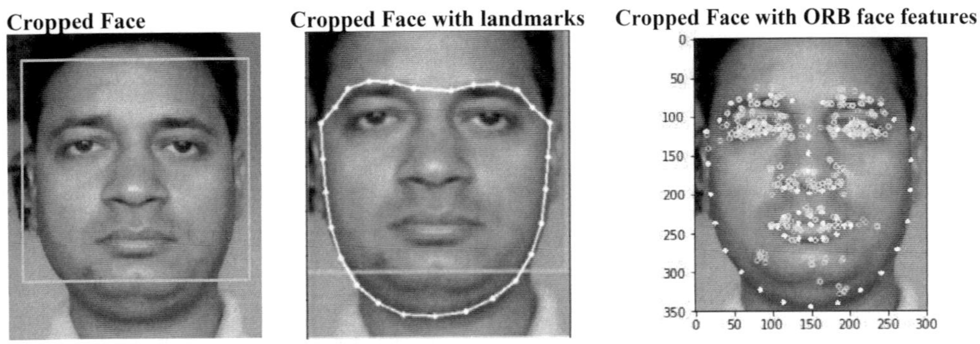

Figure 2. Shows the detection of facial features for mapping

3.1 Face Features Detection

Given a face image, the face is detected using Haar Cascade method (P Viola and M J. Jones, 2001). Once the face is detected, one thousand facial features are extracted using ORB (Rublee et al., 2011). It is an efficient and better alternative to the state-of-the-art methods for detecting the facial features. Given a pixel P in an array, it compares the brightness of P to surrounding 16 pixels that are in a small circle around P. Pixels in the circle are then sorted into three classes (lighter than P, darker than P or similar to P). If more than 8 pixels are darker or brighter than P than it is selected as a keypoint. It uses a multiscale image pyramid at different scales. After locating key points at different scales, it assigns an orientation to each keypoint like left or right facing depending on how the levels of intensity change around that keypoint. Next, we use the method (V. Kazemi & J. Sullivan, 2014) to detect the facial landmarks as shown in Figure 1. A convex hull covering the first 27 facial landmarks is considered for confining the facial features. That is, the facial features that fall within the convex hull are used further for mapping with the Big-Five personality indicators. Although the face contains around one thousand features, there are facial features range in 500-600 are falling within the convex hull. We consider only 500 facial features for mapping in order to collect a uniform number of features from each face as shown in Figure 2. The extra facial features if any are ignored from dense regions (e.g., eyes).

3.2 Mapping Face Features to Personality Indicators

The face features are mapped to personality indicators using PLSR (Ng, K.S., 2013). PLSR reduces the predictors to a smaller set of uncorrelated components and performs least squares regression on these components, instead of on the original data. It is especially useful when your predictors are highly collinear, or when having more predictors than observations and where ordinary least-squares regression either produces large standard errors. The ORB features are composed of the coordinate point, size, response, and orientation of the feature point. In our model, the response value of each feature point is considered as a facial feature.

Table 2 shows the sample dataset. The columns F1, F2 ...F500 represent the facial features obtained from ORB. The values in the corresponding columns represent the response values of facial features. The last five columns of the dataset are the personality indicators data which are target (or dependent) variables for PLSR. These are values obtained by getting the participants to fill the online form for the Big-Five personality indicators.

Table 2. Sample Dataset

Face ID	F1	F2	F3	…	F500	O	C	E	A	N
1	15	11	13	…	11	0.31	0.51	0.26	0.14	0.17
2	15	11	13	…	11	0.64	0.8	0.96	0.73	0.26
3	9	23	21	…	7	0.51	0.57	0.85	0.73	0.71
.	.	.	.	.	.	.	.	.	.	.
.	.	.	.	.	.	.	.	.	.	.
.	.	.	.	.	.	.	.	.	.	.
200	15	20	30	…	20	0.2	0.57	0.72	0.61	0.31

F1 to F500 = Facial Features, Big-Five Personality indicators: O = Openness, C = Conscientiousness, E = Extraversion, A = Agreeableness, N = Neuroticism.

As the data set contains more features than the number of observations (or records) which is likely to contain multicollinearity problem, the Ordinary Least Square (OLS) regression is not preferred. Further, to extract latent features or reduce the dimensions of the ORB facial features obtained, it is observed that PCA is not suitable because it does not consider the correlation of features with the Personality indicators and shows random behavior as shown in Figure 3. Therefore, we use PLSR for mapping the facial features with the values of the personality indicators.

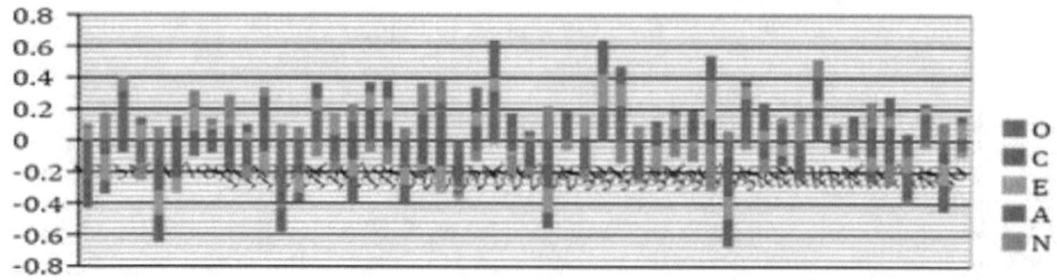

Figure 3. Correlation between the first 50 Principal Components (PCs) (on X-axis) and Personality Indicators (Y-axis)

4. EXPERIMENTS

The experiments are done on a synthetic dataset, containing the face images of 200 students. The corresponding Big-Five personality indicators of all students are collected based on their responses to the online standard questionnaire. The performance of the proposed model is evaluated based on two main metrics; coefficient of determination (R2 goodness of fit) and MSE. The values of these two metrics of the proposed model are collected on a varied number of principal components. The result of MSE and R2 corresponding to the Big-Five personality indicators on varying numbers of the principal components is shown in Figure 4.

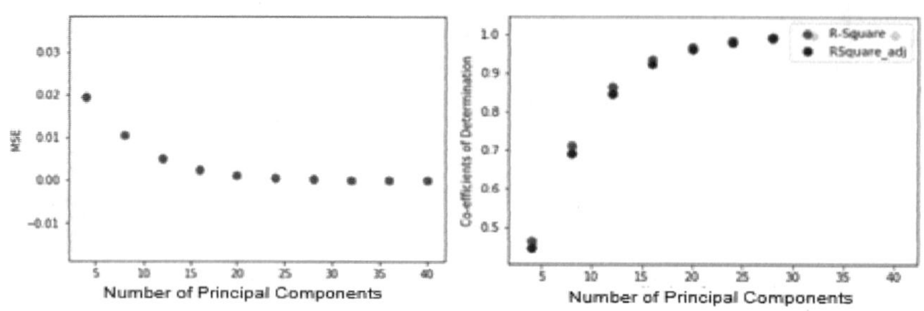

Figure 4. Plots of MSE and coefficients of determination corresponding to varied numbers of PCs

Figure 4 shows that the goodness of fit (>0.95) and MSE (<0.03) are satisfactory at the number of principal components greater or equal to 25. The 95% confidence interval of the score estimate of MSE is given by 0.001 (+/- 0.0028). The convergence of MSE, R-square, and R-square adjusted (RSquare_adj) with the increasing number of components in PLSR considering ORB face features as input show the significance of regression coefficients and so we can say that it is not an intercept-only model (Null Hypothesis).

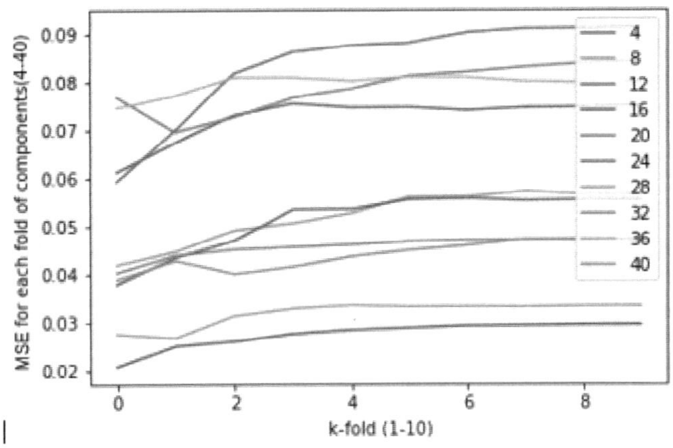

Figure 5. MSE corresponds to each iteration of the k-fold cross-validation corresponding to a varying number of PCs

The proposed model is further evaluated in terms of the variation of MSE by applying the 10-fold cross-validation. The variation of MSE corresponding to each iteration of the cross-validation is captured and is shown in Figure 5. It is observed that there is not much variation in MSE on a varying number of PCs across the 10-iterations.

5. DISCUSSION AND CONCLUSION

This work proposes FFPA for mapping facial appearance into the Big-Five personality indicators. A combination of both geometric-based and appearance-based approaches is used to extract facial features. The extracted facial features are mapped into the Big-Five personality indicators using PLSR. The performance of the proposed FFPA is demonstrated on a synthetic dataset, consisting of 200 face images. The results show that the proposed FFPA predicts the personality indicators with 0.95 coefficient of determination and MSE is 0.001. The convergence of MSE, R-square, and R-square adjusted with an increasing number of PCs in PLSR shows the significance and acceptance of the model.

However, a huge dataset and deep learning based face features extraction may provide better performance. Therefore, as an extension of this work, the proposed approach will be investigated with more data and deep learning based feature extractions to improve the performance in future.

REFERENCES

Aparna Sateesh Kini, Ravi Kumar, 2014. Personality Identification using Facial Features, *The International Journal of Engineering And Science (IJES)*, Volume-3, Issue-12, pp 39-47.

B. Rammstedt and O. John, 2007. Measuring personality in one minute or less: A 10-item short version of the Big Five Inventory in English and German. *Journal of Research in Personality*, 41(1):203–212.

Bruce Ferwerda and Marko Tkalcic, 2018. Predicting Users' Personality from Instagram Pictures: Using Visual and/or Content Features? *In Proceedings of the 26th Conference on User Modeling, Adaptation and Personalization (UMAP '18). ACM*, New York, NY, USA, 157–161. DOI:https://doi.org/10.1145/3209219.3209248.

Cristina Segalin, Fabio Celli, Luca Polonio, Michal Kosinski, David Stillwell, Nicu Sebe, Marco Cristani, and Bruno Lepri, 2017. What your Facebook Profile Picture Reveals about your Personality. *In Proceedings of the 25th ACM international conference on Multimedia (MM '17). Association for Computing Machinery*, New York, NY, USA, 460–468. DOI:https://doi.org/10.1145/3123266.3123331.

Dasa, D.G., 1999. The vedic personality inventory. An analysis of the gunas. Retrieved from Bhaktivedantacollege. org.

Ethan Rublee Vincent Rabaud Kurt Konolige Gary Bradski, 2011. "ORB: an efficient alternative to SIFT or SURF", *IEEE International Conference on Computer Vision, ICCV 2011*, Barcelona, Spain, November 6-13.

Guntuku, Sharath Chandra, Daniel Preotiuc-Pietro, Johannes C. Eichstaedt, and Lyle H. Ungar, 2019. "What twitter profile and posted images reveal about depression and anxiety." *In Proceedings of the international AAAI conference on web and social media*, vol. 13, pp. 236-246.

John, O. P., & Srivastava, 1999.The Big-Five trait taxonomy: History, measurement, and theoretical perspectives. *In L. A. Pervin & O. P. John (Eds.), Handbook of personality: Theory and research*, New York: Guilford Press. Volume-2, pp. 102–138.

Julio C. S. Jacques Junior, et al., 2019. "First Impressions: A Survey on Vision-based Apparent Personality Trait Analysis", *Spanish Ministry projects* TIN2016-74946-P.

Moreno-Armendáriz, Marco A., Carlos Alberto Duchanoy Martínez, Hiram Calvo, and Miguelangel Moreno-Sotelo, 2020. "Estimation of Personality Traits From Portrait Pictures Using the Five-Factor Model." *IEEE Access 8 (2020)*: 201649-201665.

Ng, K.S., 2013. A simple explanation of partial least squares. *The Australian National University*, Canberra.

Noura Al Moubayed, Yolanda Vazquez-Alvarez, Alex McKay, Alessandro Vinciarelli, 2014. "Face-Based Automatic Personality Perception", *ACM*.

P Viola and M J. Jones, "Rapid object detection using a boosted cascade of simple features [C]", *Proceedings of the 2001 IEEE Computer Society Conference on Computer Vision and Pattern Recognition (ICCVPR 2001)*, vol. 1, pp. 1-511-1-518, 8-14 Dec. 2001.

Sharat Chandra et al., 2015. "Do Others Perceive You As You Want Them To? Modeling Personality based on Selfies", *ACM*. ISBN 978-1-4503-3750.

Shu Liao, Wei Fan, Albert C. S. Chung and Dit-Yan Yeung, 2006. "Facial Expression Recognition Using Advanced Local Binary Patterns, Tsallis Entropies And Global Appearance Features", *IEEE International Conference on Image Processing*, pp. 665-668.

Urvashi Bakshi, Rohit Singhal, 2014. "A Survey on Face Detection Methods and Feature Extraction Techniques of Face Recognition", *International Journal of Emerging Trends & Technology in Computer Science (IJETTCS)*, Volume 3, Issue 3.

V. Kazemi and J. Sullivan, 2014. One millisecond face alignment with an ensemble of regression trees. *In IEEE Conference on Computer Vision and Pattern Recognition*, pages 1867–1874.

Wolffhechel K, Fagertun J, Jacobsen UP, Majewski W, Hemmingsen AS, et al. Interpretation of Appearance: The Effect of Facial Features on First Impressions and Personality. *PLoS* ONE 9(9): e107721. doi:10.1371/journal.pone.0107721.

ANALYSIS OF CAPSULE NETWORKS FOR IMAGE CLASSIFICATION

Evgin Goceri
Biomedical Engineering Department, Engineering Faculty
Akdeniz University, Dumlupinar Boulevard, 07058, Antalya, Turkey

ABSTRACT

Recently, the interest in convolutional neural networks have grown exponentially for image classification. Their success is based on the ability to learn hierarchical and meaningful image representation that results in a feature extraction technique which is general, flexible and can encode complex patterns. However, these networks have some drawbacks. For example, they need a large number of labeled data, lose valuable information (about the internal properties, such as shape, location, pose and orientation in an image and their relationships) in the pooling and are not able to encode deformation information. Therefore, capsule based networks have been introduced as an alternative to convolutional neural networks. Capsules are a group of neurons (logistic units) representing the presence of an entity and the vector indicating the relationship between features by encoding instantiation parameters. Unlike convolutional neural networks, maximum pooling layers are not employed in a capsule network, but a dynamic routing mechanism is applied iteratively in order to decide the coupling of capsules between successive layers. In other words, training between capsule layers is provided with a routing-by-agreement method. However, capsule networks and their properties to provide high accuracy for image classification have not been sufficiently investigated. Therefore, this paper aims (i) to point out drawbacks of convolutional networks, (ii) to examine capsule networks, (iii) to present advantages, weaknesses and strengths of capsule networks proposed for image classification.

KEYWORDS

Image Classification, Capsule Network, Dynamic Routing, Deep Network, Convolutional Neural Networks

1. INTRODUCTION

In recent years, the importance of deep neural networks has increased due to their great success in many fields. Particularly, Convolutional Neural Networks (CNNs) have been widely implemented for classification of images because of their learning ability by using convolution filters and non-linearity units (Seeland and Mader, 2021; Guoqing et al., 2021; Abbas et al., 2021). However, their architectures lead to two important issues. One of them is about the robustness of these architectures for affine transformation (e.g., shifting in pose). This problem is usually alleviated by various image augmentations. However, the testing dataset can present some unpredictable shifts. Therefore, CNNs need a huge amount of training dataset. The other problem is about the spatial relationships between features. CNNs have a tendency to memorize data instead of understanding it and they do not have the capability to learn the relationships between required features (Hinton et al., 2018). Several pooling algorithms can provide a little translation invariance. However, pooling methods do not store information about the location of features since they maintain only the presence information and ignore the pose information (Szegedy et al., 2013). To be able to overcome these two drawbacks in CNNs, Capsule Networks (CapsNets) (Sabour et al., 2017), new architectures based on the capsule concept (Hinton et al. 2011; Kosiorek et al.,2019; Wang and Liu, 2018), have been proposed.

Unlike CNNs, CapsNets can store information at a vector level not as scalar values. These capsule vectors (groups of neurons) represent richer information in the architecture. Also, to classify objects in an image, CapsNets use routing-by-agreement method. The routing process enables each capsule to maintain information, which is obtained from the parent (previous) capsules, and provides classification agreement by comparing the information. Therefore, CapsNets can store the orientation and location of components in an image. For example, a CapsNet can learn to decide whether a flower does exist in the image, and also whether it is rotated or located to the right/left. This property is called as equivariance. The authors in

(Jimenez-Sanchez et al., 2018) reported that this property reduces the requirement of huge data in the training stage. Therefore, CapsNets are promising for image classification.

CapsNets are new architectures and explorations in the literature about capabilities of CapsNets are focused on designing of capsule layers (Hinton et al., 2018; Rajasegaran et al., 2019; Deliege et al, 2018) and containment of extra convolutional layers to feed primary capsules for feature extraction (Nair et al., 2018; Phaye et al., 2018). However, the performance of CapsNets in classification of images have not been sufficiently investigated. Therefore, this paper aims (i) to point out drawbacks of CNNs, (ii) to examine CapsNets, (iii) to present advantages, strengths and weaknesses of the CapsNets proposed for image classification.

This paper has been organized as follows: Fundamentals of a CapsNet architecture and comparison with convolutional networks are explained in Section 2. CapsNet based image classification approaches are given in Section 3. Finally, discussion and conclusion are presented in Section 4.

2. FUNDEMANTALS OF A CAPSNET ARCHITECTURE AND ITS DIFFERENTIATIONS FROM A CNN

In the original CapsNet architecture (Sabour et al., 2017), capsule vectors have been used in the convolutional network. Also, instead of conventional down-sampling algorithms (e.g., maximum pooling), a dynamic routing mechanism has been implemented to link units within a capsule. This original CapsNet structure has been extended and its various models have been designed to achieve image classifications with high performance (Section 3).

Like CNNs, a CapsNet constructs a hierarchical representation of an image by passing it in layers. On the other hand, unlike deeper CNNs including many layers, the CapsNet in the original form includes merely 2 layers called as primary and secondary capsule layer. The primary layer captures low-level features. The secondary layer has the ability to predict the existence of an object and its pose information in the image (Figure 1). The main properties of a CapsNet and differentiations from a CNN architecture can be summarized as follows:

(i) Convolution is solely applied in the primary capsule layer as the first operation.

(ii) A series of feature channels are grouped to construct tensors in a CapsNet rather than performing a non-linear operation with scalar values obtained from convolutional filters. A squashing process is applied to increase non-linearity of the capsules. By the squashing process, a longer capsule is shrunk to a length less than 1 and a short capsule is shrunk to a length close to zero. In other words, squashing algorithm uses j *th* vector s_j and bounds its limit to [0.1] interval for probability modelling and preservation of vectoral-orientations. This process produces a vector v_j indicating the probability value about the presence of an object. The direction of this vector (that is also the output value of the capsule *j)* presents information about the pose of the object.

(iii) Routing by agreement is applied to optimize the weight values (w_{ij}) in a CapsNet rather than a back-propagation as it is usual in a CNN model. In the routing process, a capsule in a low-level transmits its input value into a capsule in the upper level. Therefore, these weights provide connections between the i*th* primary capsule (low level information) and j*th* secondary capsule (high level information). In other words, the weights provide affine transformation to learn part-whole relations.

(iv) Similar to a CNN model used for classification, the last layer of a CapsNet is a softmax layer, which is usually implemented by cross-entropy loss function, which can be computed for k*th* class is as (Sabour et al., 2017):

$$L_k = T_k\, max(0, r^+ - \|v_k\|)^2 + \alpha(1 - T_k) max(0, \|v_k\| - r^-)^2 \quad (1)$$

In (2), the term α (0.5) is a weight parameter which is used to guarante the final convergence. The term T_k refers to labels and gets 1 when r^- is 0.1, r^+ is 0.9 and an object, whose expected probability is greather than 0.9 (i.e., $\|v_k\| > 0.9$), does exist in k*th* class. The distance between positive samples are forced to be short by the marginal loss because 0.5 is not assigned to the threshold. Therefore a robust classifier is generated.

After the original CapsNet, discussed matrix capsules have been discussed and expectation maximization based routing have been applied (Hinton et al., 2018). Figure 1 shows connections in a standard convolutional network (Figure 1.a) and a CapsNet (Figure 1.b).

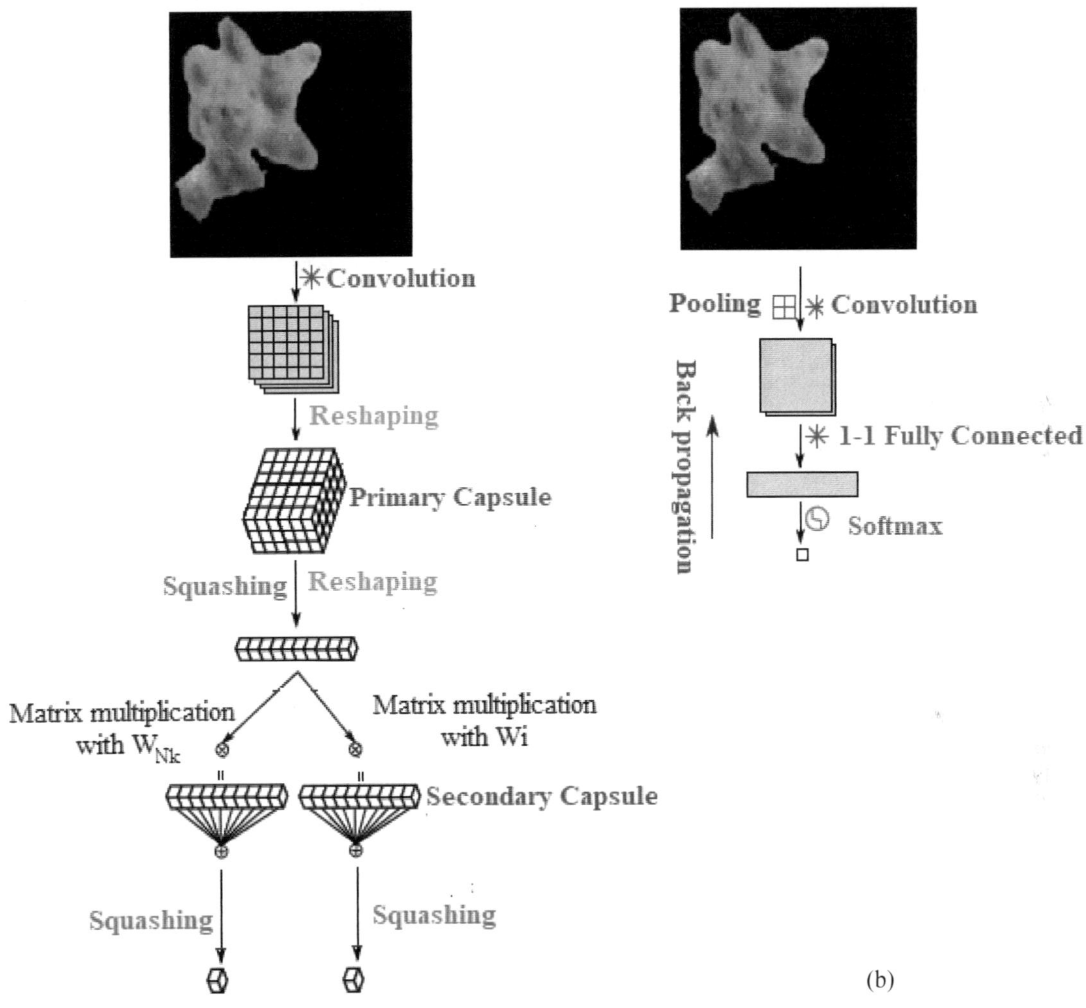

Figure 1. A CapsNet structure (a) and a covolutional network (b)

3. CAPSNET BASED IMAGE CLASSIFICATION TECHNIQUES

Various modifications of the original CapsNet architecture have been proposed to improve accuracy and to enhance the computational efficiency and representation capacity for image classification. For instance, in (Xi et al., 2017), the capacity of the network has been increased (by increasing both capsules' size and numbers of layers) according to the changes in the activation function. To generate semantic and structural information, a multi-scale feature extraction has been used in (Xiang et al., 2018). Then features' hierarchy has been encoded into primary capsule and a dropout has been applied to improve the robustness of the architecture. Another multi-scale CapsNet including five layers (input layer, convolution layer, primary and secondary capsule layer, output layer) has been proposed by the authors in (Wang et al., 2019) to classify hyper-spectral images. In (Ren 2019), different types of capsules have been grouped to reduce effects of the capsules that are useless or providing less contribution to the classification. The authors in (Mobiny and VanNguyen, 2018), modified the CapsNet architecture to use a consistent dynamic routing method to provide faster convergence. In (Neill 2018), pairwise learning has been integrated into the original CapsNet to provide better learning of relationships with a feature normalized contrastive loss. In another work (Ding et al., 2019), capsules are partitioned into several groups and corresponding high-level capsules are obtained by group reconstruction routing and then maximum pooling is used to avoid overfitting. In (Mandal et al., 2021) a hierarchical learning and two-phase dynamic routing approach has been used in multi-column CapsNet to provide macro and micro-level equivariance. In (Long et al., 2021) feature extraction has been provided by three convolutional layers instead of one in the modified CapsNet model. The authors in (Iesmantas and Alzbutas 2018) used five convolutional layers before the primary capsule layer. They also used margin loss and a multi-dimensional squashing function. In (Afshar et al., 2018) early-stopping algorithm has been used to increase generalization capability of the architecture for tumor types classification from magnetic resonance images.

The CapsNet models proposed recently to solve several image classification problems are presented in Table 1 with their properties, data sets and conclusions.

Table 1. Data sets, CapsNet models proposed for image classification and their conclusions

Reference	Data set	Model Property	Conclusion
(Mandal et al., 2021)	FashionMNIST, SVHN, handwritten digit datasets	A hierarchical learning and two-phase dynamic routing approach have been used in multi-column CapsNet to provide macro and micro-level equivariance	The performance of the model is higher than those performances obtained by other state-of-the-art multi-column networks
(Long et al., 2021)	8 categories of blood cells images	Feature extraction has been provided by three convolutional layers to obtain more specified feature map in order to feed the primary capsule layer	The model has a potential to assist physicians in classification of human blood cells
(Ren 2019)	Public images (e.g., MNIST, CIFAR-10)	Different types of capsules have been grouped to reduce effects of the capsules with less contribution (or useless) in classification.	Training of grouped capsules makes the model more robust and improves its generalization ability
(Xiang et al., 2018)	FashionMNIST and CIFAR-10	A multi-scale feature extraction has been used to generate semantic and structural information. Then features' hierarchy has been encoded into primary capsule and a dropout has been applied to improve the robustness of the architecture	The proposed model has competitive performance for classification of images from complex data sets with fewer number of parameters
(Xi et al., 2017)	MNIST and CIFAR-10 image data set	The capacity of the network has been increased (by increasing both capsules' size and numbers of layers) according to the changes in the function providing activation	The results indicate that integrating a convolution layer into the original CapsNet architecture increases validation accuracy by 0.41%
(Ding et al., 2019)	CIFAR-10/100 and SVHN	Capsules are partitioned into several groups and corresponding high-level capsules are obtained by group reconstruction routing and then maximum pooling is used to avoid overfitting	Computational complexity is reduced and recognition ability is increased compared to the the original model
(Wang et al., 2019)	Hyperspectral images from Indian pine and University of Pavia datasets	The network has been designed with five layers including a multi- and single-scale convolutional layer, a primary and secondary capsule layer	The model can manage spatial and spectral features and extract more relevant and hyper-spectral information from images

(Lei et al., 2019)	Hyperspectral images from Kennedy Space Center, Salinas and Pavia University datasets	An extra convolutional layer (before the primary capsule layers) has been integrated into the architecture to extract features from high-level layers and to increase the speed of the dynamic routing-by-agreement process	The model can provide isolation of invalid information and capture the long-distance dependencies of hyper-spectral images using.
(Neill 2018)	AT&T face recognition and verification dataset, labeled faces in the wild dataset	Pairwise learning has been integrated into the original CapsNet to provide better learning of relationships with a feature normalized contrastive loss	The learning ability of the network has been improved and faster convergence has been observed.
(Mobiny and VanNguyen , 2018)	Chest images obtained by computed tomography	A consistent routing, which enforces primary capsules matching with the same pixels to get the same coefficients, has been integrated into the original CapsNet.	The model is powerful in reconstructing the input from the final capsules and increases the network's efficiency.
(Afshar et al., 2018)	Magnetic resonance images showing brain tumors	Early-stopping algorithm has been used to increase generalization capability of the architecture	The model can outperform CNNs in tumor classification problem
(Iesmantas and Alzbutas, 2018)	Breast cancer histological images (stained with eosin and hematoxylin)	The architecture with seven layers has been constructed using five convolutional layers before the primary capsule layer, margin loss and multi-dimensional squashing function	The model can achieve classification of biopsy images to distinguish four types of breast tissue with high accuracy
(Wang et al., 2021)	Hyperspectral images from Kennedy Space Center, Salinas and Pavia University	The architecture has been designed with adversarial networks and used the information obtained by dual-channel spectral and spatial fusion to encode more relationships of the features in an image	Although promising results can be obtained from the proposed model, it leads to increase the computational complexity and needs optimization for this purpose
(Afshar et al., 2018)	Two chest X-ray datasets and external datasets of X-ray images	The original routing algorithm has been modified to extract more helpful features and also the original margin loss has been modified to set more penalty values for misclassified cases	The model presents satisfying performance and needs less number of parameters for training than its counterparts.
(Tsuji et al. 2020)	Optical coherence tomography images	Primary capsules have been fed with the outputs of five convolutional layers to be able to extract more features and leaky rectified linear unit has been used	High accuracy has been obtained. However, the model can classify only four types of cases. It should be trained and tested with other types of images
(Chang and Liu, 2020)	MNIST, affNIST and CIFAR-10	A multi-lane CapsNet by using strict-squashing function and optimizing dropout implementation to be able to classify images with complex background	The proposed model provides better results when they are compared to the results obtained from the original CapsNet
(Panigrahi et al., 2020)	Oral biopsy images	The secondary capsules in the original CapsNet have been modified as cancer capsules and parameters have been adapted according to the characteristics of the images to obtain high accuracy	The model can efficiently classify histopathological image data sets as benign or malignant to help detection of oral cancer
(Jia and Huang, 2020)	CIFAR-10, F-MNIST	The hierarchical CapsNet model has been constructed using residual convolutional layers, diverse enhanced primary capsules and adapting the sigmoid function in the routing algorithm	The model presents higher accuracy than its seven ensembles, but its computational cost should be reduced

(Xiang et al., 2021)	Breast ultrasound images	A three-dimensional residual-CapsNet (i.e., Res-CapsNet) model has been implemented to diagnose tumors using tumor masks obtained with U-Net from the images that have been cropped and resized.	The proposed approach has the potential to reduce mis-diagnosis and achieve better accuracy compared with the other CNN models.
(Koresh et al., 2021)	Optical coherence tomography images	Images have been classified using the CapsNet architecture after removing speckle noises with a hybrid noise reduction filter.	The proposed method can be applied to provide efficient corneal thickness measurements.
(Cruz et al., 2020)	Dermoscopy images (HAM10000 and BioGPS image datasets)	After re-sizing of the images to 28x28, the original CapsNet has been used with the Softmax function and the number of epochs, batch size learning rate, which have been chosen experimentally as 50, 10 and 0.001, respectively.	According to the results of experimental works, the proposed approach is more sensitive than the recent classifiers and presents high classification performance.
(Xue 2020)	Hyperspectral images from Indian pine and University of Pavia datasets	A generative adversarial network architecture has been implemented with three-dimensional capsules, batch normalization and the Tanh function. The routing mechanism does merely exist between capsule layers.	The proposed conditional generative adversarial training algorithm has the potential to increase the generalization ability for classification of hyperspectral images.
(Paoletti et al., 2020)	Hyperspectral images from Indian pine and Kennedy Space Center	To integrate spatial and spectral features, training of the CapsNet architecture has been provided with active learning by using a small set of labeled images.	The proposed method presents robust results even if the network is trained with small data sets.
(Maurya et al., 2021)	Indirect immune fluorescence images	The proposed CapsNet model containing a decoder and encoder section provides classification with the Sigmoid function in the final layer	The proposed approach produces results with better performance compared with the results of CNN based architectures.
(Santos et al., 2020)	Retinal fundus images in healthy and glaucomatous	The original CapsNet has been implemented with the appropriate parameters that have been selected experimentally for the images obtained by histogram equalization.	The proposed network has the potential to classify healthy and glaucoma cases from images.

4. DISCUSSION AND CONCLUSION

CNNs have been considered as efficient feature extractors. However, pooling layers in them lead to loss of spatial relations of pixels. Also, they are not always robust to affine transformations. Therefore, CapsNet have been proposed recently as a novel architecture to overcome those disadvantages of CNNs by encoding not only the presence of features but also their spatial relationships.

A CapsNet can learn both desired weights to extract features and pose parameters from the image. Multi-dimensional vectors (with entries indicating spatial changes like skewness, shifting, rotation and thickness) are used for pose modeling. For instance, in a medical case, an image can show different patterns leading to a diagnosis of a disease. To diagnose the disease, while a CNN architecture detects the existence of the features, a CapsNet architecture performs the same detection and also finds information about relationships between the features.

The dynamic routing algorithm in the CapsNet provides efficiency in mapping of low- and high-level capsules. Since a capsule contains collections of neurons and the routing process includes all capsules, the CapsNet has an ability for stronger representation when it is compared to conventional networks, which ignore some neurons in the pooling layer. Therefore, CapsNets achieve successful results using less images and provide more robustness to an affine transformation. However, redundant features can be collected with the dynamic routing. Also, if low-level capsules' information is too much, then the corresponding high-level capsules may lead to interference due to noise or other ir-relevant or redundant information. In addition, computational complexity is an important issue to deal with a large data network. Therefore, a CapsNet architecture should be designed carefully according to the problem handled to have a reasonable generalization capability and further researches are still needed to improve CapsNet based classifiers.

REFERENCES

Abbas, A., Abdelsamea, M.M., Gaber, M.M. 2021. Classification of COVID-19 in Chest X-ray Images Using DeTraC Deep Convolutional Neural Network. *Application Intelligence*, Vol.51, No.1, pp. 854–864

Afshar P., Mohammadi A., Plataniotis K.N. 2018. Brain Tumor Type Classification via Capsule Networks. *The 25th IEEE International Conference on Image Processing (ICIP),* Athens, Greece, pp. 3129–3133

Afshar P., Heidarian S., Naderkhani F., Oikonomou A., Plataniotis K.N., Mohammadi A. 2020. COVID-CAPS: A Capsule Network-based Framework for Identification of COVID-19 Cases from X-ray Images. *Pattern Recognition Letters,* Vol.138, No.1, pp.638-643

Chang S., Liu J. 2020. Multi-Lane Capsule Network for Classifying Images with Complex Background. *IEEE Access,* Vol. 8, No.1, pp. 79876-79886

Cruz M.V., Namburu A., Chakkaravarthy S., Pittendreigh M., Satapathy S.C. 2020. Skin Cancer Classification using Convolutional Capsule Network (CapsNet). *Journal of Scientific and Industrial Research (JSIR)*, Vol. 79, No. 11, pp.994-1001

Deliege A, Cioppa A, Van droogenbroeck M. 2018. Hitnet: A Neural Network with Capsules Embedded in A Hit-or-Miss Layer, Extended with Hybrid Data Augmentation and Ghost Capsules. *arXiv:1806.06519,* pp.1-19

Ding X., Wang N., Gao X., Li J., Wang X. 2019. Group Reconstruction and Max-Pooling Residual Capsule Network. *Proceedings of the Twenty-Eighth International Joint Conference on Artificial Intelligence*, Macao, China, pp. 2237-2243

Guoqing Li, Xuzhao Shen, Jiaojie Li, Jiuyang Wang. 2021. Diagonal-Kernel Convolutional Neural Networks for Image Classification. *Digital Signal Processing*, Vol.108, No.1, pp.1-8

Hinton G., Sabour S., Frosst N. 2018. Matrix Capsules with EM Routing. *The 6th Int. Conference on Learning Represent*ation, Vancouver, Canada, pp. 1-15.

Hinton G., Krizhevsky A., Wang S.D. 2011. Transforming Auto-Encoders. *International Conference on Artificial Neural Networks (ICANN),* Espoo, Finland, pp 44–51

Iesmantas T., Alzbutas R. 2018. Convolutional Capsule Network for Classification of Breast Cancer Histology Images. *International Conference on Image Analysis and Recognition*. Varzim, Portugal, pp. 853–860

Jia B., Huang Q. 2020. DE-CapsNet: A Diverse Enhanced Capsule Network with Disperse Dynamic Routing. *Applied Sciences,* Vol. 10, No.3, pp.1-13

Jimenez-Sanchez A., Albarqouni S., Mateus D. 2018. Capsule Networks Against Medical Imaging Data Challenges. *International Workshop on Computer Assisted Stenting,* Granada, Spain, pp.1-10

Koresh H.J.D., Chacko S., Periyanayagi M. 2021. A Modified Capsule Network Algorithm for Oct Corneal Image Segmentation. *Pattern Recognition Letters*, Vol. 143, No.1, pp.104-112

Kosiorek A., Sabour S., Teh Y.W., Hinton G. 2019. Stacked Capsule Autoencoders. *The 33rd Conference on Neural Information Processing Systems (NeurIPS 2019),* Vancouver, Canada, pp 15486–15496

Lei R., Zhang C., Du S., Wang C., Zhang X., Zheng H., Huang J., Yu M. 2021. A Non-local Capsule Neural Network for Hyperspectral Remote Sensing Image Classification. *Remote Sensing Letters*, Vol. 12, No.1, pp. 40-49.

Long F., Peng J.J., Song W., Xia X., Sang J. 2021. BloodCaps: A Capsule Network Based Model for the Multiclassification of Human Peripheral Blood Cells. *Computer Methods and Programs in Biomedicine*, Vol. 202, No.105972, pp.1-10

Mandal B., Sarkhel R., Ghosh S., Das N., Nasipuri M. 2021. Two-phase Dynamic Routing for Micro and Macro-level Equivariance in Multi-Column Capsule Networks. *Pattern Recognition*, Vol. 109, No. 107595, pp.1-10

Maurya R., Pathak V.K., Dutta M.K. 2021. Computer-aided Diagnosis of Auto-immune Disease Using Capsule Neural Network. *Multimed Tools Applications*, Vol. 72, No.1, 1-22

Mobiny A., VanNguyen H. 2018. Fast Capsnet for Lung Cancer Screening. *International Conference on Medical Image Computing and Computer-Assisted Intervention*. Granada, Spain, pp. 741–749

Nair P, Doshi R, Keselj S. 2018. Pushing the Limits of Capsule Networks. *Technical note*, Vol.1, No.1, pp.1-16

Neill J.O. 2018. Siamese Capsule Networks. *arXiv:1805.07242*, pp.1-10.

Phaye S.S.R., Sikka A., Dhall A., Bathula D. 2018. Dense and Diverse Capsule Networks: Making the Capsules Learn Better. *arXiv:1805.04001,* pp.1-10

Panigrahi S., Das J., Swarnkar T. 2020. Capsule Network Based Analysis of Histopathological Images of Oral Squamous Cell Carcinoma. *Journal of King Saud University - Computer and Information Sciences*, Vo.1, No.1, pp.1-8

Rajasegaran J., Jayasundara V., Jayasekara S., Jayasekara H., Seneviratne S., Rodrigo R. 2019. Deepcaps: Going Deeper with Capsule Networks. *The International Conference on Computer Vision and Pattern Recognition (CVPR),* California, USA, pp 10725–10733

Paoletti M.E., Haut J.M., Plaza J., Plaza A.. 2020. Training Capsnets via Active Learning for Hyperspectral Image Classification. *IEEE International Geoscience and Remote Sensing Symposium (IGARSS 2020),* Waikoloa, HI, USA, pp. 40-43

Ren Q. 2019. Grouping Capsules Based Different Types. *arXiv:1911.04820v1*, pp.1-15

Sabour S., Frosst N., Hinton G. 2017. Dynamic Routing Between Capsules. *The 31st Conference on Neural Information Processing Systems (NIPS 2017),* Long Beach, USA pp 3856–3866

Santos P.R.S., Carvalho Brito V., Carvalho Filho A.O., Araújo F.H.D., Lira Rabêlo R.A., Mathew M.J. 2020. A Capsule Network-based for Identification of Glaucoma in Retinal Images. *IEEE Symposium on Computers and Communications (ISCC),* Rennes, France, pp. 1-6

Seeland M., Mader P. 2021. Multi-view Classification with Convolutional Neural Networks. *Plos One*, Vol. 16, No.1, pp.1-17.

Szegedy C., Zaremba W., Sutskever I., Bruna J., Erhan D., Goodfellow I., Fergus R. 2013. Intriguing Properties of Neural Networks. *arXiv:1312.6199,* pp.1-10

Tsuji T., Hirose Y., Fujimori K., Hirose T., Oyama A., Saikawa Y., Mimura T., Shiraishi K., Kobayashi T., Mizota A., Kotoku J. 2020. Classification of Optical Coherence Tomography Images Using a Capsule Network. *BMC Ophthalmology,* Vol. 20, No.114, pp.1-9

Wang D., Liu Q. 2018. An Optimization View on Dynamic Routing Between Capsules. The 6th International Conference on Learning Representations (ICLR 2018), Vancouver, Canada, pp.1-4

Wang D., Xu Q., Xiao Y., Tang J., Luo B. 2019. Multi-scale Convolutional Capsule Network for Hyperspectral Image Classification. *Chinese Conference on Pattern Recognition and Computer Vision (PRCV 2019)*, Nanjing, China, pp. 749-760

Wang J., Guo S., Huang R., Li L., Zhang X., Jiao L. 2021. Dual-Channel Capsule Generation Adversarial Network for Hyperspectral Image Classification. *IEEE Transactions on Geoscience and Remote Sensing,* (in press), pp.1-16

Xi E., Bing S., Jin Y. 2017. Capsule Network Performance on Complex Data. *arXiv:1712.03480*, pp.1-7

Xiang C., Zhang L., Tang Y., Zou W., Xu C. 2018. MS-CapsNet: A Novel Multi-Scale Capsule Network. *IEEE Signal Processing Letters, Institute of Electrical and Electronics Engineers*, Vol. 25, No. 12, pp.1850-1854

Xiang H., Huang Y.S., Lee C.H., Chien T.Y.C., Lee C.K., Liu L., Li A., Lin X., Chang R.F. 2021. 3-D Res-CapsNet Convolutional Neural Network on Automated Breast Ultrasound Tumor Diagnosis. *European Journal of Radiology,* Vol. 138(109608), No.1, pp.1-10.

Xue Z. 2020. A General Generative Adversarial Capsule Network for Hyperspectral Image Spectral-Spatial Classification. Remote Sensing Letters, Vol. 11, No.1, pp.19-28

ANALYSIS AND VISUAL EXPLORATION OF PREDICTION ALGORITHMS FOR PUBLIC BICYCLE SHARING SYSTEMS

Alexandra Cortez Ordoñez and Pere-Pau Vázquez
ViRVIG, Universitat Politècnica de Catalunya
Carrer Llorens I Artigas, 4-6, 08028 Barcelona, Spain

ABSTRACT

Public bicycle sharing systems have become an increasingly popular means of transportation in many cities around the world. However, the information shown in mobile apps or websites is commonly limited to the system's current status and is of little use for both citizens and responsible planning entities. The vast amount of data produced by these managing systems makes it feasible to elaborate and present predictive models that may help its users in the decision-making process. For example, if a user finds a station empty, the application could provide an estimation of when a new bicycle would be available. In this paper, we explore the suitability of several prediction algorithms applied to this case of bicycle availability, and we present a web-based tool to visually explore their prediction errors under different time frames. Even though a quick quantitative analysis may initially suggest that Random Forest yields a lower error, our visual exploration interface allows us to perform a more thorough analysis and detect subtle but relevant differences between algorithms depending on variables such as the station's behavior, hourly intervals, days, or types of days (weekdays and weekends). This case illustrates the potential of visual representation together with quantitative metrics to compare prediction algorithms with a higher level of detail, which can, in turn, assist application designers and decision-makers to dynamically adjust the best model for their specific scenarios.

KEYWORDS

Visualization Systems and Tools, Visual Analytics, Bike Sharing Systems, Forecasting Algorithms

1. INTRODUCTION

During the last decades, the popularity of public bicycle sharing systems (BSS) has been significantly increased in many medium and large cities. Not only have these transportation systems brought about a noticeable reduction in traffic congestion, noise, and pollution but also have had a considerable positive impact on user's health (Ricci, 2015). Despite their substantial benefits, local governments often delegate the management of their operations to contractors through public tenders. These operators are compensated independently of the number of users, thus having little incentive to promote, improve, or increase its use. As a result, BSS management and end-user applications are not quite sophisticated and provide a very limited amount of information, sometimes even erroneous, harming user's enthusiasm towards this public service (Chen et al., 2020). The advance of Information Technologies (IT) and the Internet of Things (IoT) has enabled the collection of richer data to a greater extent which is unfortunately not used today and could be leveraged to include modern features such as predictions with manifold benefits.

In our previous paper (Cortez & Vázquez, 2021) we created a web-based visualization system for the exploratory analysis of Barcelona's BSS. Our system offers novel features not existing in others such as the prediction of slots or bicycles of each type (mechanical or electrical), analysis of docking stations suffering outages, or a prioritized list of stations close to a point of interest. Its development was based on the requirements and input from regular users and experts in policy-making, system operation, and urban planning, collected through several semi-structured interviews. The visualization system, showed in Figure 1, allows the first group to obtain precise information on the future availability of bicycles or drop-off slots to assist them in deciding whether to wait for a bicycle, walk to a nearby station or use other means of transportation. Besides, the system helps the second group understand patterns of usage and get deeper insights. For instance, policymakers could take decisions regarding resizing, changing the placement of docking stations, or reinforcing other public transport systems. Managers, on their side, could use the information to improve re-balancing operations. After the evaluation of the system, we found that both groups of users considered highly useful the availability prediction of mechanical and electrical bikes and free slots in the following two hours. This has been the initial motivation that drives us to investigate various prediction models and the best way to evaluate them easily and efficiently.

In this paper, we seek to close the gap in extant research by analyzing the suitability of different prediction algorithms and their most influential variables using Barcelona's BSS as a use case. Our innovative interactive application is useful for bike-sharing visualization systems developers. It facilitates the rapid comparison and understanding of the strengths and weaknesses of different prediction algorithms by visually presenting the information. This tool was initially conceived to compare the performance of four forecasting models: Random Forest, Linear Regression, ARIMA, and Prophet. However, the application was developed in a modular way to ensure transferability to other similar data sources.

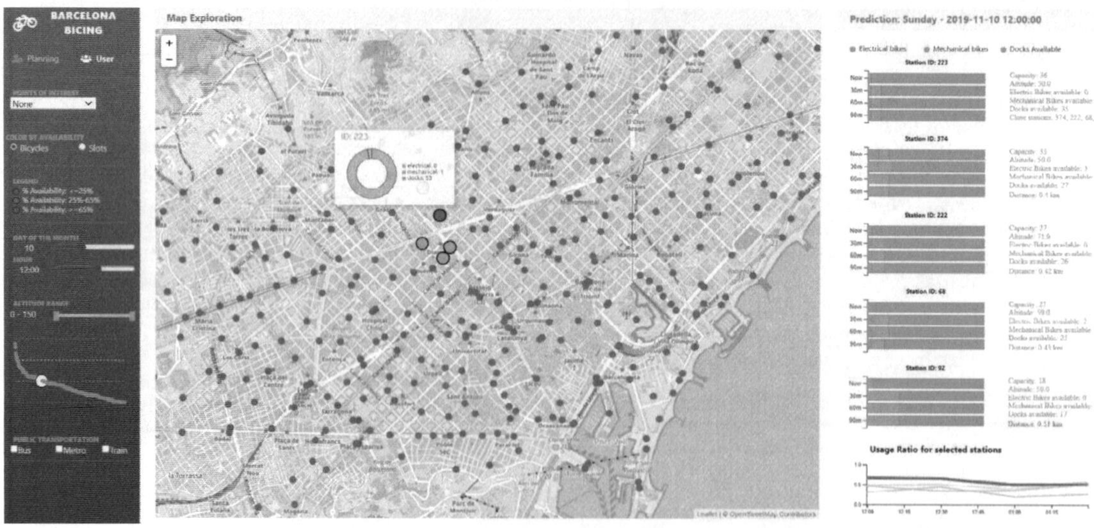

Figure 1. The initial web-based visualization system was applied to Barcelona's Bicing. The map shows the availability of bicycles in stations (red colors indicate low availability). The right view displays the prediction for the next two hours for the selected station and the closest ones prioritized by difficulty to access (altitude + distance)

2. RELATED WORK

Large studies for comparing different prediction models have been developed in the last years in a variety of domains, for instance on economics (Alon et al., 2001), urban traffic (Vázquez et al., 2020), health (Lim et al., 2000) or more recently COVID propagation (Appadu et al., 2021). Other investigations try to focus on a more general domain such as time series (Bontempi et al., 2012; Sharda & Patil, 1992) or classification problems (Caruana & Niculescu-Mizil, 2006; King et al., 1995). We have found few extensive studies for the general comparison of prediction algorithms (Ahmed et al., 2010; Fischer et al., 2018; Nguyen & Park, 2020). These investigations mainly concentrate on the analysis of novel machine learning algorithms vs traditional forecasting methods. Their results are presented using tables or the default plots provided by the software employed. We share with them the interest in the comparison of traditional and novel forecasting techniques; however, we also focus on a specific domain, BSS, and provide bike-sharing visualization developers with a novel visual interface to compare the outcomes of the selected models easily and dynamically.

The analysis of BSSs usage has been addressed in multiple ways. One common approach is to study the effect of urban configuration on bicycle flows and destination preferences (Faghih-Imani et al., 2014; Faghih-Imani & Eluru, 2015). Other investigations analyze how the elevation of stations may affect the trips

(Frade & Ribeiro, 2014; I. Kim et al., 2020). The influence of important events (Xie & Wang, 2018), and the correlation to weather data (Gebhart & Noland, 2014) and other variables, such as the calendar events (El-Assi et al., 2017; K. Kim, 2018; Younes et al., 2020) have been also studied. Therefore, building on a common focus to characterize bicycles' availability and use, this study presents suitable prediction algorithms and thorough comparison.

Other studies evaluate the pickup and drop-off events applying regression to model the counts of bicycles (Holmgren et al., 2017, 2018). However, they only provide numerical measurements from which is difficult to get deeper insights such as the algorithms performance on weekdays and weekends, or how the amount of activity may affect them. We also evaluated regression and compared it with other prediction models. More sophisticated algorithms have been applied to BSS scenarios, such as Graph Convolutional Neural Networks (Lin et al., 2018), hierarchical prediction model and Gradient Boosting Regression Tree (Li et al., 2015), among others. These papers propose a single model to analyze the bikes' demand. In contrast, we are interested in bike availability and we evaluate four different prediction algorithms that are commonly used, easy to understand, and available through various libraries in R or Python. The comparison between different forecasting algorithms in the BSS context has also been investigated (Feng & Wang, 2017; Hulot et al., 2018a; Wang & Kim, 2018; Xu et al., 2018), but these studies mainly illustrate their findings with tables and static charts, and no visual tool is developed to help users to drill down the data and gather a deeper understanding of the prediction algorithms' behavior.

Finally, this work is a continuation of a previous paper (Cortez & Vázquez, 2021) where we created a visualization system for the exploratory analysis of Barcelona's BSS. From our interviews with users, system operators, and policymakers, we found that even if the prediction of bike availability for the following two hours was considered highly useful, it was not present in official applications, mainly focused on usage patterns analysis (Dai et al., 2020; Froehlich et al., 2009; Shi et al., 2019) and availability status (Meddin et al., 2020; Oliveira et al., 2016; Oppermann et al., 2018). These interviews motivated our interest to further investigate and compare different prediction algorithms that can be applied to BSS scenarios for which we developed a visual interface that facilitates a quick and effective evaluation of their performance.

3. METHODS AND RESULTS

In this section, we present the process followed to collect the data and select the features, a description of the models used, and the results. The forecasting and initial data processing are performed using R. The visual interface is built using D3 and Flask, and data management is carried out in Python.

The first step we need to perform is the **data gathering and processing**. Given that the information needed for this type of analysis differs among public BSS, we concentrate on Barcelona's BSS named Bicing. Its data is available through the Open Data BCN website which is updated monthly. For each month there are more than 3.5 million records since data collection occurs approximately every 5 minutes. For this study, only information from 2019 is used to train and evaluate the models since 2020 had an abnormal behavior due to the lockdown and several mobility restrictions. Moreover, the company that provides the bike service in Barcelona was gradually changed during 2019, which caused a lack of continuity in the information. Thus, we focus on the last months of 2019 from September to November.

The Barcelona BSS has 424 docking stations, however, after data cleaning only 409 stations are kept. Data treatment includes deleting information of docking stations, that even when appearing in the set, are still not used, as well as others that were not working properly. Besides, garbled information such as dates outside the analyzed range or negative data availability is removed. From these data, the additional information necessary to train the models is computed: day of the week (and month), total docks available in each station, and the number of pickups and drop-offs (absolute and relative) per hour. Considering that we want to get further insights into the behavior of the algorithms, we also calculate usage ratios by hour.

Usage Ratios are derived from the frequency of pickups and drop-offs and help us differentiate between static and dynamic docking stations. It is calculated as follows:

$$use_{ijk} = \sum arrivals_{ijk} + \sum departures_{ijk} \text{ , } where\ i = StationID, j = day, k = hour$$

To better interpret this ratio and have a common scale we re-scale these values between 0 and 1:

$$UsageRatio_{ijk} = \frac{(use_{ijk} - MinUse)}{MaxUse - MinUse}, where\ i = StationID, j = day, k = hour$$

Once our data is clean, we proceed with the **selection of features** to train the prediction algorithms. It is based on the information available in Barcelona's BSS and previous studies (Lin et al., 2018; Wang & Kim, 2018; Xu et al., 2018) which have contributed with valuable knowledge to understand the factors that might affect the bike-sharing demand. These attributes can be classified as station-related or weather features. The first group is composed by day of the week (from Monday to Sunday), time slot, number of available bikes (mechanical and electrical), and station's capacity. Weather features are temperature, wind, humidity, atmospheric pressure, and overall weather classified in four categories: sunny, cloudy, light rain, and heavy rain. The features day of the week, time slot, and weather are categorical variables while the others are numerical.

Then, we analyze the performance of different **prediction algorithms**. Several models to predict bike sharing demand have been tested by different authors (Lin et al., 2018; Wang & Kim, 2018; Xu et al., 2018), some of them are quite sophisticated and developed specifically for this scenario while others are extensively used in many domains. For this study, we focus on prediction algorithms that are popular among data scientists because of their ease of use and interpretation, their availability through libraries in R and Python and their low computational resources requirements. Besides, similar to several studies (Alon et al., 2001; Sharda & Patil, 1992), we test the performance of traditional methods (**Linear Regression,** and **Autoregressive integrated moving average**) and new machine learning techniques (**Random Forest,** and **Prophet**). We have considered Linear regression as a base model because of its common use in predictive analysis. The Autoregressive integrated moving average is widely used to predict events that happen over time. Given that interpretability of the models and their parameters is not a concern for this study, Random Forest is chosen due to its ability to avoid overfitting. Previous works (Hulot et al., 2018b; Wang & Kim, 2018; Xu et al., 2018) show how these models have been broadly used in the BSS field. Finally, we also test Prophet as an example of novel methods developed by private companies which are gaining more relevance in recent years. The description of the models applied is presented as follows:

Linear Model is one of the most popular and studied forecasting methods. It can be defined as an approach to modeling the relationship between two or more variables by fitting a linear equation to observed data (Darlington & Hayes, 2017). One variable is known as the dependent variable and the others are considered as explanatory or independent variables. The relationship between them is constructed using linear predictor functions and a disturbance term or error that adds "noise" to this relationship. Linear models are widely used since their unknown parameters and their statistical properties are easier to estimate from the data itself.

Autoregressive integrated moving average or Arima is one of the most widely used approaches to time series forecasting. It can be considered as a combination of the differenced autoregressive model with the moving average model (Hillmer & Tiao, 1982). Its components are: *i)* Autoregression (AR) which shows that the time series variable is regressed on its own lagged or past values. *ii)* Integrated (I) part represents the differenced values of d order necessary for the time series to become stationary, it means raw values are replaced by the difference between data and the previous values. *iii)* Moving average (MA) indicates the dependency between an observation and its residual error, i.e., the forecast error can be represented as a linear combination of past errors. Each component is represented as a parameter with a standard notation: *i)* p: the lag order, *ii)* d: the degree of difference, *iii)* q: the order of the moving average.

Random Forest is a supervised learning algorithm that consists of randomly generating multiple decision trees and training them using the bagging method (Feng & Wang, 2017; Ho, 1995). As individual decision trees mainly suffer from overfitting, Random Forest trains decision trees with different parts of the training set by creating random subsets of the features and building smaller trees using those subsets. Then, the subtrees are combined reducing the variance. One of the advantages of this method is to increase the overall result as the combination of many learning models will outperform any individual model. Its main limitation its slowness and the high need of computational resources for many trees.

Prophet is open-source software released by Facebook in 2017 and implemented in R and Python (Taylor & Letham, 2017). It is specifically developed for time series and based on an additive model where non-linear trends are fitted with different seasonality (yearly, weekly, and daily), and holiday effects. Lately,

Prophet has gained popularity due to its simplicity as it allows users to adjust parameters intuitively without knowing the details of the underlying model. Moreover, it is robust to outliers, missing data, and dramatic trend shifts.

For each station, all models are trained using September and October data and both mechanical and electrical bikes' availability are predicted for November 2019. Furthermore, the natural logarithm of the predicted variable (availability) is also computed to check if results could be improved, but it did not improve the performance of the original variables. We also evaluate several error measures to compare the models. Our primary choice is the root-mean-square error (RMSE) as others (e.g., MAE, MAPE) were strongly correlated and did not add any valuable insights.

The **error measures** comparison for the four models described is shown in Table 1. Results suggest that electrical bikes' availability prediction has the smallest levels of error as a result of low variance. In general, using non-transformed data in both mechanical and electrical forecasting, Random Forest is giving the lowest RMSE levels using an optimal amount of 500 trees. Similarly, the Multiple Linear Regression model also exhibits good data fitting, while requiring less computational resources. In contrast, Arima and Prophet do not adequately capture the characteristics of bicycle trips and cannot make an accurate prediction. A possible explanation is their better suitability for time series data with strong seasonal effects and several seasons of historical data, which is not our case for the reasons abovementioned. Table 1 also displays the RMSE for the time slot from 7:00 to 21:00, when the Bicing usage ratio is higher compared with other periods when it is close to zero. Moreover, data is divided into weekdays and weekends since their usage patterns are quite different. The analysis using different time frames allows us to discover interesting insights. For instance, the error is smaller when we focus on the period with the highest usage ratio (from 7:00 to 21:00). Likewise, the error on weekends tends to be higher than on weekdays. Another interesting result is the similar performance of some algorithms during weekends.

Table 1. RMSE results. Random Forest seems to be more suitable for capturing trips characteristics. However, a deeper analysis shows some interesting outcomes

	Mechanical / Electrical					
	RMSE	RMSE 7:00-21:00	RMSE weekdays	RMSE weekdays 7:00-21:00	RMSE weekends	RMSE weekends 7:00-21:00
Random Forest	5.11 / 0.60	5.00 / 0.57	4.99 / 0.57	4.90 / 0.54	5.27 / 0.66	5.20 / 0.65
Linear Model	5.44 / 0.66	5.34 / 0.63	5.33 / 0.63	5.10 / 0.59	6.02 / 0.73	5.85 / 0.71
Prophet	5.98 / 0.65	5.86 / 0.62	5.85 / 0.62	5.63 / 0.58	6.54 / 0.72	6.36 / 0.71
Arima	6.48 / 0.69	6.65 / 0.67	6.70 / 0.67	6.84 / 0.65	6.23 / 0.73	6.36 / 0.71

4. VISUAL TOOL

Obtaining numerical performance measures for prediction algorithms is not enough if we want to fully understand the complete behavior of the system. It is well known that descriptive statistics such as the average or the median, overly simplify information. In our context, users may be interested in investigating whether the prediction algorithms have larger errors at certain moments of the day, or whether they are influenced seasonally or by the day of the week. These values could be difficult to analyze in tables, therefore, it is very useful to visualize the output of the prediction algorithms against each other, as well as with different configurations.

Overview. We have designed a web-based multiple-view application that facilitates the analysis of these algorithms through a set of heatmaps as shown in . There are three linked views. The control panel (1) is used to select the parameters to analyze. The larger portion of the screen (3) is devoted to four different heatmaps that encode the RMSE results for each prediction algorithm. Details can be accessed using the details-on-demand view (2) named Maximum errors. It provides contextual information about maximum errors, the id of the station where it is produced, and when these values are found.

Filtering and interaction techniques. To facilitate the exploration, we provide several filtering modes. The default mode shows the ***Hour view*** where all stations are arranged along the X-axis and hours in the Y-axis. Through the control panel, users can switch between different days of the month, group information by time ranges, or hide early hours which usually have usage ratios close to zero. This configuration can also be changed to the ***Day view***, where users can visualize the summary of RMSE per station and the day of the week (from Monday to Sunday). It also allows users to display data for the whole week, filtered by weekdays or grouped by weekend/weekday. Given that the Bicing system has both electrical and mechanical bikes, and their specific availability is a strong decision factor (Cortez & Vázquez, 2021) (e.g. uphill trips), it becomes interesting to analyze whether their prediction algorithms errors exhibit different behavior. Therefore, we also let the user toggle between electrical or mechanical bikes.

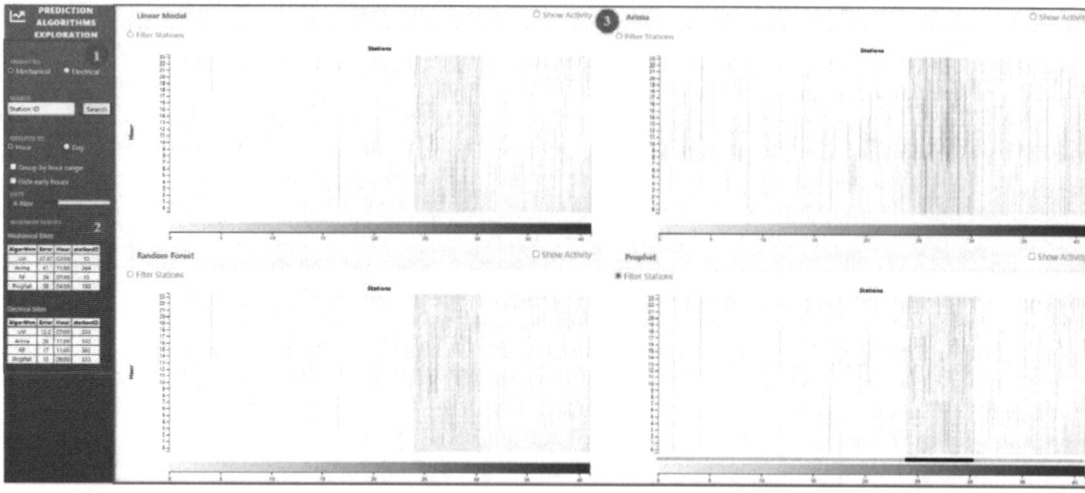

Figure 2. Visual Interface. The control panel (1) lets the user control what variables are shown in the heatmaps (3). (2) shows the maximum errors in all algorithms, as well as the stations and when these errors are produced

As we explain in the next section, a smaller number of bicycles picked and dropped off might result in higher errors in the prediction. Hence, each error heatmap can be transformed into an activity heatmap by toggling its top-right checkbox labeled *Show Activity*.

We have implemented some cross-highlighting methods to facilitate the analysis and allow users to identify patterns that cannot be easily detected through tables or general numerical measures:

- Similar behavior between prediction algorithms.
- Larger prediction errors on certain days or hours.
- Relationship between errors and usage ratios.
- Stations that exhibit larger errors for all algorithms.

This way, instead of inspecting a single algorithm, users can analyze the four of them at once and check if they behave similarly for distinct parameters such as day of the month, time of the day, etc. Upon hovering on any heatmap, the station under the mouse is highlighted in all the heatmaps and users can compare easily the RMSE performance. It is also possible to select a particular station by looking for its ID using the *Search button* or emphasize a set of stations using the *Filter stations* button. As the number of stations is high (more than 400), just labeling them would pose difficulties to the user to relate the same position in different heatmaps.

5. USE CASES

This section presents two of the more significant use cases that we have found.

Use case 1. Our visual tool allows us to easily identify different patterns that can be useful to select or discard a model, or to dynamically choose the best algorithm for different time frames. Using the heatmaps it is possible to identify a similar behavior between Random Forest and Multiple Linear Regression algorithms, as shown in . Even though the error is slightly larger in the case of regression, both models show similar results. Switching between the activity and the RMSE also reveals interesting discoveries. For instance, during weekdays, Arima tends to be less accurate between 10 a.m. and 6 p.m. when the activity is high (-top right). From 12 a.m. to 6 a.m., the activity is very low in all stations, thus, the application offers an option to remove this time range and focus only on the hours with the highest activity and, therefore, the greatest interest to analyze. Moreover, it can be inferred that stations with lower usage ratios usually have higher prediction errors and Prophet is especially sensitive to this situation as shown in Figure 3.

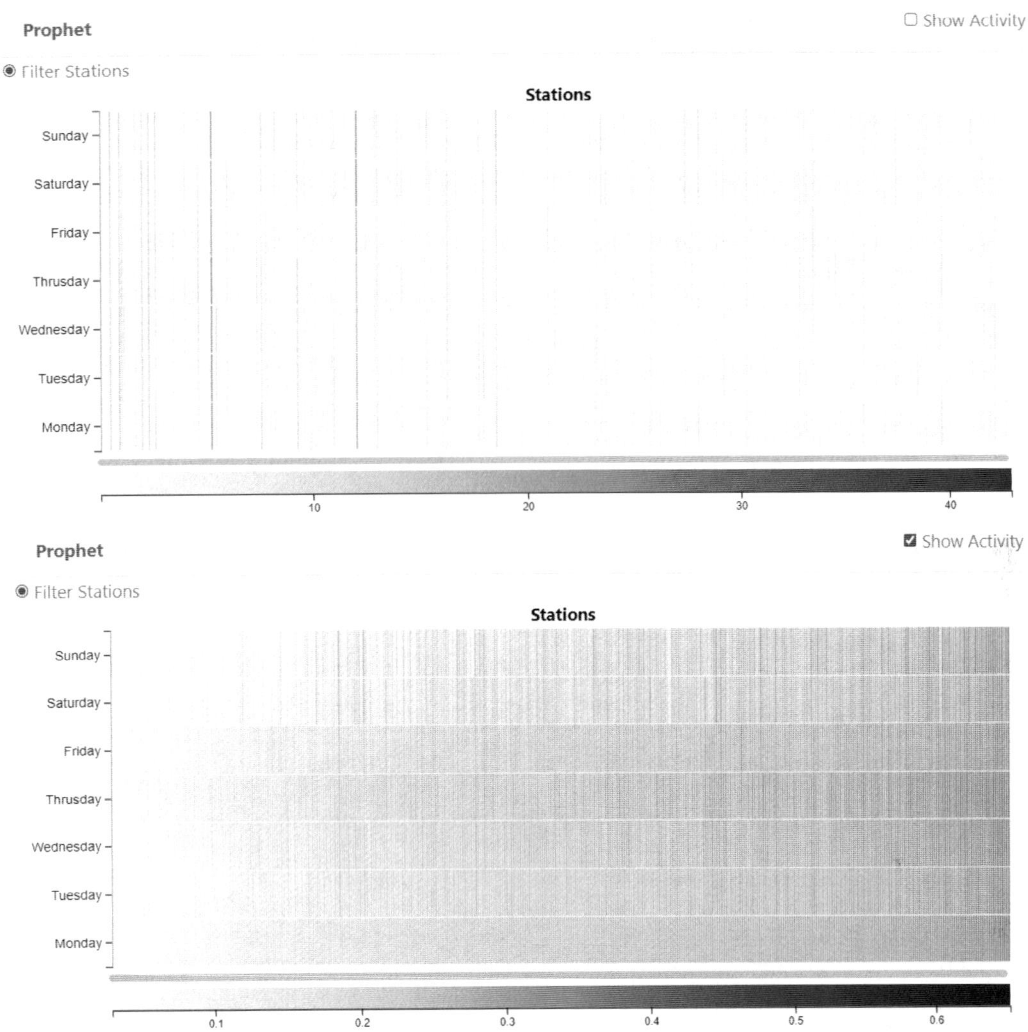

Figure 3. The *Show Activity* checkbox allows the user to toggle between error data (top) and activity data (bottom). Stations with higher usage ratios are predicted better than the stations with a lower amount of activity

Use case 2. The need for different prediction models for the same station in different time frames can be rapidly identified using our tool. For example, when aggregating RSME results and sorting them by day of the week (*Day view*), both Random Forest and Prophet show that station 171 presents the biggest prediction error for mechanical bicycles on November 30 (Figure 4-top right). If we only consider working days, station 171 continues to be the one with the greatest error on November 22. If the *Hour view* is selected and station 171 is highlighted, the behavior of the RMSE for each algorithm and day of the month can be inspected. In fact, this station presents higher levels of RMSE error during several days. On November 22, the visual analysis and the exploration of the tables presented on the details on-demand view (Figure 4-top left), allows us to identify that each model performs better in a different time frame, which may suggest choosing a different algorithm depending on the range of hours to improve the prediction.

MAXIMUM ERRORS:

Mechanical Bikes

Algorithm	Error	Hour	stationID
LM	35.12	06:00	171
Arima	46	01:00	171
RF	32	07:06	171
Prophet	68	06:00	171

Electrical bikes

Algorithm	Error	Hour	stationID
LM	12.78	09:00	273
Arima	23	12:00	302
RF	12	08:00	273
Prophet	13	08:00	273

MAXIMUM ERRORS:

Mechanical bikes

Algorithm	Error	Day	stationID
LM	45.1	02-Nov	13
AR	49	03-Nov	364
RF	39	30-Nov	171
PR	76	30-Nov	171

Electrical bikes

Algorithm	Error	Day	stationID
LM	22.3	20-Nov	421
AR	34	13-Nov	302
RF	22	13-Nov	302
PR	23	20-Nov	421

Figure 4. The details-on-demand view shows the maximum errors for each algorithm. On the left, the *Hour view* displays the hours with the largest errors for the selected day. The *Day view*, on the right, shows the day with the largest RMSE

6. CONCLUSION

In this study, a novel approach for the selection of prediction algorithms through visual exploration has been presented. Several widely used prediction algorithms have been analyzed in the context of public Bicycle Sharing Systems (BSS) using Barcelona's open data. For this purpose, an interactive full web-based visualization system was developed to represent in an easy and intuitive manner the forecasting error (RMSE) obtained from the application of the following four prediction algorithms to our dataset: Multiple Linear Regression, Arima, Random Forest, and Facebook's Prophet. A quick quantitative analysis suggests that Random Forest performs better and gives the smallest RMSE to predict the availability of both mechanical and electrical bikes, which often display distinct patterns. Nonetheless, a single metric does not usually represent the whole picture in such dynamic systems and can lead to sub-optimal decisions. For example, we observe that algorithms perform differently depending on the station's behavior and other variables such as hourly intervals, days, or types of days (weekdays and weekends). In addition, a relationship between the station's usage ratio (activity) and the prediction error has been found. Therefore, the proposed type of visual representation clearly allows for a more thorough analysis which can assist BSS application designers and decision-makers to select the best model for their specific scenarios.

Among the research limitations, the irruption of the COVID pandemic and a change of operator in Barcelona's BSS were the most restricting factors. As a result, the data used was time-constrained to those months without a strict lockdown, leaving not enough data for more advanced prediction models or the exploitation of seasonality. Besides, Barcelona's Open Data website provides only monthly updates for its BSS, thus the impossibility to perform real-time analysis. Hence, we believe that the real potential of this visualization comparison method can be further explored in a more optimal situation. This work has been partially motivated by the interviews with a government official responsible for monitoring the BSS performance. In the future, we want to evaluate the system together with various BSS stakeholders so as to improve its user-friendliness and the comprehension of the represented information.

ACKNOWLEDGEMENT

Partially supported by project TIN2017-88515-C2-1-R(GEN3DLIVE), from the Spanish Ministerio de Economía y Competitividad, by 839 FEDER (EU) funds.

REFERENCES

Ahmed, N. K., Atiya, A. F., El Gayar, N., & El-Shishiny, H. (2010). An empirical comparison of machine learning models for time series forecasting. *Econometric Reviews*, *29*(5), 594–621. https://doi.org/10.1080/07474938.2010.481556

Alon, I., Qi, M., & Sadowski, R. J. (2001). Forecasting aggregate retail sales: *Journal of Retailing and Consumer Services*, *8*(3), 147–156. https://doi.org/10.1016/s0969-6989(00)00011-4

Appadu, A. R., Kelil, A. S., & Tijani, Y. O. (2021). Comparison of some forecasting methods for COVID-19. *Alexandria Engineering Journal*, *60*(1), 1565–1589. https://doi.org/https://doi.org/10.1016/j.aej.2020.11.011

Bontempi, G., Taieb, S. B., & Borgne, Y. (2012). Machine Learning Strategies for Time Series Forecasting. *EBISS*.

Caruana, R., & Niculescu-Mizil, A. (2006). An empirical comparison of supervised learning algorithms. *ICML 2006 - Proceedings of the 23rd International Conference on Machine Learning*, *2006*, 161–168.

Chen, H., Zhu, T., Huo, J., & Andre, H. (2020). Sustainable co-governance of smart bike-sharing schemes based on consumers' perspective. *Journal of Cleaner Production*, *260*, 120949. https://doi.org/10.1016/j.jclepro.2020.120949

Cortez, A., & Vázquez, P.-P. (2021). Advanced Visual Interaction with Public Bicycle Sharing Systems. *Journal of WSCG*, *29*, ??

Dai, H., Tao, Y., & Lin, H. (2020). Visual analytics of urban transportation from a bike-sharing and taxi perspective. *Journal of Visualization*, *23*(6), 1053–1070.

Darlington, R. B., & Hayes, A. F. (2017). Regression analysis and linear models. *New York, NY: Guilford.*

El-Assi, W., Mahmoud, M. S., & Habib, K. N. (2017). Effects of built environment and weather on bike sharing demand: a station level analysis of commercial bike sharing in Toronto. *Transportation*, *44*(3), 589–613. https://doi.org/10.1007/s11116-015-9669-z

Faghih-Imani, A., & Eluru, N. (2015). Analysing bicycle-sharing system user destination choice preferences: Chicago's Divvy system. *Journal of Transport Geography*, *44*, 53–64.

Faghih-Imani, A., Eluru, N., El-Geneidy, A. M., Rabbat, M., & Haq, U. (2014). How land-use and urban form impact bicycle flows: evidence from the bicycle-sharing system (BIXI) in Montreal. *Journal of Transport Geography*, *41*, 306–314.

Feng, Y., & Wang, S. (2017). A forecast for bicycle rental demand based on random forests and multiple linear regression. In G. Zhu, S. Yao, X. Cui, & S. Xu (Eds.), *16th {IEEE/ACIS} International Conference on Computer and Information Science, {ICIS} 2017, Wuhan, China, May 24-26, 2017* (pp. 101–105). {IEEE} Computer Society. https://doi.org/10.1109/ICIS.2017.7959977

Fischer, T. G., Krauss, C., & Treichel, A. (2018). *Machine learning for time series forecasting - a simulation study*.

Frade, I., & Ribeiro, A. (2014). Bicycle sharing systems demand. *Procedia-Social and Behavioral Sciences*, *111*, 518–527.

Froehlich, J. E., Neumann, J., & Oliver, N. (2009). Sensing and predicting the pulse of the city through shared bicycling. *Twenty-First International Joint Conference on Artificial Intelligence*.

Gebhart, K., & Noland, R. (2014). The impact of weather conditions on bikeshare trips in Washington, DC. *Transportation*, *41*, 1205–1225. https://doi.org/10.1007/s11116-014-9540-7

Hillmer, S. C., & Tiao, G. C. (1982). An ARIMA-Model-Based Approach to Seasonal Adjustment. *Journal of the American Statistical Association*, *77*(377), 63–70. https://doi.org/10.1080/01621459.1982.10477767

Ho, T. K. (1995). Random Decision Forests. *Proceedings of the Third International Conference on Document Analysis and Recognition (Volume 1) - Volume 1*, 278.

Holmgren, J., Aspegren, S., & Dahlströma, J. (2017). Prediction of bicycle counter data using regression. *Procedia Computer Science*, *113*, 502–507.

Holmgren, J., Moltubakk, G., & O'Neill, J. (2018). Regression-based evaluation of bicycle flow trend estimates. *Procedia Computer Science*, *130*, 518–525.

Hulot, P., Aloise, D., & Jena, S. D. (2018a). Towards station-level demand prediction for effective rebalancing in bike-sharing systems. *Proceedings of the ACM SIGKDD International Conference on Knowledge Discovery and Data Mining*, 378–386. https://doi.org/10.1145/3219819.3219873

Hulot, P., Aloise, D., & Jena, S. D. (2018b). Towards Station-Level Demand Prediction for Effective Rebalancing in Bike-Sharing Systems. *Proceedings of the 24th ACM SIGKDD International Conference on Knowledge Discovery & Data Mining*, 378–386. https://doi.org/10.1145/3219819.3219873

Kim, I., Pelechrinis, K., & Lee, A. J. (2020). *The Anatomy of the Daily Usage of Bike Sharing Systems: Elevation, Distance and Seasonality*.

Kim, K. (2018). Investigation on the effects of weather and calendar events on bike-sharing according to the trip patterns of bike rentals of stations. *Journal of Transport Geography*, *66*, 309–320.

King, R. D., Feng, C., & Sutherland, A. (1995). STATLOG: COMPARISON OF CLASSIFICATION ALGORITHMS ON LARGE REAL-WORLD PROBLEMS. *Applied Artificial Intelligence*, *9*(3), 289–333. https://doi.org/10.1080/08839519508945477

Li, Y., Zheng, Y., Zhang, H., & Chen, L. (2015). Traffic prediction in a bike-sharing system. *GIS: Proceedings of the ACM International Symposium on Advances in Geographic Information Systems*, *03-06-Nove*. https://doi.org/10.1145/2820783.2820837

Lim, T.-S., Loh, W.-Y., & Shih, Y.-S. (2000). A Comparison of Prediction Accuracy, Complexity, and Training Time of Thirty-Three Old and New Classification Algorithms. *Machine Learning*, *40*(3), 203–228. https://doi.org/10.1023/A:1007608224229

Lin, L., He, Z., & Peeta, S. (2018). Predicting station-level hourly demand in a large-scale bike-sharing network: A graph convolutional neural network approach novel Graph Convolutional Neural Network with Data-driven Graph Filter (GCNN-DDGF) model. *Transportation Research Part C: Emerging Technologies*, *97*, 258–276. https://doi.org/10.1016/j.trc.2018.10.011

Meddin, R., DeMaio, P., O'Brien, O., Rabello, R., Yu, C., Gupta, R., & Seamon, J. (2020). *The Meddin Bike-sharing World Map*.

Nguyen, S., & Park, A. (2020). *A Comparison of Machine Learning Algorithms of Big Data for Time Series Forecasting Using Python*.

Oliveira, G. N., Sotomayor, J. L., Torchelsen, R. P., Silva, C. T., & Comba, J. L. D. (2016). Visual analysis of bike-sharing systems. *Computers \& Graphics*, *60*, 119–129.

Oppermann, M., Möller, T., & Sedlmair, M. (2018). Bike sharing Atlas: visual analysis of bike-sharing networks. *Int. J. Transp*, *6*, 1–14.

Ricci, M. (2015). Bike sharing: A review of evidence on impacts and processes of implementation and operation. *Research in Transportation Business \& Management*, *15*, 28–38.

Sharda, R., & Patil, R. B. (1992). Connectionist approach to time series prediction: an empirical test. *Journal of Intelligent Manufacturing*, *3*(5), 317–323. https://doi.org/10.1007/BF01577272

Shi, X., Wang, Y., Lv, F., Liu, W., Seng, D., & Lin, F. (2019). Finding communities in bicycle sharing system. *Journal of Visualization*, *22*(6), 1177–1192.

Taylor, S., & Letham, B. (2017). Forecasting at Scale. *The American Statistician*, *72*. https://doi.org/10.1080/00031305.2017.1380080

Vázquez, J. J., Arjona, J., Linares, M., & Casanovas-Garcia, J. (2020). A Comparison of Deep Learning Methods for Urban Traffic Forecasting using Floating Car Data. *Transportation Research Procedia*, *47*, 195–202. https://doi.org/https://doi.org/10.1016/j.trpro.2020.03.079

Wang, B., & Kim, I. (2018). Short-term prediction for bike-sharing service using machine learning. *Transportation Research Procedia*, *34*, 171–178. https://doi.org/10.1016/j.trpro.2018.11.029

Xie, X.-F., & Wang, Z. (2018). Examining Travel Patterns and Characteristics in a Bikesharing Network and Implications for Data-Driven Decision Supports: Case Study in the Washington DC Area. *Journal of Transport Geography*, *71*, 84–102. https://doi.org/10.1016/j.jtrangeo.2018.07.010

Xu, C., Ji, J., & Liu, P. (2018). The station-free sharing bike demand forecasting with a deep learning approach and large-scale datasets. *Transportation Research Part C: Emerging Technologies*, *95*(July), 47–60. https://doi.org/10.1016/j.trc.2018.07.013

Younes, H., Zou, Z., Wu, J., & Baiocchi, G. (2020). Comparing the Temporal Determinants of Dockless Scooter-share and Station-based Bike-share in Washington, DC. *Transportation Research Part A: Policy and Practice*, *134*, 308–320.

HELLO, MY NAME IS SMARTTRAM, HUMAN FACTORS IS ON BOARD, ENJOY THE RIDE! DEVELOPING A HUMAN FACTORS PROGRAM FOR AUTOMATIC TRAMS

Hanna Koskinen, Susanna Aromaa and Vladimir Goriachev
VTT Technical Research Centre of Finland Ltd
Tekniikantie 21, PL1000, 02044 VTT, Finland

ABSTRACT

Our transport system is currently undergoing fundamental change due to increasing use of automation. New automation solutions are introduced in all sectors of transportation, for example automated metros and autonomous ships are in the visions of technology developers. There are many reasons for this ongoing trend of higher use of automation such as demands for sustainability and efficiency to mention some. In this paper, we present a research and development effort aiming at introducing an automatic tram, that is to say SmartTram. In particular, we concentrate on how the changing role of human (as driver, passenger and member of other stakeholder groups) is acknowledged in the design of a new automatic tram. For this reason, we present a human factors engineering program for automated trams. This approach can be utilized also in other sectors when increasing automation.

KEYWORDS

Public Transport, Automatic Tram, Human Factors Engineering

1. INTRODUCTION

There is a worldwide initiative to increase use of automation solutions in transport systems and enable new kind of mobility services that are in the center of the smart city concepts. Even though the research and development of automated cars may have gain more attention (Cohen et al., 2017; Kyriakidis et al., 2019; Merat & Jamson, 2009) the same automatization trend impacts all other aspects of transportation (e.g., public transportation and cargo) (Beiker, 2014; Karvonen et al., 2011; Wahlström et al., 2016). In this paper, our focus is on public transportation and in particular developing automatic solutions for trams. The design task, that is to say, the development of automatic tram, is challenging because the tram needs to operate in an open infrastructure opposite to the closed-rail systems that most of the introduced automatic transport systems has been earlier. Moreover, apart from few exceptions, not many reference cases about automatic trams may be found (see e.g., Hofmann, 2020). The urban city environments that the trams often operate are, from the automation design point of view, the most challenging ones. In these urban environments, advanced sensor networks and high connectivity are demanded to reliable detect variety of objects (e.g., pedestrians and other vulnerable road users [VRU]) and aspects of the driving environment (e.g., weather and lighting conditions or traffic density).

From the operation and human point of view, the automatic tram will change the tram driver's work substantially. The tram driver will no longer be expected handling all the operative level driving tasks (e.g., driving by sight, controlling driving speed and stopping at tram stops as well as monitoring the situation in the cabin and the tram stops) and the main task shifts toward supervising the automatic driving system. Thus, even with the increasing levels of automation, the human operator is still needed at least to supervise and monitor that the system operates as intended. The driver may also be expected to intervene in the operation in case of an emergency or some complex driving situation (e.g., handling moving to detour or passing a traffic work site). From the passengers' point of view, the automatic tram is a notable change, as well. There may be issues such as can it be trusted in the functioning of the automatic tram (Karvonen et al.,

2011) or uncertainty how to behave and use the tram if there is no human driver to ask help. There are many studies that have been investigating the interaction of the pedestrians and other VRUs with the automatic vehicles (Hulse et al., 2018; Parkin et al., 2016; Rasouli & Tsotsos, 2018). In these studies, different visualization and signaling concepts have been presented and evaluated in order to communicate the intentions of the automatic vehicle to the other road users. In addition, there are also other stakeholders to consider during the design of automatic trams for example maintenance technicians. Due to several stakeholder/user groups with varying needs and expectations, driving a tram and the human interaction with the automated tram will remain as an important human factors issue to be taken under careful investigation.

In this paper, we introduce the human factors engineering (HFE) program including iterative evaluation of future solution that have been developed for the SmartTram project in order to acknowledge appropriately the human and social aspect in the design of the automatic tram. We first discuss the importance of developing proper HFE program in safety-critical design projects. After which we introduce the specific HFE activities planned for the SmartTram project. A particular emphasis has been put on laying out the verification and validation (V&V) plan and the related simulator and training facilities.

2. HUMAN FACTORS ENGINEERING IN SAFETY-CRITICAL DESIGN PROJECTS

A systematic approach and human factors practices are needed in the design of safety-critical systems such as control rooms of nuclear power plants, cockpits of aircrafts and operating theatres in hospitals where many technical but also social and organizational aspects need to be seamlessly integrated. In addition, maintaining holistic and life cycle perspective are also important in order to reach a proper socio-technical understanding of the design task at hand. It has been suggested in the literature, that at least the following list of HFE activities should be included in design of complex systems: screening, management and planning, operating experience (OE) review, development of concept of operations (ConOps), function allocation and analysis, task analysis, human reliability analysis, personnel selection, training and qualifications, system design and development, design of maintenance activities, V&V, and commissioning and in-time operation monitoring. All these HFE activities should be carried out in a coordinated manner and at the same time, there should be a continuous, effective and timely dialogue between the human factors representatives and the other engineering specialists working in the project. This is not a straightforward task to do. Consequently, the importance of HFE integration in complex engineering projects is widely recognized (Hale et al., 2007; Hugo, 2000) The benefits of HFE integration may be, for example, that the problems can be avoided or mitigated and, design relevant information and feedback from the evaluations can be more effectively fed back to the design. Thus, drafting a more formal HFE program within which all the HFE activities, their deliverables and main interactions with the other design parties in a project are described is one way to address the integration problem and create a base for high quality HFE practices. The HFE program should cover all the phases of the design process from the initial clarification and analysis phase to the final implementation of the system. Because of the different starting points and contextual circumstances in different design projects it is expected that the HFE program will need to be tailored and customized individually to each project even though the basic structure of the HFE program would be much alike. Based on these requirements, we present a HFE program for safety-critical system design and SmartTram (Table 1).

Table 1. A HFE program for SmartTram system design

Input	Design process	Output
• Need for change (e.g., growing amount of passengers, sustainable and environmentally friendly public transport solutions) • Existing concepts (e.g., proofs of concept, level of automation) • Operational experience (other automated traffic solutions e.g., metro)	**Initial clarification and analysis** Impact, needs and constraints HFE goals	• Human factors input to project plan • HFE program/ activities (i.e., tasks and responsible persons, schedule and resources) • Preliminary evaluation schema (i.e., Systems Usability Case based evaluation of concept, subsystems and integrated system)
• Operating environment description • User and safety requirements • Standards	**Requirements and concept design** Concept of operation Task analysis User requirements	• SmartTram concept (documentation of ConOps, level of automation, user interactions) • Project requirement set • HSI style guide (e.g., main design principles, HSI guidance on layout, navigation, color-coding, alarms etc.)
• I&C architectures • Standards	**Detail/integrated design** User interface, training design	• Tram interior and user interface design solution
• V&V plan (e.g., users groups, scenarios, acceptance criteria) • Standards	**Verification & validation (V&V)** Simulations Validation tests	• V&V record (e.g., identified human engineering discrepancies and design feedback, decisions on further design iterations)
	Implementation & commissioning	• Accumulated evaluation record (careful documentation of implantation and early operating experiences)

3. HUMAN FACTORS ENGINEERING IN SMARTTRAM PROJECT

The social and human aspect is important in the SmartTram project as the tram will operate in our everyday living environment and thus should be sensitive to how it is perceived also by the general public not to mention the tram drivers whose work is anyway going to change radically. For that reason a HFE program and a specific plan for the iterative evaluation of the SmartTram from human factors point of view was prepared and implemented as a part of the development process.

3.1 Human Factors Engineering Program

The HFE activities summarized in the Table 1 are the main responsibility of the HFE experts working in the SmartTram project. At the moment, the project is in its initial clarification and analysis phase, that is to say, a lot of analytical research work is carried out (e.g., options for technical platform are investigated.) The relevant information from the HFE perspective is also collected (e.g., identifying and analyzing the different user groups), and benchmarking on, for example, about the existing human-system interaction concepts in tram driving are conducted. In addition, operating experiences of similar systems are of interest in this phase. It may be that not many directly comparable solutions (i.e., automatic trams) can be found, however, operating experiences on other automatic transport and machinery may offer relevant background information as well. This information serves as an input for planning the SmartTram project and drafting the specified HFE program (i.e., planned HFE activities within the project) and preliminary evaluation schema (i.e., V&V plan).

3.2 Verification and Validation Plan

Iterative evaluation and testing is an integral part of designing complex safety-critical systems (see Figure1) and the continuous engineering paradigm that promote improvements throughout the product life cycle. Thus, the HFE evaluation schema should be considered already from the very beginning of any development project. That is also why in the SmartTram project, the V&V plan was drafted in the first phase of the project (i.e., initial clarifications and analysis phase in the Table 1). Typical for complex system engineering projects, like the SmartTram-project, are that they are long and therefore the design work is often divided into several stages or manageable parts that follow each other's. A concept of subsystem validation (SSV) (Laarni et al., 2014) has been introduced to carry out evaluations throughout the design whenever a part of a whole get completed and ready for testing. For example, a modernization of a control room may be realized in stepwise and thus the evaluation of different subsystems (i.e., normal operation and safety systems) become timely in different time windows in the project. Following the SSVs, an integrated system validation (ISV) is conducted before the commissioning phase of the new system. It is also essential that when the system is in its operative state, the operating experiences are systematically collected, and used as an input for identifying further places of improvements for the system.

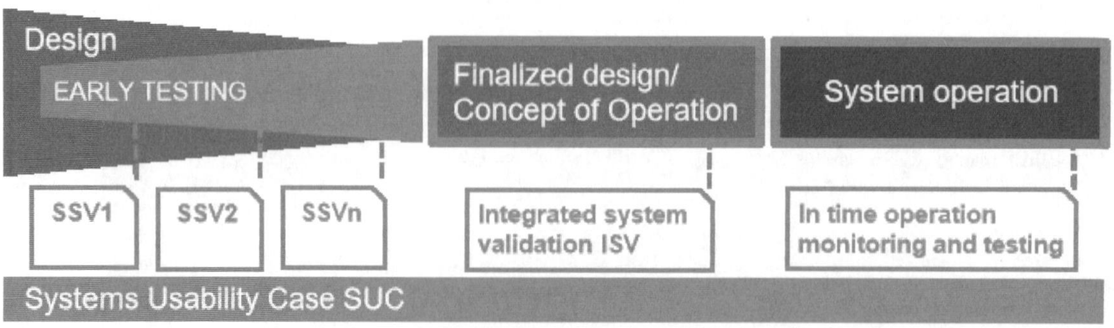

Figure 1. Iterative evaluation throughout the life cycle of a complex safety-critical system

Moreover, it is expected that a huge amount of HFE data being gathered even within one complex system engineering project and the life cycle of system. An evaluation approach called Systems Usability Case (SUC) (Koskinen et al., 2017; Liinasuo & Norros, 2007) has been used as a methodical starting point in the SmartTram project for managing and organizing the system evaluation. A safety case (Bishop & Bloomfield, 1998) is required in many safety standards and therefore produced in variety safety-critical domains as a part of their normal qualification procedure. SUC approach bases on Systems Usability (SU) construct (Savioja, 2014) and the safety case thinking and it exploits the design requirements in forming the set of criteria for the HFE evaluations. The SUC approach is considered to be especially well suited to evaluation of systems that are complex and unique by their nature. In the first part of the SUC procedure called as a goal structure, the project specific design requirements are organized thematically with regards to the more generic usability and HFE requirements and the high-level acceptance goal set for the project. Through this construction, a more specified set of acceptance criteria and the test occasions (e.g., scenarios) in which the fulfilment of the requirements may be tested are derived. Going through the design rational and the documentation helps also the HFE evaluators to become better acquainted with the system and thus be able to ask more specific and detailed questions concerning the systems usability. After constructing the goal structure, an evaluation session is realized to collect evidence. These evaluation sessions may be carried out with different type of mockups and prototypes or in more advanced simulator environments depending on the maturity of the design solution and the project phase. In the second part of the SUC, called as a claim structure, a reasoning process takes place. The claim structure comprises of a set of evidence, arguments and claims. Constructing the claim structure aims to create a documented body of evidence providing a valid argument of the degree of systems usability of the system under consideration. Often it is so that in the early phase evaluations many human engineering discrepancies (HEDs) are still identified. Each identified HED needs to be handled individually and give an appropriate resolution. Solving one HED may require redesign to take place whereas for other HED training of personnel may be the most effective way to handle the identified issue. When coming closer to the implementation phase and the ISV of the system it is expected that the amount of HEDs is lower as many of the HFE issues are already been able to solve and act upon earlier in the V&V process. No critical HEDs should be existing in the system at the time of implementation. Using SUC helps to conduct the V&V process in a systematic, transparent and longitudinal fashion.

3.3 SmartTram Simulator Facility for User Testing

One useful approach to be applied during an HFE program in a safety-critical system design is virtual reality (VR) based models and simulators. In VR, digital technology provides simulation of reality typically through visual, auditory, and haptic interfaces. By using VR simulators in the context of safety-critical system design, it is possible to immerse users to their future operating tasks in a safe environment. The VR simulators exist realized with varying technical solutions (e.g., from visualizations on a PC screen to immersive virtual environments experienced with head mounted displays) and they can be used for different purposes during the HFE program. For example, by using a simulator it is possible to train new operators / tram drivers to cope hazard traffic situations. In general, there are several reasons contributing to VR simulators' usefulness, such as converting the abstract to the concrete (e.g., making some specific concept idea illustratively tangible) and making hands-on training possible in situations where it is still impossible to train things in the real world setting.

In the SmartTram project, a virtual environment was created for the SmarTram system (see Figure 2). A virtual prototype visualizes quite a conventional tram cockpit but it has been enhanced with new SmartTram features and control panels. The tram driver may now experience how it would be to operate a tram enhanced with advanced automatic features. In building the VR simulator, the results of an earlier research study and interviews with conventional tram drivers was used to detect challenging situations faced in tram operators' daily work. For example, the tram diver reacting to sudden movements of pedestrians, cars or trams ahead, maintaining the planned tram schedule, and maintaining the speed and adjusting it according to the varying breaking distance in different weather conditions. The SmartTram simulator system was build based on this contextual understanding of the work of the tram drivers and the VR simulator was aimed at depict the tram driving conditions as realistically as possible. Consequently, the VR simulator offers a high fidelity simulator environment for iterative design and evaluation of the SmartTram project.

Figure 2. A virtual reality based SmartTram simulator. Tram operator's view in an autumn-evening lighting conditions in an urban city environment. The rain and fallen leaves on the tramlines affect acceleration and stopping distance of the tram

The SmartTram simulator system includes 3D models of a tram and a city, road event visualizations (other trams, cars, pedestrians, etc.), different weather conditions (e.g., summer, autumn and winter specific circumstances such as high or low intensity of sunlight and slippery tramlines) and a new SmartTram visual-assistance system. The SmartTram visual-assistance system is based on the three core components: 1) precise model of the tramlines for the current route (e.g., all the turns and altitude changes),

2) tram localization on the route (i.e., GPS/ sensors on the track), and 3) self-awareness system similar to the ones used in the self-driving cars (including sensors for obstacle detection, braking performance calculations, environment conditions monitoring etc.). For example, related to the driving situation in autumn visualized in Figure 2, the SmartTram visual-assistance system is aware of the temperature, humidity and the tramline conditions (e.g., wet). The SmartTram system also uses computer vision to detect presence of leaves on the rails and by using above information, the SmartTram concludes that the rails are very slippery. Depending on the set level of automation, the SmartTram may notify or if needed even transfer the full control to the tram driver to handle the difficult driving situation. Even though the human operator would not have any more the main responsibility of operative driving of the tram, it would still be necessary to have the human in the loop at operating the tram system. In representing information to support human operator's situation awareness about the slippery trail conditions the SmartTram visual-assistance system could, for example change color of the rails and display warning signs on the road surface to indicate the hazard. Similarly, the system may modify corner speed limits or form braking distance estimations, and visualize these for the tram driver. Consequently, the tram driver would then be better aware of the prevailing driving situation and thus be better prepared to take over the control in case needed. Making design decisions on the level of automation and the different visualization, human-system interaction concepts and the different automatic functionalities of the SmartTram may benefit greatly from the possibility to study and explore the qualities of different design solutions (possibly even with the future users) beforehand in a safe simulator environment.

In addition, two hazardous traffic situations (i.e., pedestrians running across the street unexpectedly and a car stopping in front of the tram) were initially introduced in the SmartTram simulator in order to be able to create realistic and challenging test scenarios. Through the scenarios that are based on possible real-life traffic situations in tram driving, it would be also possible to carry out more formal evaluations (e.g., ISV) about the interaction between the human operator and the automatic tram (i.e., the new concept of operation) when the design project is approaching to its end point. A realistic simulator environment is also essential in training the new tram drivers as the imagined role of human operator in operation of SmartTram is substantially different from the role that the dram drivers have today. The build SmartTram simulator system also includes data collection features (e.g., total time, collisions and stopping distance from the tram stop) which are useful when collecting evidence and evaluating the system with the users.

4. CONCLUSIONS AND FUTURE WORK

In the modern smart city environments, many technologically advanced mobility services and solutions are expected to be in place. Thus, increasing levels of automation is also central in developing the public transportation. This paper describes development efforts to introduce automatic tram, that is, the SmartTram. The change from the conventional tram operation to the automatic operation is expected to bring many advances (e.g., efficiency and safety) but also some challenges (e.g., radical change in the human operator's role in driving the tram). Many complex and safety-critical design projects has suffered with lack of proper socio-technical understanding leading costly mistakes in later phases of the system operation. In the SmartTram project, the aim has been to integrate the human and social aspects in the design engineering from the very beginning of the development project. For this purpose, a dedicated HFE program with a V&V plan and a VR based simulator environment was introduced in the project.

In the following phases of our SmartTram project, the most critical HFE activities are to set the user requirements and design an initial concept of operation for the SmartTram. Following the SUC approach the initial goal structure will be formed to support the SmartTram V&V process as well. User studies should be conducted with the SmartTram simulator in order to refine the user requirements and validate the SmartTram operation concept. These activities in the requirements and concept design phase will create a foundation for the later design phases of the development of SmartTram and enables monitoring that the SmartTram project is proceeding favorable direction also from the social and human point of view. Because, in the end, it begins from the smart ´integrative´ design that can make the cities and the transport services of our future smart and sustainable.

ACKNOWLEDGEMENT

We want to thank all researchers and partners in cooperation working within the SmartTram project for working together towards the common goal of well-functioning and safe traffic systems in smart cities. We also want to thank the interviewed tram drivers for sharing their valuable insights about their work.

REFERENCES

Beiker, S. (2014). Road Vehicle Automation. *Road Vehicle Automation, January*, 61–70. https://doi.org/10.1007/978-3-319-05990-7

Bishop, P., & Bloomfield, R. A. (1998). Methodology for Safety Case Development. *Safety-Critical Systems Symposium.*

Cohen, T., Jones, P., & Cavoli, C. C. (2017). *Social and behavioural questions associated with automated vehicles: scoping study: final report. January*, 1–124.

Hale, A., Kirwan, B., & Kjellén, U. (2007). Safe by design: where are we now? *Safety Science*, *45*, 305—327.

Hofmann, M. (2020). Siemens Mobility and Transport Company VIP Postdam : On the path to an autonomous tram. *Bahn Manager Magazin.*

Hugo, J. (2000). Towards a unified HFE process for the nuclear industry. *Proceedings of NPIC& HMIT.*

Hulse, L. M., Xie, H., & Galea, E. R. (2018). Perceptions of autonomous vehicles : Relationships with road users , risk , gender and age. *Safety Science*, *102*(April 2017), 1–13. https://doi.org/10.1016/j.ssci.2017.10.001

Karvonen, H., Aaltonen, I., Wahlström, M., Salo, L., Savioja, P., & Norros, L. (2011). Interacting with Computers Hidden roles of the train driver : A challenge for metro automation. *Interacting with Computers*, *23*(4), 289–298. https://doi.org/10.1016/j.intcom.2011.04.008

Koskinen, H., Laarni, J., Liinasuo, M., Norros, L., & Savioja, P. (2017). Systems Usability Case in Stepwise Control Room Validation. *10th International Topical Meeting on Nuclear Plant Instrumentation, Control and Human Machine Interface Technologies NPIC&HMIT 2017.*

Kyriakidis, M., de Winter, J. C. F., Stanton, N., Bellet, T., van Arem, B., Brookhuis, K., Martens, M. H., Bengler, K., Andersson, J., Merat, N., Reed, N., Flament, M., Hagenzieker, M., & Happee, R. (2019). A human factors perspective on automated driving. *Theoretical Issues in Ergonomics Science*, *20*(3), 223–249. https://doi.org/10.1080/1463922X.2017.1293187

Laarni, J., Savioja, P., Norros, L., Liinasuo, M., Wahlström, M., & Salo, L. (2014). Conducting multistage HFE validations - constructing Systems Usability Case. *ISOFIC/ISSNP 2014*, 1–10.

Liinasuo, M., & Norros, L. (2007). Usability case – integrating usability evaluations in design. In E. Law, K. Larusdottir, & M. Norgaard (Eds.), *COST294-MAUSE Workshop on Downstream Utility*. Institute of Research in Informatics of Toulouse IRIT.

Merat, N., & Jamson, A. H. (2009). How Do Drivers Behave in a Highly Automated Car? *Driving Assesment Conference*, 514–521.

Parkin, J., Clark, B., Clayton, W., Ricci, M., & Parkhurst, G. (2016). *Understanding interactions between autonomous vehicles and other road users: A Literature Review.*

Rasouli, A., & Tsotsos, J. (2018). Autonomous Vehicles that Interact with Pedestrians A Survey of Theory and Practice. *THE IEEE TRANSACTIONS ON INTELLIGENT TRANSPORTATION SYSTEMS.*

Savioja, P. (2014). *Evaluating Systems Usability in Complex Work: Deeloping of a Systemic Usability Concept to Benefit Control Room Design*. Aalto University.

Wahlström, M., Karvonen, H., Kaasinen, E., & Mannonen, P. (2016). Designing user-oriented future ship bridges: An approach for radical concept design. *Ergonomics in Design: Methods and Techniques*, *August*, 219–233. https://doi.org/10.1201/9781315367668

A NEW SERVICE MODEL FOR VEHICLE SENSING DATA COLLECTION

Christian Prehofer[1] and Preeta Abbasi[2]
[1]*DENSO AUTOMOTIVE Deutschland GmbH, Germany*
[2]*Technische Universität München, Munich, Germany*

ABSTRACT

Vehicles are equipped with more and more sensors like cameras and radar system. These can collect lots of useful data, e.g. for road monitoring, high-definition map updates and for information about accidents or other emergencies. To access and utilize this data, key challenges are the huge amount of data and also the different application needs. We present a new solution to coordinate the vehicle data collection, offering different service models and reducing data uploads by avoiding similar data. We use an architecture with a central coordination scheme to avoid redundant image uploads. It has been successfully evaluated with data from 30 cars driving in Munich, created from a simulator. This includes realistic scenarios with dynamic changes and different services.

KEYWORDS

Connected Vehicles, Data Collection, Connected Mobility

1. INTRODUCTION

Current vehicles are evolving into a sensing platform, generating a large amount of real-time data about the vehicles and their surroundings with cameras, radars and other sensors. This has led to a huge demand for data-driven mobility services, such as traffic management, predictive maintenance, smart cities and driving behavior analysis.

In this work, we focus on the collection of vehicle data for applications which require large data volumes. Examples are collecting pictures in case of an emergency, but also for road surveillance or map updating based on pictures. Our vehicular data dissemination architecture follows the idea of reverse content delivery networks (R-CDN), (Moustafa, Schooler, and McCarthy 2017), yet focuses specifically on vehicle data.

A main challenge is the amount of data to be transmitted, from connected vehicles over cellular data connections or Wifi networks. As the capacity of wireless networks is limited, especially in more remote areas, this is a major bottleneck. Secondly, there are different kinds of services with different needs. For instance, in case of an emergency, all efforts should be taken instantly, while road monitoring for a big road network should be done in a highly efficient way to reduce costs.

To address these challenges, we present a new service model for vehicle data collection, which differentiates several service classes according to different criteria, including time, cost and reliability. We assume a central entity to support the upload of vehicle data of an area, and vehicles first upload metadata of their content which is very small. As vehicles increasingly use connected services like navigation and traffic warnings, it is reasonable to assume that there is a continuous connection for such additional metadata upload. For instance, (Khan and Prehofer 2020) has shown in simulations that redundancy reduction and Wifi off-loading for vehicle data collection can reduce traffic by a factor up to 20 in larger systems. Here, we present a new service model for different kinds of services and a distributed implementation of our model, including dynamic reaction to changes like service class upgrades or leaving vehicles. We present an architecture and a system concept which can also handle changes, both in the demand side as well as changes in vehicles. For instance, vehicles may drop out. This is evaluated with realistic traffic data and shows the different behavior of our services.

2. APPROACH AND SERVICE MODEL

In the following, we present our approach and the service model for efficient data collection from vehicles. The goal is to find a service model which is generic and flexible for different applications, and also permits efficient implementation.

There exist many applications for connected vehicles, from remote diagnosis, fleet management to new kinds of user-supporting services (Zeng, Balke, Songchitruksa, et al. 2012; Siegel, Erb, and Sarma 2017). Here, we focus on services which require considerable upload of sensor data from the environment, such as camera and radar sensors. Camera data from the environment can be used to analyse the road, e.g. other traffic including pedestrians, as well as the roadside areas. We first classify these use cases as follows, depending on their urgency and data needs:

- **(Roadside) Monitoring**: to document in regular intervals, e.g. every 30 minutes, at least one picture from the concerned area shall be uploaded, at minimal cost.
- **Urgent need**, e.g. for an accident we need data urgently to plan rescue personnel.
- **Evidence**: all available data is needed to detect or to document an incident, but not urgent.

A typical example of roadside monitoring is to scan for damages on a road or to detect changes in construction areas, traffic signs or similar. Depending on the specific case and road, pictures are only needed at specific intervals. While many vehicles may pass a segment of a road during the interval, only one of them may be needed.

The case of urgent data describes cases where data is needed as soon as possible to evaluate a roadside situation. For instance, for an accident it is important to know how much rescue personnel and what equipment is needed.

In the third case, evidence or documentation needs to be collected, and all available data is needed. In contrast to the above case, the urgency is lower but the reliability is more important. An important difference to the above is that this service may also be initiated after an incident has occurred, as vehicles may store data for a short period of time. For instance, a request for such evidence could ask for all data (for an area) from the last 30 minutes.

Based on the above challenges and the analysis of different kinds of services, we propose a service model for vehicle data collection. The goal of a service model is to find a simple set of services which can accommodate the typical applications of connected vehicles.

To optimize the data collection, we assume a coordination of the pictures from the cloud side. As current vehicles are connected to some cloud services, e.g. for collecting traffic data, we consider this as a natural extension. We assume that cars continuously upload the metadata of pictures, including time and location to the cloud. The service in the cloud assigns priorities and sends requests to vehicles. Vehicles upload the requested pictures based on priorities.

For the case of a roadside monitoring service, the goal is to upload only one pictures from an area in case multiple images exist. Here, we need to define how to capture the notion of similarity. The observation is that pictures, including radar and lidar images, from roughly the same location at same point in time should be very similar, hence only one is considered sufficient.

In order to accommodate different kinds of scenarios here, we define the notion of a **similarity group**. If pictures are in the same similarity group, this means that their content overlaps significantly. There can be different ways to determine this similarity, depending on the sensor data but also on the accuracy of the location and target application needs. A rigorous method would be to use the geographic area covered by a picture. Then, similarity can be determined mathematically by matching these areas. A less accurate, but computationally easier method is to use just a square model of the area, where pictures of the same area are considered similar.

The Service Model includes the following service classes:

- **Urgent:** data is sent immediately, with higher priority than the service classes below.
- **Priority Select:** for each similarity group, the goal is to upload at least one picture for a defined time period.
- **Bulk Select:** as above, one picture is uploaded for each similarity group, but with lower priority than the above, and also permitting higher delays. This includes a possible wait for a Wifi network with lower cost of transmission.

- **Reliability**: all data shall be transmitted in a reliable fashion. Waiting for Wifi networks or regions with better network coverage is possible, but deletion of the data is to be avoided.

We assume that for different parts of a road network, different services model can be applied. A typical case would be to start with roadside monitoring, with Priority- or Bulk Select services, and then switch to Urgent or Reliability as needed.

Figure 1 illustrates the properties of the service classes regarding time, reliability and cost. For cost, we assume cost increases with the data volume and the required speed. Time refers to the delay of a successful upload, whereas reliability means the probability that a picture from a similarity group is transmitted successfully. For all, we only give qualitative scale.

Our service model is aimed to be independent of different implementation options. We do assume that metadata is collected in a coordination unit as discussed above. This refers to the management of the data in the vehicle, as well as to the data transmission. For the upload of the full contents, there exist different kinds of approaches, including roadside networks (Siegel, Erb, and Sarma 2017) and peer-to-peer networks (Rahman et al. 2018). Our approach focuses on direct upload to the cloud for several feasibility reasons. First, roadside networks or other participants may not be available, especially on less travelled roads. Secondly, relaying to other entries create considerable coordination overhead and has several intrinsic issues like reliability, cost sharing, as well as privacy issues.

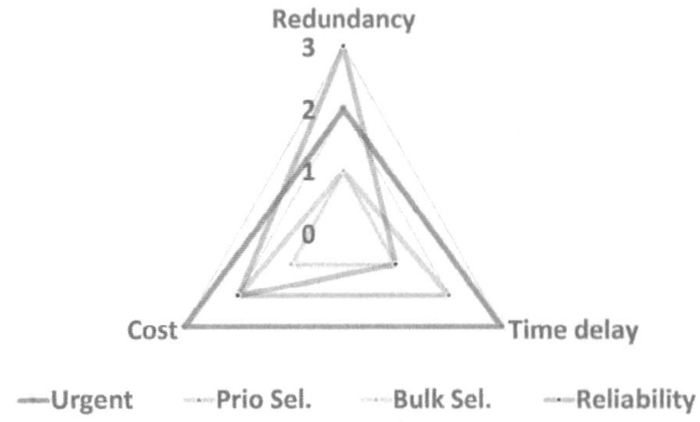

Figure 1. Dimensions of R-CDN Service Classes

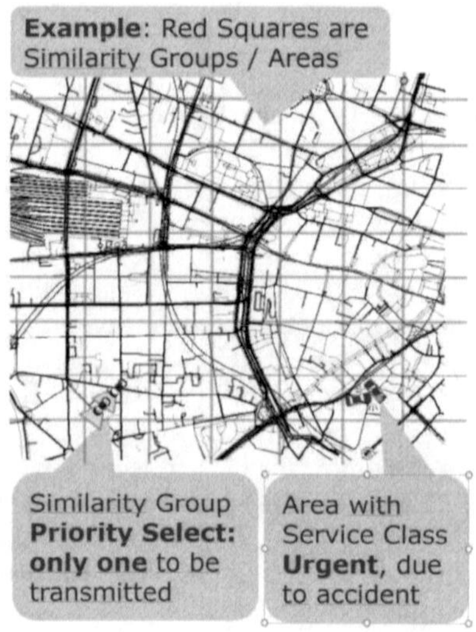

Figure 2. Example of R-CDN Service Classes

3. SYSTEM ARCHITECTURE

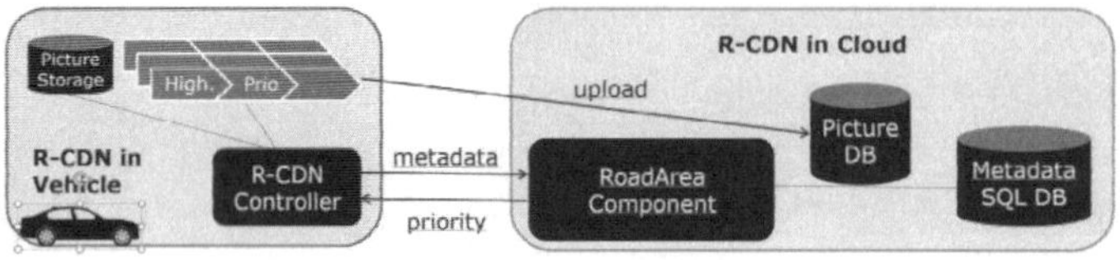

Figure 3. Architecture of R-CDN

In the following, we discuss our system architecture and basic operation. The high-level architecture is shown in Figure 3. There are three main components in the connected vehicle architecture.

1. **R-CDN Controller:** This is an in-vehicle service which manages the data and uploads. It sends image metadata to Road Area service and in the response, it gets back priority. Based on the priority, the vehicle service stores the image in the queue which resides in the local storage of vehicle. Vehicle service is continuously sending them to Road Area service.

2. **RoadArea Component:** This cloud side component manages the priorities and service classes for different areas. This means to calculate priorities of an image, and to manage changes. For instance, RoadArea is also capable of updating an image's priority based on service class. The RoadArea component is connected to image metadata database to manage the metadata of the images. It should also store images in image database.

3. **Database (DB):** There are two databases which support connected vehicle architecture. The metadata of image is stored and manipulated in relational database i.e. PostgreSQL. The images are stored in MongoDB, which is a document-oriented database.

On the vehicle side, the images are locally stored in 3 queues, indicating the priority:

- Highest
- Regular
- Lowest

In addition to the above, there are several other cases not shown in the figure above.

- In the cloud side, there is a REST API to manage the service class for each area.
- In case the priority of a picture changes, the RoadArea component can notify the vehicle.
- If vehicles drop out, e.g. are turned off, this is noticed in the cloud side and priorities are adapted.

More details on managing priorities are discussed below.

The RoadArea Component is in charge of managing the service class for each area. For simplicity as discussed above, we divide the map into squares which we use for both similarity groups and also for areas to assign service models. Thus, every similarity group has one of the above services, e.g. Urgent. In our evaluation system, the road network is divided into similarity groups (about 50x50m). This is illustrated in Figure 2.

Overall, a key assumption of the R-CDN architecture is that the CS is aware of a complete road network that it overlooks. The participating vehicles in this road network are connected to it and continuously transmit metadata like location of pictures taken.

Furthermore, we assume that the RoadArea component is in charge of managing picture priorities and uploads for a specific area. For a scalable architecture, multiple RoadArea components for different regions are possible. In this case, vehicles may have pictures from different RoadArea components and must manage uploads accordingly.

The RoadArea component is in charge of managing the priorities of the pictures for uploading. We assume here the following:

- Vehicles can change route or drop out any time
- Uploads are unpredictable
- Vehicles have regular connection for control data, low volume

Our approach gives guidance to vehicles which data is important by assigning priorities. The main mechanism is that for Priority Select and Bulk Select service classes, only one picture from the corresponding area gets the highest priorities, and all others get lower priority. This can be seen as selecting one candidate for priority upload. While these are uploaded faster in most cases, it is possible that pictures with lower priority come first. There can be several reasons. The vehicle with the higher priority picture may have some overload, poor network connection or even drop out and stop.

For the Urgent service class, the goal is to put all pictures into the highest queue. On the other hand, for the reliability service class, the lower priorities are sufficient, but vehicles are instructed not to delete these pictures.

In summary, there are several cases where priorities are assigned or changed:

- Initial upload of metadata is the initial assignment.
- Successful upload of one picture. In case of Priority and Bulk Select, the others are not needed any more and are downgraded.
- Change in service class leads to changes, e.g. upgrade to highest priority for the Urgent service class.
- Picture timeout means that after a certain lifetime, pictures are considered outdated and are not suited for upload. In case some of them are selected as the upload candidate with Urgent in the Select service classes, then another candidate needs to be found.
- Vehicle drops out. In this case, we have check the upload candidates for the Select service classes as in above case.

4. EVALUATION

We have evaluated our system based on a test case generated from realistic traffic data with the Sumo simulator (Lopez et al. 2018). The scenario includes 31 vehicles driving in an area of Munich for a few minutes and send 4540 times picture metadata to the RoadArea service. We assume vehicles take pictures every 3 seconds. Overall, there are 849 distinct similarity groups in this area.

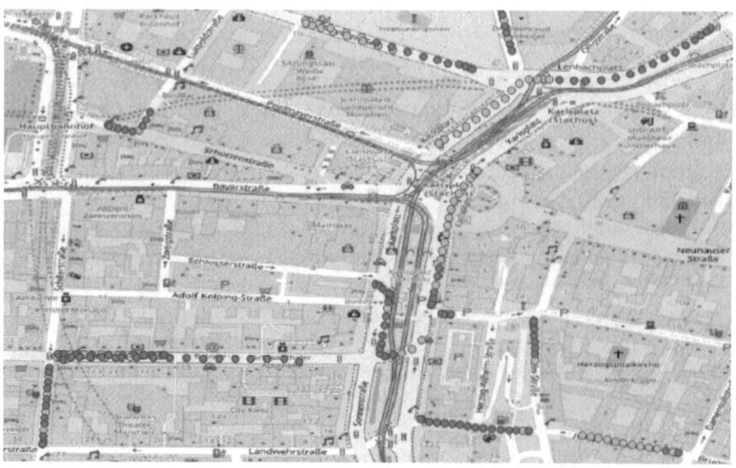

Figure 4. Example Scenario after 150 Uploads, where green dots indicate uploaded images and yellow dots are images for possible upload

Table 1. Table depicts similarity group coverage for Priority Select

Number of uploads	200	400	600	800
Similarity Groups Covered	167	275	375	462
High Priority Images	164	274	375	462
Regular Priority Images	36	126	225	338

The goal of our proposed approach is to upload the images efficiently while considering redundant images. We run the system for evaluation purposes and observe the behaviour of the system in terms of similarity group coverage for uploaded images. For example, we would like to find out how many similarity groups have been covered while uploading 500 images. Also, we plan here to gather the results after changing the state of the system. A change is considered when a vehicle is disconnected, or the service class of a similarity group is updated etc.

As an example, Figure 4 shows our evaluation scenario after a few minutes when 150 images have been uploaded (assuming all pictures are Priority Select and 2 second upload delay).

Our main evaluation criterion is the **similarity group coverage** for the Priority Select service group, which indicates for how many similarity groups we have at least one picture. We assume Priority Select as the starting point for all areas in the evaluation, unless stated otherwise. The similarity coverage is considered as after a specific image upload count. Table 1 presents coverage of similarity group at specific upload image count, where all areas are Priority Select. In this evaluation, vehicles start driving and upload medata data every three seconds. Once the priority from the RoadArea component is received, uploads start according to the priority queues. We use a simple scheme for priorities where higher queues need to be empty for transmission of lower ones.

Figure 5 compares the case of all pictures in Priority Select vs Urgent classs, with a delay of 2 seconds for upload. This delay is useful to permit some coordination of the uploads. The setup is otherwise as above. Even for our small example, running just 800 uploads, in case of Priority Select 585 similarity groups are covered, while in the same setup, Urgent service class for all areas uploads just 396, pictures. Thus, Priority Select service class yields a 50% improvement of service class coverage compared to Urgent. For larger, longer running examples, the prior work in (Khan and Prehofer 2020) has shown much higher values. The scenario in (Khan and Prehofer 2020) is similar, but considers higher number of pictures with more upload congestion and Wifi-offloading.

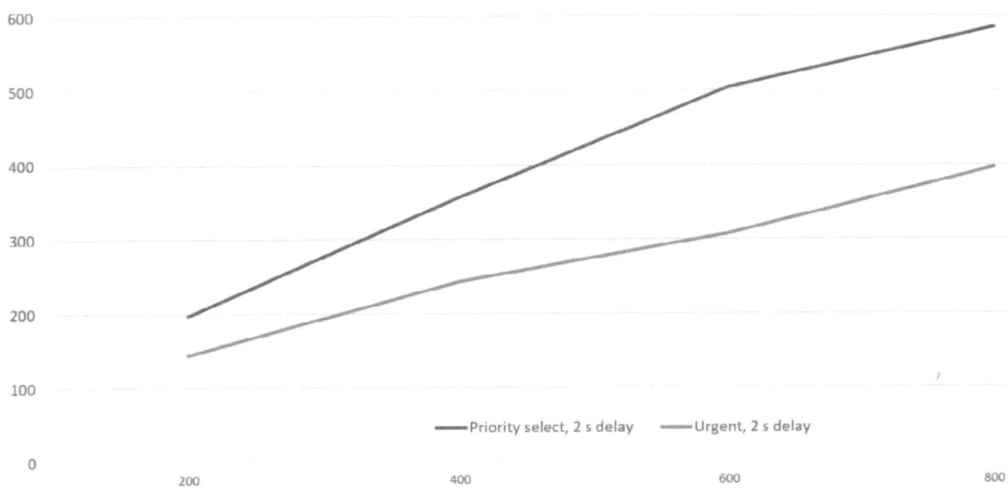

Figure 5. Similarity Group Coverage for Priority Select and Urgent

Next, we evaluate the impact on the system when **vehicles are disconnected** or drop out in some way. For this evaluation and also in the next one, we use a different way for uploads. We first let the vehicles collect all the pictures in our scenario (4540), then the vehicles start upload in a round robin fashion. This simplifies the analysis, as no new pictures are added during evaluation phase. In particular, smaller differences are easier to detect.

After running the system on the test data, we have disconnected 5 random vehicles out of 31 vehicles in the system. These 5 vehicles constitute about 20% of the vehicles in the system. The service class of all similarity groups is set to Priority Select. We have employed a round robin upload strategy here, which created 175 rounds of uploads for the data from the remaining 26 vehicles. The 5 vehicles were disconnected from the system with the help of a REST endpoint for disconnecting vehicles which resides in Vehicle service. The mentioned vehicles cover 390 distinct similarity groups in the system.

For comparison, we have gathered results without disconnection of vehicles and compare this with the case where 5 vehicles are dropped out after data collection. This is shown in Table 2.

Table 2. Table depicts similarity group coverage when 20% vehicles are disconnected with Priority service class

Number of uploads	Similarity Group Coverage (without Disconnecting Vehicles)	Similarity Group Coverage with Disconnecting Vehicles
200	187	185
400	355	339
600	488	467
800	602	574
1000	696	645

We observed that after disconnecting 5 vehicles out of 31 vehicles on the running system, on upload of first 1000 images, 645 similarity groups are covered as depicted in the table. The graph also shows that the system handles vehicle dropouts quite well and vehicle dropout does not impact the reliability of the system.

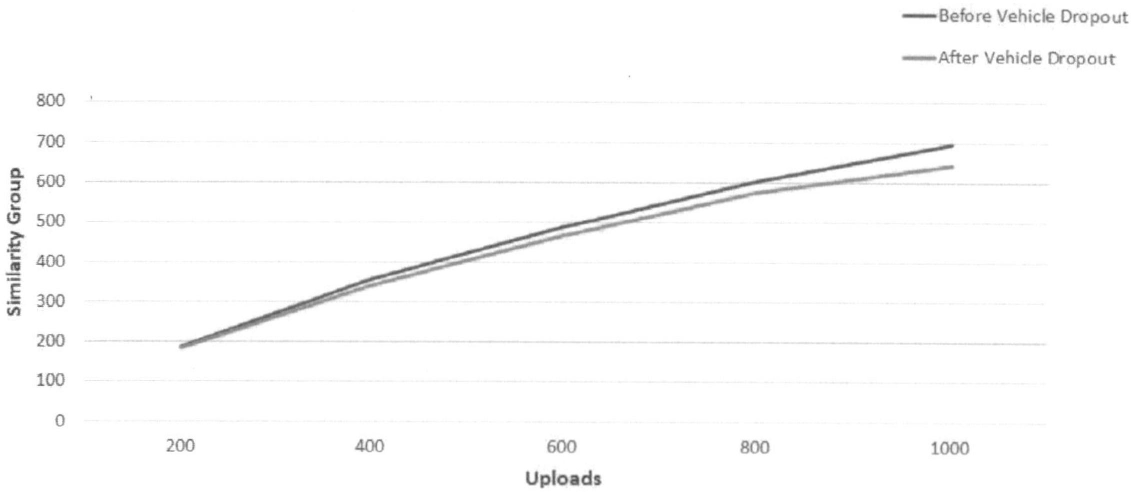

Figure 6. Illustrates coverage of Similarity Group before and after vehicle dropout

Another evaluation considers **outdated images**. After running the system on the testdata, while uploading the images, we slow down the rate of uploading images. Every image should be uploaded after 1 second. In the meantime, the Road Area service has started out-dating the images. The images which are 3 minutes old in the database are considered to be outdated. We also slow down the rate of image outdate by 1 second. Below mentioned table describes the behaviour of the system when images were outdated. Service class of all similarity groups is set to Urgent.

The duration of this test run depends on the number of images uploaded and image outdate threshold. For example, 1 second delay is introduced to upload each image and in addition to that, we wait for three minutes so that the images in the database are being outdated. The first 200 images will take 6 minutes 20 seconds in which 3 minutes are taken by images to be outdated and 3 minutes 20 seconds to upload images.

Table 3. Table depicts similarity group coverage when images are being outdated

Number of uploads	Similarity Groups Coverage without Image Outdating	Similarity Groups Coverage with Image Outdating
200	125	110
400	254	180
600	346	219

5. RELATED WORK

An evaluation of data collection with an approach similar to the Priority Select in realistic city traffic simulations with 100.000 cars has shown a data reduction by factor of 20 (Khan and Prehofer 2020). Here, we have presented and evaluated a more extensive service model, including dynamic changes and updates.

Regarding WiFi offloading, (Lee et al. 2010) shows that a significant amount of mobile data can be offloaded for pedestrians using smartphones. Here, we analyze the offloading behavior in vehicles that cover distances much faster than pedestrians and show similar results for this aspect. For WiFi traffic other works show that congestion and transfer latency usually result from poor allocation of WiFi resources (Hossain et al. 2010). Other approaches like Cabernet (Eriksson, Balakrishnan, and Madden 2008), Drive-Through Internet (Ott and Kutscher 2004) and Shared Wireless Infostation Model (SWIM) (Small and Haas 2003) consider fairness among users. The above works could complement our findings here, but do not consider the offloading as such in realistic scenarios. For road monitoring with smartphone sensors, the work in (Freschi et al. 2014), describes techniques to reduce the data volume, but this is specific to the data analysis applied in their case.

The general idea of selective data upload has also been investigated in sensor networks. Data selection techniques, also known as suppression-based techniques, have been proven useful and accurate in monitoring physical phenomena while significantly reducing the amount of transferred data (Kulik, Tanin, and Umer 2008; Puggioni and Gelfand 2009). The most basic method is temporal suppression where connected vehicle data is only transmitted when the data is different from what the vehicle and the central server expect. The main difference is that in our case, the mobile vehicles continuously transmit metadata to a central server which coordinates the data collection.

6. SUMMARY

We have presented a new approach, R-CDN, where connected vehicles efficiently upload the images in the cloud according to our novel service model. The service model differentiates between redundancy (or reliability), time delay as well as cost in terms of upload effort. For this model, we have devised a demand management strategy, where an image will be assigned a priority for uploading to the cloud. We also manage these in case of changes on demand or vehicle side.

For evaluation, we have implemented a flexible solution which can also handle changes like vehicles dropping out. The system was tested on a data set generated by SUMO, with a dataset of 4540 images from 31 randomly moving vehicles. In particular, we have shown the benefit of the Priority Select service class, which yields a 50% improvement of service class coverage.

REFERENCES

Eriksson, Jakob, Hari Balakrishnan, and Samuel Madden (2008). “Cabernet: Vehicular Content Delivery Using WiFi”. In: *Proceedings of the 14th ACM International Conference on Mobile Computing and Networking*. MobiCom ’08. San Francisco, California, USA: Association for Computing Machinery, pp. 199–210. isbn: 9781605580968. doi: 10.1145/1409944.1409968.

Freschi, Valerio et al. (2014). “Geospatial data aggregation and reduction in vehicular sensing applications: The case of road surface monitoring”. In: *2014 International Conference on Connected Vehicles and Expo (ICCVE)*. IEEE, pp. 711–716.

Hossain, Ekram et al. (May 2010). “Vehicular telematics over heterogeneous wireless networks: A survey”. In: *Computer Communications* 33.7, pp. 775–793. doi: 10.1016/j.comcom.2009.12.010.

Khan, Zaryab and Christian Prehofer (2020). “Efficient and Selective Upload of Data from Connected Vehicles”. In: *Proceedings of the 6th International Conference on Vehicle Technology and Intelligent Transport Systems - Volume 1: VEHITS*, INSTICC. SciTePress, pp. 559–566. doi: 10.5220/0009790105590566.

Kulik, Lars, Egemen Tanin, and Muhammad Umer (2008). “Efficient Data Collection and Selective Queries in Sensor Networks”. In: *GeoSensor Networks*. Springer Berlin Heidelberg, pp. 25–44. doi:
10.1007/978-3-540-79996-2_3.

Lee, Kyunghan et al. (2010). "Mobile Data Off-loading: How Much Can WiFi Deliver?" In: *ACM CoNEXT 2010*.

Lopez, Pablo Alvarez et al. (Nov. 2018). "Microscopic Traffic Simulation using SUMO". In: *2018 21st International Conference on Intelligent Transportation Systems (ITSC)*. IEEE.

Moustafa, Hassnaa, Eve M. Schooler, and Jessica McCarthy (2017). "Reverse CDN in Fog Computing: The Lifecycle of Video Data in Connected and Autonomous Vehicles". In: *2017 IEEE Fog World Congress (FWC)*.

Ott, J. and D. Kutscher (n.d.). "Drive-thru internet: IEEE 802.1 1b for "automobile" users". In: *IEEE INFOCOM 2004*. IEEE. doi: 10.1109/infcom.2004.1354509.

Puggioni, Gavino and Alan E. Gelfand (June 2009). "Analyzing space-time sensor network data under suppression and failure in transmission". In: *Statistics and Computing* 20.4, pp. 409–419. doi: 10.1007/s11222-009-9133-z.

Rahman, Sawsan Abdul et al. (2018). "A novel on-demand vehicular sensing framework for traffic condition monitoring". In: *Vehicular Communications* 12, pp. 165–178.

Siegel, Joshua E, Dylan C Erb, and Sanjay E Sarma (2017). "A survey of the connected vehicle landscape—Architectures, enabling technologies, applications, and development areas". In: *IEEE Transactions on Intelligent Transportation Systems* 19.8, pp. 2391–2406.

Small, Tara and Zygmunt J. Haas (2003). "The shared wireless infostation model". In: *Proceedings of the 4th ACM international symposium on Mobile ad hoc networking & computing - MobiHoc 03*. ACM Press. doi: 10.1145/778415.778443.

Zeng, Xiaosi, Kevin Balke, Praprut Songchitruksa, et al. (2012). *Potential connected vehicle applications to enhance mobility, safety, and environmental security.* Tech. rep. Southwest Region University Transportation Center (US).

DEVELOPMENT OF A SMART CITY SERVICE CATALOGUE FOR SENSOR-BASED DIGITAL SERVICES

Yusuf Bozkurt, Jan Fauser, Reiner Braun, Dieter Hertweck and Alexander Rossmann
Department of Computer Science, Reutlingen University,
72762 Reutlingen, Germany

ABSTRACT

The increasing urban population growth leads to challenges in cities in many aspects: Urbanisation problems such as excessive environmental pollution or increasing urban traffic demand new and innovative solutions. In this context, the concept of smart cities is discussed. An enabling element of the smart city concept is applying information technology (IT) to improve administrative efficiency and quality of life while reducing costs and resource consumption and ensuring greater citizen participation in administrative and urban development issues. While these smart city services are technologically studied and implemented, government officials, citizens or businesses are often unaware of the large variety of smart city service solutions. Therefore, this work deals with developing a smart city services catalogue that documents best practice services to create a platform that brings citizens, city government, and businesses together. Although the concept of IT service catalogues is not new and guidelines and recommendations for the design and development of service catalogues already exist in the corporate context, there is little work on smart city service catalogues. Therefore, approaches from agile software development and pattern research were adapted to develop the smart city service catalogue platform in this work.

KEYWORDS

Smart City, Service Catalogue, IoT Service, Smart City Service Catalogue Platform, Transparency, Governance

1. INTRODUCTION

The shift of populations to cities and urban areas creates complex problems, for instance, environmental impacts, rapid urbanisation, traffic etc. (Alberti et al., 2019). Cities play a significant role in the social and economic development of any country. Digitalisation has a major impact on society and the economy nowadays and in the future. According to Stolterman & Fors (2004), digitalisation, or digital transformation, refers to "the changes associated with the application of digital technology in all aspects of human society". Digitisation enables a wide range of opportunities to develop new services in smart cities to address different challenges related, e.g., climate change or urbanisation. Harakal'ova (2018) defines a smart city as the main element of the smart city concept: the use of information technology to improve management efficiency and standard of living while reducing costs and use of resources and ensuring greater participation of citizens in matters of management and urban development. Many smart city services are available based on Internet of Things (IoT) technology (Perera et al., 2014; Zanella et al., 2014). For example, the monitoring of CO2 and NOx concentration in the cities with IoT sensors. That could provide city developers information regarding the identification of green areas that have a significant impact on air quality (OKLab Köln, 2021). According to Peng et al. (2017), little research has been done on the awareness of such smart city services and user participation. Government officials, policymakers or SMEs are often unaware of the existing large variety of smart city service solutions (Kramers et al., 2014). Additionally, another barrier in enterprises or cities is their uncertainty about which technologies exist or to choose from to address the requirements for a concrete use case. Another issue is implementing the service effectively and determining the maturity of available service (Rachinger et al., 2019). In addition, high implementation costs and lack of technical experts in municipalities and enterprises are often a barrier.

To address these problems, the paper at hand deals with developing a smart city services catalogue that documents best practice services to create a platform to bring citizens, city government, and businesses together. A smart city service catalogue platform structures and describes existing services, supports developing new ideas and identifying and implementing new smart city services. Such a service catalogue represents the first point of contact to the service. It facilitates the contact between interested parties and providers, and users/cities that have already implemented this service. Vice versa, this leads to time and cost savings when implementing smart city services (Yuaca et al., 2019). We formulated the following research question for this paper: *What are the components to develop a smart city service catalogue platform?*

To answer this research question, we developed a concrete implementation of the smart city service catalogue platform iteratively, described in this paper and available online at www.smartcity-services.de. The rest of this paper is structured as follows: In section 2, we will introduce some background information and discuss related work. Section 3 describes our development process for the smart city service catalogue platform, and in section 4, we present the implemented service catalogue platform. In the last section, we summarise the main findings and discuss future research.

2. BACKGROUND

The urban population today makes up 56 % of the world's population. By 2050, the population is expected to increase to 68 % (United Nations, Department of Economic and Social Affairs, 2018). This growth leads to multiple challenges in different areas of a city (e.g. waste management, traffic management, public transportation). The European Commission (Catriona et al., 2014) structures smart cities in following six dimensions: Smart governance, smart environment, smart mobility, smart living, smart people and smart economy (Bozkurt et al., 2020; Caragliu et al., 2011; Catriona et al., 2014; Giffinger & Gudrun, 2010). Bozkurt et al. (2020) analyse these six dimensions and rank them according to their popularity in the scientific literature. According to this work, smart environment represents the most studied dimension, while smart economy ranks last. According to Bozkurt et al. (2020), the dimensions cover the following topics: 1) Smart environment focuses on sustainable and environmentally friendly urban development using information and communications technology (ICT). Activities range from smart buildings to energy-saving measures for IoT services. 2) Smart governance deals with, e.g., smart city strategy development, transparency and necessary framework conditions for digitalisation projects and smart city initiatives. 3) Intelligent transport systems, optimisation and creation of mobility services are discussed in smart mobility. Citizen participation, social justice, education and co-creation are discussed in 4) smart people. Literature on 5) smart living deals mainly with e-health, but also with smart home topics. Finally, the last dimension, 6) smart economy deals with data-driven business models and business generation in different data life cycle layers.

Despite some dimensions of smart cities are already visible and studied, it is still difficult to give an all-accepted definition of smart cities. For example, Caragliu et al. (2011) emphasise economic growth and high quality of life through the combination of traditional urban infrastructure and ICT and the investment in human and social capital and participatory governance. Lombardi et al. (2012) share a similar view, linking social and environmental issues with the application of ICTs. Cretu (2012) emphasises integrating ICT into every aspect of human life and new thinking paradigms in governance and economy. Washburn & Sindhu (2010) supported a more technological perspective considering smart cities as a collection of ICTs applied to urban infrastructure and services. In contrast, Kourtit et al. (2012) advocate a knowledge-intensive and creative perspective on human and social capital, infrastructure and entrepreneurial capital. Despite numerous definitions and views, the role of ICT as an enabler of smart city activities appears as a common element.

Smart city applications and services are deployed across the city to address challenges such as pollution, ageing society and resource scarcity. Government agencies and businesses are interested in using ICT as an enabler of new smart services. Mainly discussed smart city service areas are transportation (e.g. smart parking, smart traffic lights), healthcare (e.g. patient monitoring systems), energy (e.g. smart grids), public safety services (e.g. smart surveillance), building management, waste management and education (Peng et al., 2017). There is a general understanding that the proper use of smart city services can sustainably improve a city's liveability (Lee & Lee, 2014; Peng et al., 2017; Piro et al., 2014; Yeh, 2017; Yigitcanlar & Lee, 2014). While these smart city services are being technologically studied and implemented, little research has been done on the awareness of such services and user participation (Peng et al., 2017). To better understand the users of smart city services, Lytras & Visvizi (2018) conducted a qualitative study and questioned 102 participants on the usage of smart city services. One of the aspects of the study addressed the main concerns of citizens when using smart city services. It resulted that 45% of the respondents were concerned about security and privacy. This concern was followed by data protection (25%), lack of transparency (8%), ethical concerns (6%), required soft skills (5%), third party awareness (5%) and complexity of services (4%). These concerns can be overcome through a high level of transparency of smart city services. Therefore, a smart city service catalogue platform with best practices worldwide is the first approach to bring citizens, city administration and businesses together.

The concept of a service catalogue is not new and has been addressed and discussed by companies for years as part of IT governance frameworks such as ITIL or COBIT. Many articles deal with this topic and state the necessity and the advantages of service catalogues for companies (e.g. transparent communication of existing IT services) (Horvat et al., 2013; Taconi et al., 2014; Xu et al., 2010). There is no standard design for a service catalogue. Still, the ITIL framework describes some mandatory components: 1) A general list of all services offered, 2) a sufficient description of each service, 3) the alignment between IT and business, 4) the operation level agreement, 5) the service level agreement and 6) the underlying contract (Sembiring & Surendro, 2016). Such a catalogue is primarily used to communicate services transparently and create a consistent picture of the service portfolio (Horvat et al., 2013; Meriwether, 2014; Sembiring & Surendro, 2016; Sipina, 2011; Taconi et al., 2014; Xu et al., 2010). Although first smart city service catalogues are already visible (IoT Collaborative, n.d.; OASCITIES, 2021; UNPARALLEL Innovation, 2021), the topic of smart city service catalogues has remained almost unaddressed in the scientific community.

3. DEVELOPMENT PROCESS

Although various publications already exist, there is no consensus on what a service catalogue should look like. These publications and guides are primarily for businesses to assist them in designing and creating service catalogues (Horvat et al., 2013). Hubbers et al. (2007), for example, emphasise the decomposition of all business processes and the analysis of the IT infrastructure as well as the business goals as a starting point of creating a service catalogue. Kieninger et al. (2011) propose an approach to classify IT services into ten groups (e.g. standard application services, intranet services, backup services). A similar approach is described by Arcilla et al. (2013) by grouping services into hardware, email, backup. Taconi et al. (2014) propose a framework for identifying services and creating service catalogues structured in 9 phases and provides a step by step workflow for identifying available IT services in the company. However, all this valuable work is not directly applicable to creating a smart city service catalogue platform. An enterprise service catalogue, for example, lists and describes the IT services available in the company and the connected business processes. Nevertheless, in the case of the smart city service catalogue platform, we intend to present best practices from different cities to provide ideas for implementing new services and enable an exchange of services between various stakeholders.

Fehling et al. (2015) describe a three-phase model for 1) identification, 2) authoring, and 3) application of patterns in different domains with multiple actors. They describe the approach by referring to patterns in cloud computing, cloud data, application management, costumes in films and green business process. These domains are characterised by their high diversity, making a homogenised general description of patterns complex (Fehling et al., 2015). The basic approach of this methodology proved to be suitable for our project, as the topic of smart cities is also a strongly interdisciplinary field with a multi-stakeholder structure (Albino et al., 2015; Bozkurt et al., 2020; Giffinger & Gudrun, 2010; Lombardi et al., 2012). We were able to adopt the approach of Fehling et al. (2015) to identify and describe smart city services and create the service catalogue platform with minor modifications. That led to the development framework shown in Figure 1, which is the foundation of our work. The framework's core is the agile work approach of the research team, which develops and synchronises the service catalogue in regular sprints. Theoretical findings from the literature represent the foundation of the framework. In addition, the entire work is supported by the "Best Practices" and "Requirements" pillars, which represent findings from existing references and potential user groups.

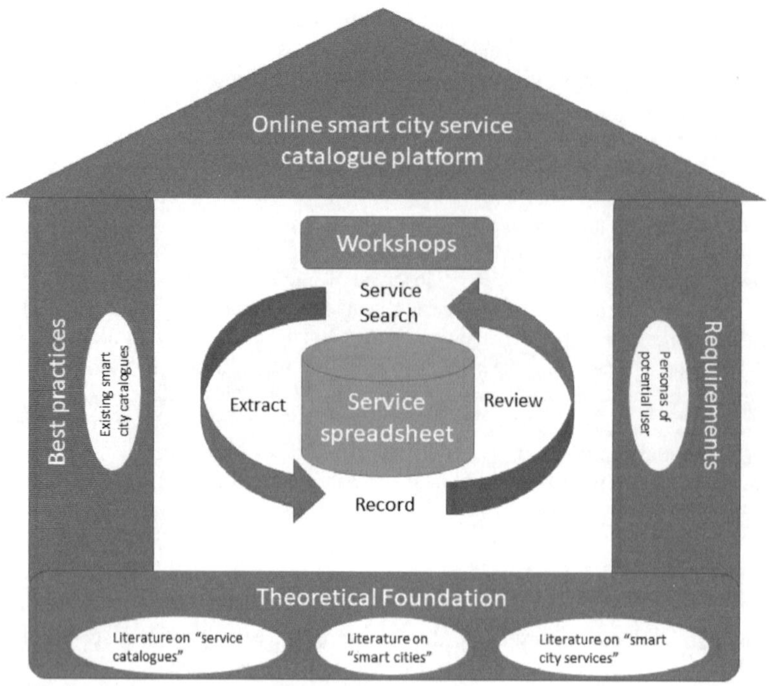

Figure 1. Development Framework

We needed to consider the fundamental question of who the potential users of the online smart city service catalogue platform are. Therefore, potential users were identified initially in a workshop with graduate students and experts from the smart city field. As a result, the following personas were developed: 1) City administration (decision-makers and employees), 2) citizens and communities, 3) companies, 4) teaching and research institutions. Besides developing the personas, the theoretical foundation was established by the scientific literature on smart cities, service catalogues and smart city services (see Chapter 2). These findings were continuously taken into account. A smart city service catalogue platform flourishes through its multitude of existing services and also stimulates the expansion of services through its abundance. Therefore, it was essential for us to offer many services in the very first version of the service catalogue.

For this reason, the research team conducted an extensive search for existing smart city services. That involved a detailed review of existing service catalogues, smart city IoT communities and smart city service providers (e.g. eco curious, 2021; element14, 2021; Smart City Solutions, 2021; TTN Ulm, 2021). Each research member recorded the services at a detailed level to create a collective pool of smart city services in a first step. In the subsequent step, the research group reviewed the collection of smart city services in a workshop to identify relevant and universal categories to describe smart city services. In the second iteration, missing information was completed, and new services were included. Subsequently, the services were categorised according to the six smart city dimensions and resulted in a first version of the service catalogue as an Excel file.

The service catalogue was supposed to be available as an online service catalogue platform from the beginning, easily accessible and transparent for different users. But before developing the service catalogue as a platform, we created mock-ups based on the previously created service catalogue (Excel file) and considering the personas. Mock-ups helped us understand at an early stage that categorising the service catalogue platform according to the six smart city dimensions is not the right design for our target group. Especially the dimensions smart economy, smart living and smart people are not intuitive for general readers. Therefore, we decided to adopt five easily understandable high-level dimensions for the service catalogue platform as the entry point, namely 1) mobility, 2) environment, 3) public, 4) living and 5) industry. These five dimensions are still based on Catriona et al. (2014), but the understanding is easier for the general readers. After this revision, a preliminary version of the online service catalogue platform was implemented and filled with the first pilot services. The insertion of these pilot services helped us to gain new insights for further improvements. After implementing these insights, the remaining services were uploaded.

4. SERVICE CATALOGUE

We used the content management system (CMS) Word Press [1]to implement our smart city service catalogue platform. Word Press is one of the most used CMS worldwide (Schäferhoff & WebSiteSetup, 2021; W3Techs, 2021). The platform aims to provide open source and commercial available best practice examples of IoT network services to different actors. Moreover, the platform offers a service catalogue for sensor-based, digital services (IoT services) and enables the exchange of services. The implemented smart city service catalogue is available on www.smartcity-services.de.

In Chapter 3, we described the five main categories in which we structured the different services, which supports the navigation and identification of relevant services for different user groups. We defined the category "Environment" as services that are monitoring environmental changes and used in, e.g., agriculture, buildings and energy savings etc. "Mobility" is defined as services in public or private transportation and traffic management. The category "Public" describes services for optimising the management of public infrastructure, city administration, citizen participation or education. Services in health, society and home were categorised in the category Living. In the category Industry, services for industrial usage such as condition monitoring or predictive maintenance were assigned. A service can be assigned to more than one category. For instance, the service "Vehicle / Asset Tracking" (LoRa Alliance, 2021). It is a LoRaWAN-based (The Things Network, 2021) GPS tracker for tracking products or material of a company. It supports optimising (intra-) logistic processes in container and asset management, warehouse and inventory scenarios, outdoor tracking, theft protection. Another scenario of "Asset Tracking" can also be in the public area, such as tracking bicycles of a sharing provider. To strengthen the community and the platform idea, we implemented a form that allows everyone to add a service to the service catalogue platform in a predefined structure. After a successful review, the service will be published on the service catalogue platform. In Table 1, we have listed the 32 services, which are currently available on the service catalogue platform. In addition, each service has a short description, and the assigned categories of the service are shown.

We developed a standardised format for describing the services to increase comprehensibility and address the users' different requirements. Inspired by Alexander et al. (1977) pattern description, we developed a structure to describe the individual services. To identify the service, each service has a title. A visualisation of a service on our smart city service catalogue platform is shown in Figure 2 ("DIY Fine Dust Sensor"). For quick visual identification of a service, we use cover images, which we assigned to the different categories, for example, environment or mobility. In which category a service was assigned is listed under the title. For further filter and description purposes, we assigned tags to every service. This should enable users to search the service catalogue beyond the different categories, such as a specific technology or keyword. We used the following tags to describe further the service "DIY Fine Dust Sensor": #Air #citizenscience #sensor. Below the tag section is a short description of the service. A short description should not exceed 30 words and summarises the key value proposition of the service. The short description aims to communicate the main idea of the service effectively and efficiently to the reader. In order to better understand the service, especially readers with non-IT background, a video, if available, is embedded in the service description. The category "Abstract" offers a detailed explanation of the service, structured in use case, functionality and benefits. This is intended to achieve a deeper understanding of the service for a user. The category "Place of operation" shows the country or the city where the service is already in usage. This should enable the user to evaluate the implementation in the context of regional factors, especially regarding data protection laws, which differ significantly between different countries and impact the implementation of a service. The "Licensing Model" category describes how a service is licensed, such as commercial licensing or open source. This is a piece of relevant information for evaluating any costs incurred by implementing the service. In addition, open-source services may also have specific implementation requirements. For the category "Technological Architecture", we used a toolchain approach to visualise the architecture components and their relationships, such as hardware, software, and communication protocols. Additionally, we give a short description of the technological architecture. This provides the user with an overview of technical implementation details.

---

[1] https://wordpress.com/

Table 1. Smart City Services (E=Environment; M=Mobility; P=Public; L=Living; I=Industry)

Service title	**Short description**	**Categories**				
		E	M	P	L	I
Connected Beehive for beekeeping	This service provides temperature and humidity monitoring of connected beehives to save bees and make life easier for beekeepers.	x				
District heating monitoring	The service describes the implementation for district heating monitoring based on LoRaWAN.			x		x
DIY Fine Dust Sensor	This service describes how to build an own open source based fine dust sensor and measure air pollution.	x		x		
DIY Noise Measuring Sensor	This service describes how to build an open source based digital noise measurement system and measure noise pollution in your urban area.				x	
DIY Pax Counter ESP32	This service describes how to build a mini Pax counter, a proof-of-concept device for people monitoring in real-time and anonymously.	x	x	x	x	x
DIY Radiation Measurement	This service describes how to build an open-source Geiger counter, which measures radiation to contribute your data to the community.	x				
Door & Window event monitoring	This service describes how to integrate a system for door & windows event monitoring based on LoRaWAN or Zigbee.				x	
DYI NO2 Sensor	This open-source-based project offers a sensor-based service for monitoring air quality.	x		x	x	
Earthquake/ground vibrations for construction sites	The application is used to analyse earthquakes and their magnitude. The purpose is to ensure the accuracy of sensitive measuring devices during construction work.	x				x
Energy Management System (EMS)	The Energy Management System (EMS) is based on LoRaWAN that can be used in measurements of energy consumption in private and public institutions.			x	x	x
Feedback Buttons	Wireless customer feedback buttons can be used to request customer opinions with low energy consumption.			x		x
Flood water tracking	With the support of Flood Network, live data can be displayed showing where water levels are high, or flooding is imminent.	x		x		
General Tracing	Basic asset tracing based on LoRaWAN and GPS for localisation.		x	x		x
Ground sensors for frost and snow	The sensors implemented in the ground can provide helpful information to local road maintenance services to optimise the winter services.	x		x		
Parking sensors	Smart parking sensor solutions reduce the amount of traffic searching for a free parking space and reduce noise and air pollution emissions.		x	x		x
Recognition of structural damage	The service provides a condition monitoring and anomaly detection of small and hardly visible structure damages in bridges or walls.			x	x	x
Smart Health: Infrared Temperature Sensor	Real-time data from the temperature sensors enables healthcare workers to screen individuals with a high temperature efficiently.				x	
Smart home sensor empowered by LoRaWAN	This room-sensor service enables the monitoring of temperature, humidity or CO2.			x	x	x
Smart Lighting Indoor	A smart LED light bulb with which the lighting can be adjusted to different activities.			x	x	
Smart metering	This service enables the monitoring of gas, water and heat in households by using LoRaWAN.				x	
Smart pest traps	This service describes the implementation of condition monitoring of the traps status and toxin amount for rats and mouse traps.	x		x		x
Smart Smoke Detector	Smoke detector with radio interface for LoRaWAN and Wireless M-Bus. These small but effective devices are an essential early warning system for fire safety.			x	x	x
Smart Traffic Lights	This service enables the automatisation of the traffic flow based on data analytics.		x	x		x x
Smart Waste	This service describes the implementation of a network of sensor-based smart garbage containers, which enables the monitoring of the waste level. This data can be used to optimise the routing of waste collection tours.	x		x		
Soil Moisture Sensor	The soil moisture sensor connected to LoRaWAN enables the monitoring of soil parameters for optimal plant care.	x			x	
Street Lighting empowered by	Intelligent street lighting based on LoRaWAN optimises infrastructure management and energy consumption.	x		x		

LoRaWAN						
Traffic Counter empowered by LoRaWAN	This service provides a traffic counter based on LoRaWAN, transmitting and recording the number of incoming vehicles in urban areas.		x	x		
Vehicle / Asset Tracking	LoRaWAN based GPS can track vehicles or other assets in a long-range.		x	x		
Vibration monitoring empowered by LoRaWAN	Real-time monitoring of individual machines with LoRaWAN sensors to alert users of defects or malfunctions.					x
Water Flow Monitoring System	The flow measurement station allows users to detect abnormal water flow rates that indicate leaks and blockages.	x		x		x
Water flow velocity measuring system	System for measuring water flows within autonomous water systems can be used for predictive/planned maintenance.	x		x		
Water Quality/monitoring	Drinking water monitoring allows monitoring the quality of tap water in cities.	x		x	x	x

Furthermore, the user gains an idea about the service's functionality on a technical level and can identify potential gaps in infrastructure or knowledge. In the category "Link / Repository / References," we provided the links of the concrete services, e.g. from a service provider or, in the case of a prototype to a GitHub repository. This provides the user with additional information and allows them to explore the specific service further.

Figure 2. Smart city services description

5. CONCLUSION

The goal of this work was to describe the development of a smart city service catalogue platform based on an actual implementation. Despite multiple perspectives on smart cities and different definitions, the application of ICT as an enabler of smart city services is visible. Existing city services are optimised through ICT by integrating sensors into the physical world. But also new and innovative services for cities are developed with the use of ICT. An online catalogue of such services and best practices from cities worldwide can foster innovation in other cities. Driven by this motivation, we developed a platform for smart city services that helps cities develop new ideas and identify and implement new smart city services. However, the service catalogue platform is not only addressed to the city government but also to businesses, individual interested citizens, communities, and educational and research institutions. Although the concept of IT service catalogues is not new and guidelines and recommendations for the design and development of service catalogues already exist in the corporate context, there is little work on smart city service catalogues. Therefore, we have adapted approaches from agile software development and pattern research to develop the smart city service catalogue platform. This systematic approach has made it possible to develop the service catalogue iteratively in a project team with several researchers and students.

The results of this work provide practical and theoretical contributions. Practitioners can use this paper and the developed service catalogue as a guideline for creating smart city service catalogues in their region or their specific domain. Furthermore, the service catalogue is a valuable opportunity to share services and use it as a platform with different stakeholders. In this way, interested parties and providers can easily find each other. We hope that this will lead to a high level of transparency, innovation and stimulation of smart city activities by making it easier to get started. The theoretical contribution is that researchers can use this work to enhance the methodology and conduct further research on smart city service catalogues. Service catalogues are discussed in science and practice, but only from a business perspective. This work shows that there is no framework or guideline for the creation of service catalogues for smart city services, although smart city services are often discussed, and service catalogues are an essential element for transparency and open exchange. Furthermore, the service catalogue provides a basis for developing patterns in the smart city domain by conducting the phases 2) and 3) described by (Fehling et al., 2015). In addition to patterns, reference architectures for ICT-supported smart city services can also be developed, and business models for smart city services can be analysed using the smart city service catalogue platform.

The services have only been researched and prepared by one team. That means that there may be some human bias in the search for services, and we may have considered only limited aspects. Furthermore, due to the Corona pandemic, regular workshops with interested citizens and other stakeholders could not be held throughout the development of the service catalogue. Consequently, the workshops were mostly limited to the core research team. Nevertheless, these limitations also indicate the direction of further research. As the smart city service catalogue platform is already online, it will be possible to bring it to the public on a large scale and collect feedback for further improvements. Besides the continuous development, it is also important to upload more services, as a large number of services simulates further ideas. For this purpose, we have contacted several European partner institutions that will upload services from their countries. In this way, a continuous increase in awareness and in the number of services with the self-service functionality will be achieved.

ACKNOWLEDGEMENT

Experts from the Working Group on Digitisation (PA8) from countries such as Austria, Bulgaria, Croatia, Germany, Romania, Slovenia supported by the State Ministry of Baden-Württemberg. Finally, we would like to thank the students Ibrahim Sevik, Benjamin Nußer, Andreas Knoll and Damiano Squillante who supported the implementation of the service catalogue platform.

REFERENCES

Alberti, V., Alonso Raposo, M., Attardo, C., Auteri, D., Ribeiro Barranco, R., Batista E Silva, F., Benczur, P., Bertoldi, P., Bono, F., Bussolari, I., Louro Caldeira, S., Carlsson, J., Christidis, P., Christodoulou, A., Ciuffo, B., Corrado, S., Fioretti, C., Galassi, M. C., Galbusera, L., … Zulian, G. (2019). *The Future of Cities: Opportunities, challenges and the way forward* (Issue JRC116711). https://doi.org/10.2760/375209

Albino, V., Berardi, U., & Dangelico, R. M. (2015). Smart cities: Definitions, dimensions, performance, and initiatives. *Journal of Urban Technology*, *22*(1), 3–21. https://doi.org/10.1080/10630732.2014.942092

Alexander, C., Ishikawa, S., & Silverstein, M. (1977). *A Pattern Language: Towns, Buildings, Construction*. Oxford University Press.

Arcilla, M., Calvo-Manzano, J. A., & San Feliu, T. (2013). Building an IT service catalog in a small company as the main input for the IT financial management. *Computer Standards and Interfaces*, *36*(1), 42–53. https://doi.org/10.1016/j.csi.2013.07.003

Bozkurt, Y., Braun, R., Rossmann, A., & Hertweck, D. (2020). Smart Cities in Research: Status-Quo and Future Research Directions. *IADIS INTERNATIONAL JOURNAL ON WWW/INTERNET*, *18*(1), 121–138.

Caragliu, A., del Bo, C., & Nijkamp, P. (2011). Smart cities in Europe. *Journal of Urban Technology*, *18*(2), 65–82. https://doi.org/10.1080/10630732.2011.601117

Catriona, M., Cochrane, G., Cave, J., Millard, J., Pederson, J. K., Kåre, R., Liebe, A., Wissner, M., Massnik, R., & Kotternik, B. (2014). Mapping Smart cities in the EU. In *European Parlament*.

Cretu, L. G. (2012). Smart Cities Design using Event-driven Paradigm and Semantic Web. *Informatica Economica*, *16*(4), 57–67.

eco curious. (2021). *eco curious*. https://ecocurious.de/

element14. (2021). *element14*. https://www.element14.com/community/welcome

Fehling, C., Barzen, J., Breitenbücher, U., & Leymann, F. (2015). *Institute of Architecture of Application Systems Authoring , and Application A Process for Pattern Identification , Authoring , and Application*.

Giffinger, R., & Gudrun, H. (2010). Smart cities ranking: An effective instrument for the positioning of the cities. *ACE: Architecture, City and Environment*, *12*(4), 7–26.

Harakal'ova, L. (2018). Smart Villages - New Concept of Rural Development of the EU. *Proceedings of the 4Th International Conference on European Integration 2018 (ICEI 2018), PTS 1-3*, 413–421.

Horvat, N., Matija, J., & Mekovec, R. (2013). Specifying Service Catalog – a Case Study. *Central European Conference on Information and Intelligent Systems*, 142–296.

Hubbers, J. W., Ligthart, A., & Terlouw, L. (2007). Ten ways to identify services. *SOA Magazine*, *2007*(Xiii), 1–7. http://www.soamag.com/I13/1207-1.pdf

IoT Collaborative. (n.d.). *Smart City Catalog Overview*. https://iotcollaborative.org/smart-city-catalog-overview/

Kieninger, A., Baltadzhiev, D., Schmitz, B., & Satzger, G. (2011). Towards service level engineering for IT services defining IT services from a line of business perspective. *Proceedings - 2011 Annual SRII Global Conference, SRII 2011*, *May*, 759–766. https://doi.org/10.1109/SRII.2011.83

Kourtit, K., Nijkamp, P., & Arribas, D. (2012). Smart cities in perspective – a comparative European study by means of self-organising maps. *Innovation: The European Journal of Social Science Research*, *25*(2), 229–246. https://doi.org/10.1080/13511610.2012.660330

Kramers, A., Höjer, M., Lövehagen, N., & Wangel, J. (2014). Smart sustainable cities – Exploring ICT solutions for reduced energy use in cities. *Environmental Modelling & Software*, *56*, 52–62. https://doi.org/10.1016/j.envsoft.2013.12.019

Lee, J., & Lee, H. (2014). Developing and validating a citizen-centric typology for smart city services. *Government Information Quarterly*, *31*(SUPPL.1), S93–S105. https://doi.org/10.1016/j.giq.2014.01.010

Lombardi, P., Giordano, S., Farouh, H., & Yousef, W. (2012). Modelling the smart city performance. *Innovation: The European Journal of Social Science Research*, *25*(2), 137–149. https://doi.org/10.1080/13511610.2012.660325

LoRa Alliance. (2021). *Why LoRaWAN is the logical choice for asset-tracking connectivitiy*. https://lora-alliance.org/resource_hub/why-lorawan-is-the-logical-choice-for-asset-tracking-connectivity/

Lytras, M. D., & Visvizi, A. (2018). Who uses smart city services and what to make of it: Toward interdisciplinary smart cities research. *Sustainability (Switzerland)*, *10*(6), 1–16. https://doi.org/10.3390/su10061998

Meriwether, W. (2014). Making the Case for Creating an IT Service Catalog. *Computer Economics*, *36*(6), 1–10.

OASCITIES. (2021). *CxC CATALOGUE*. https://catalogue.city/en/cities

OKLab Köln. (2021). *OpenAir Cologne*. https://openair.cologne/DatenFuerDieStadt/index.html

Peng, G. C. A., Nunes, M. B., & Zheng, L. (2017). Impacts of low citizen awareness and usage in smart city services: The case of London's smart parking system. *Information Systems and E-Business Management*, *15*(4), 845–876. https://doi.org/10.1007/s10257-016-0333-8

Perera, C., Zaslavsky, A., Christen, P., & Georgakopoulos, D. (2014). Sensing as a service model for smart cities supported by Internet of Things. *Transactions on Emerging Telecommunications Technologies*, *25*(1), 81–93. https://doi.org/10.1002/ett.2704

Piro, G., Cianci, I., Grieco, L. A., Boggia, G., & Camarda, P. (2014). Information centric services in Smart Cities. *Journal of Systems and Software*, *88*, 169–188. https://doi.org/10.1016/j.jss.2013.10.029

Rachinger, M., Rauter, R., Müller, C., Vorraber, W., & Schirgi, E. (2019). Digitalisation and its influence on business model innovation. *Journal of Manufacturing Technology Management*, *30*(8), 1143–1160. https://doi.org/10.1108/JMTM-01-2018-0020

Schäferhoff, N., & WebSiteSetup. (2021). *Popular CMS by Market Share*. https://websitesetup.org/news/popular-cms/

Sembiring, M., & Surendro, K. (2016). Service catalogue implementation model. *2016 4th International Conference on Information and Communication Technology, ICoICT 2016*, *c*. https://doi.org/10.1109/ICoICT.2016.7571894

Sipina, N. (2011). Universal Service Definition in the Context of Service Catalog Design. *BPTrends*, *January*, 1–9. www.bptrends.com%5Cn

Smart City Solutions. (2021). *Smart City Solutions*. https://www.smart-city-solutions.de/

Stolterman, E., & Fors, A. C. (2004). *Information Technology and the Good Life* (pp. 687–692). https://doi.org/10.1007/1-4020-8095-6_45

Taconi, L. H., Barros, R. M., & B.b, Z. (2014). GAIA Service Catalog: A Framework for the Construction of IT Service Catalogs. *Sistemas de Informação*, *1*(14), 11–25.

The Things Network. (2021). *LoRaWAN*. https://www.thethingsnetwork.org/docs/lorawan/index.html

TTN Ulm. (2021). *TTN Ulm & LoRa*. https://lora.ulm-digital.com/

United Nations, Department of Economic and Social Affairs, P. D. (2018). *World Urbanization Prospects: The 2018 Revision*. https://population.un.org/wup/Download/Files/WUP2018-F21-Proportion_Urban_Annual.xls

UNPARALLEL Innovation. (2021). *IoT Catalogue*. https://www.iot-catalogue.com/

W3Techs. (2021). *Usage statistics of content management systems*. https://w3techs.com/technologies/overview/content_management

Washburn, D., & Sindhu, U. (2010). Helping CIOs Understand "Smart City" Initiatives. In *FORRESTER*. http://c3328005.r5.cf0.rackcdn.com/73efa931-0fac-4e28-ae77-8e58ebf74aa6.pdf

Xu, D., Wang, Y., Li, X., & Qiu, X. S. (2010). ICT service composition method based on service catalogue model. *IET Conference Publications*, *2010*(571 CP), 324–328. https://doi.org/10.1049/cp.2010.0779

Yeh, H. (2017). The effects of successful ICT-based smart city services: From citizens' perspectives. *Government Information Quarterly*, *34*(3), 556–565. https://doi.org/10.1016/j.giq.2017.05.001

Yigitcanlar, T., & Lee, S. H. (2014). Korean ubiquitous-eco-city: A smart-sustainable urban form or a branding hoax? *Technological Forecasting and Social Change*, *89*, 100–114. https://doi.org/10.1016/j.techfore.2013.08.034

Yuaca, F., Backhouse, J., & University United Nations. (2019). *Smart City Applications Catalogue Checklist and Suggestions*. https://collections.unu.edu/eserv/UNU:7524/Smart_City_Applications_Catalogue_Checklist_and_Suggestions.pdf

Zanella, A., Bui, N., Castellani, A., Vangelista, L., & Zorzi, M. (2014). Internet of things for smart cities. *IEEE Internet of Things Journal*, *1*(1), 22–32. https://doi.org/10.1109/JIOT.2014.2306328

SMART CITY SOLUTIONS FOR LOCATION TRACKING

Neetesh Bhati, Sujala D. Shetty[1] and Aparna Raj
[1]Dr.
Department of Computer Science,
Birla Institute of Technology and Science, Pilani, Dubai Campus, U.A.E

ABSTRACT

With the advancement in technology cities are getting smarter and becoming more livable and responsive. In the next few years, we expect a significant rise in the use of data and technology to make better decisions and improve the quality of life. Outdoor navigation using GPS is relatively easy but finding way indoors is still considered as a frenetic task. We aim to use data from multiple sources to create a detailed profile of the geographic information for every individual which can be easily used and securely accessed whenever needed. In this paper, we propose a method for indoor navigation which guides the user to a specific spot using smart phones. Here A* algorithm is used to find the shortest path between two points on the map and ArcGIS software for creating the map data. The generated map along with the required services are hosted on Osiris, an open-source indoor map rest API server. The sever is connected to a front end using an Android application developed with Android Studio. This can be applied across large companies which are situated in sprawling campuses.

KEYWORDS

GIS, Location Tracking, Indoor Navigation, Android Application

1. INTRODUCTION

Navigation is something that people have been doing since the early days and in modern times, it has continued to develop for the outdoors with the aid of technology such as GPS (Global Positioning System). Even though it provides incredibly precise positioning, it is not accurate for indoors as it relies on satellite line of sight. Also, the main reason that lacks in obtaining the accurate indoor positions is the difficulty in creating indoor maps with minimal infrastructure.

With indoor location and navigation being a hot subject, we are trying to investigate how it can be done to a functional degree with Wi-Fi routers and ideally expanded from there by the infrastructure. This subject is being addressed by many companies including Microsoft, who have grown it into an actively developed area. Hence our goal is to develop a small version of the indoor navigation framework for Android. For the easy deployment of the system, we make use of ArcGIS platform which provides the location-based analytics.

2. RELATED WORK

Providing an indoor navigation system has its challenges. The first and foremost essential factor is the accuracy in determining the position of the device. The next challenge is in mapping the interior of the location and storing it in the database for easy access. Finally, we must find a path between the two points to display it to the user. The path must be shortest, fastest, and easiest to take. Determining this path has its computational complexity (Poply & Shetty, 2019). Though there are multitude of methods such as lateration, fingerprinting, dead reckoning etc. none of them provides actual shortest route to the user (Jackermeier & Ludwig, 2018) (He & Chan, 2016) (Palamakula, 2015). Some of the existing mechanisms are described a s follows.

In (Jamil et al., 2020), authors used RSSI (Received Signal Strength Indicator) trilateration method for determining the indoor position. It is an estimated measure of power level that an RF client device is receiving from an access point or router. This ensures that the system can get the signal from the nearest point of entry called Access point (AP), which is connected to a wired router, switch, or hub via an Ethernet cable, and projects a Wi-Fi signal to a designated area. The position of the recipient is then determined by these distances and AP co-orders. But, because of the multipath and non-line of view (NLOS) propagations, the precision and reliance on one-point positioning were low because of the non-stationary character of the RSSI.

Enhanced alteration methods based on RSS are implemented in (Wang, 2011). The paper includes a framework focused on regression and a method based on correlation. The regression-based approach uses linear regression to depart from the distance between the wireless system and the access point as well as the associated signal intensity reading from the propagating model. The correlation-based method has been used to match the long-distance model with correlated RSS measurements from a local location. The regression approach led to reducing the error for the Wi-Fi network from 21 feet to 15 feet while the correlation approach decreased the error further from 22 feet to 12 feet.

In (Satan, 2018), authors triangulate the position of a device with the aid of the signal strength of several receivers. In (Brena et al., 2017), authors used an RF method. They introduced a few methods of optimizing precision, but they found that the use of the NNSS (Nearest Neighbor in Signal Space) performed well when applying to search space collected offline, which provides an outline resolution of 2-3 meters in length.

3. DESIGN METHODOLOGY

Indoor navigation with Wi-Fi signals existed as early as the early 2000s, is no invention. In the field of device development, i.e., the real deployment, there have been several attempts to achieve it, including the Microsoft Android Route Guide, which only received 10,000+ downloads (which is in the 10,001 - 50,000 range). Also, indoor plans of certain buildings are supported by Google Maps but do not provide indoor navigation. Another example is a site mapping application that can only use cell data, and not Wi-Fi, for indoor navigation. This program has only received over 1,000 (1,001 – 5,000 range) downloads. So, we took on this challenge to create an app. for indoor navigation.

There are several components to keep in mind while designing a full stack application. It includes deciding the backend server, the frontend application client, the database server schema, the API structure which will be used to facilitate communication between the several components of the application, etc. In Figure 1. we have laid out the basic architecture of the application. It has an API for communication with Android application, web server, and data storage.

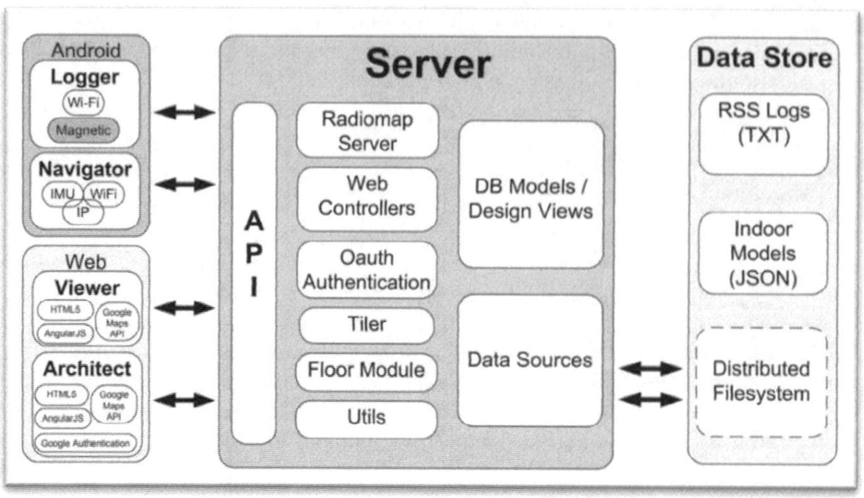

Figure 1. The application architecture

We have used several APIs that help us to overlay the floorplan image on a map with geo-tags (GeoTIFF) using data that we had previously prepared. The next move is to incorporate user location and route scanning. However, we soon discovered that in the MapBox API we could not explicitly track indoor route seeking (or that would take way too long). The MapWize API is developed on MapBox itself. We were presented with a system for overlaying a pre-processed floorplan on a real-world map, inserting our space polygons, entering additional room details (like the applicable search terms for users, for instance: 'Place',' 'Class' and '267'). The wayfinding had to be carried out by grouping various nodes between rooms over the whole floor so that potential roads could be diagramed. Besides, we were able to download the WiFi router's locations in a JSON file, which was useful at the next stage, which was to get the individual user's location, by entering every router and noticing details and place.

4. INDOOR NAVIGATION

4.1 The Navigation Algorithm

A* is like Dijkstra Algorithm for determining the shortest path. A* can be thought of as the first Greedy search and it can direct itself by using a heuristic. It is as fast as Greedy approach algorithms in a simple case. The key to its effectiveness is that it blends the pieces of information used in the Dijkstra algorithm with the information used by Greedy Best-First-Search (favoring vertices that are close to the goal). G(n) is the exact cost of the path from the starting point to any vertex n in the standard language used in A* and h(n) the approximate heuristic cost from the n vertex to the target. The yellow (h) is far from the goal and (g) is far away from the start (Sifat Hassan et al., 2020). A* balances the two as they pass from start to finish. The vertex n which is lower f(n) = g(n) + h will be tested each time through the main loop (n). Figure 2. represents the shortest path calculation between two specified points (Aydin et al., 2017).

Table 1. Different algorithms for shortest path calculation

Algorithm	Comments
A*	• Based on Heuristics • G - Exact cost of path from initial node to current node • H - admissible cost to reach the goal from current node • F = G + H • If H is overestimated, the goal node is found faster. • If H is underestimated, best results but longer processing time.
BFS	• Graph G = (V,E) • Algorithm complexity in time depends on $O(\|E\| + \|V\|)$ when every edge and every nodes is visited. • In reality, $O(\|E\| + \|V\|)$ can vary between $O(\|V\|)$ and $O(\|V\|^2)$ depending on graph edge evaluation.
Dijkstra's	• THE algorithm execution time is $O(\|E\| + \|V\|^2)$ and in worst case the performance is $O(\|E\| + \|V\| \log \|V\|)$
HPA*	• Internal edges in a cluster is obtained by running A* • HPA* is 1% optimal path finding algorithm
LPA*	• Ideal for changing networks, dervied from A*

Table 1. compares various algorithms along with their merits and demerits which are suitable for path finding application. We have tested these algorithms via a simulation to find the most efficient one for this paper. Since the proposed alogrithm computes amongst lesser nodes, optimized network is deemed more efficient (Apanaviciene et al., 2020). It often discovers the next best route also. A* maintains a priority queue of options that it's considering, ordered by how good they might be (Kotaru et al., 2015) . It keeps searching until it finds a route to the goal that's so good that none of the other options could possibly make it better.

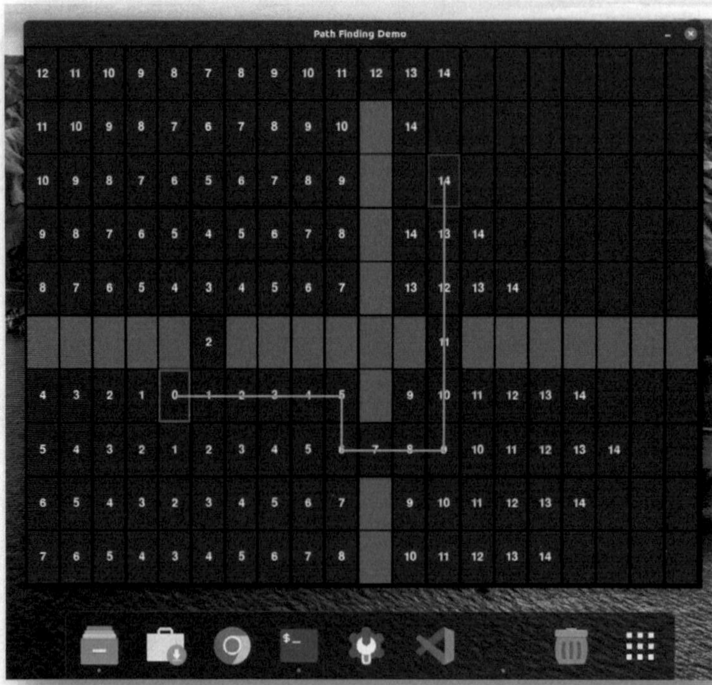

Figure 2. A* algorithm demonstration in Python

4.2 The ArcGIS Maps

There are various components on the ArcGIS platform which are communicated through the ArcGIS REST API and common file formats. To create a good application for ArcGIS, knowing the common elements of the software is important. ArcGIS Online and ArcGIS Enterprise are central to the ArcGIS network. The platform hosts GIS services and a gateway with online UIs and APIs that allows content, maps, apps, and users to be written, posted, and managed. We can interactively use the portal or provide direct access to the underlying REST facilities (Alam et al., 2018).

In addition to ArcGIS Online and ArcGIS Enterprise, ArcGIS Pro and ArcMap are part of the desktop suite that allows users to publish and manage data and charts. These desktop applications can also be expanded and written using multiple tools for comprehensive and advanced analysis. The ArcGIS Desktop website provides a rundown of the features of the ArcGIS Desktop.

There are several data formats supported by ArcGIS.

1. Shapefile – Esri's semi-open, hybrid vector data format using SHP, SHX, and DBF files. Originally invented in the early 1990s, it is still commonly used as a widely supported interchange format.
2. Enterprise Geodatabase – Esri's geodatabase format for use in a relational database system.
3. File Geodatabase – Esri's file-based geodatabase format, stored as folders in a file system.
4. Personal Geodatabase – Esri's closed, integrated vector data storage strategy using Microsoft's Access MDB format is a legacy format generally replaced by the file geodatabase in most contemporary use.

4.3 The Hosting Web Server

Osiris provides a solution for indoor mapping and APIs for indoor access to GIS data. This is developed as an easy-to-install, ready-to-use app package for small to medium projects. The building data is spread as a vector for the creation of apps that represent the pages as four of the key features of Osiris. Osiris has an additional Interest Points API to show external outside positions. Figure 3. & 4. shows the design of an ArcGIS Map and how it is hosted on a web server.

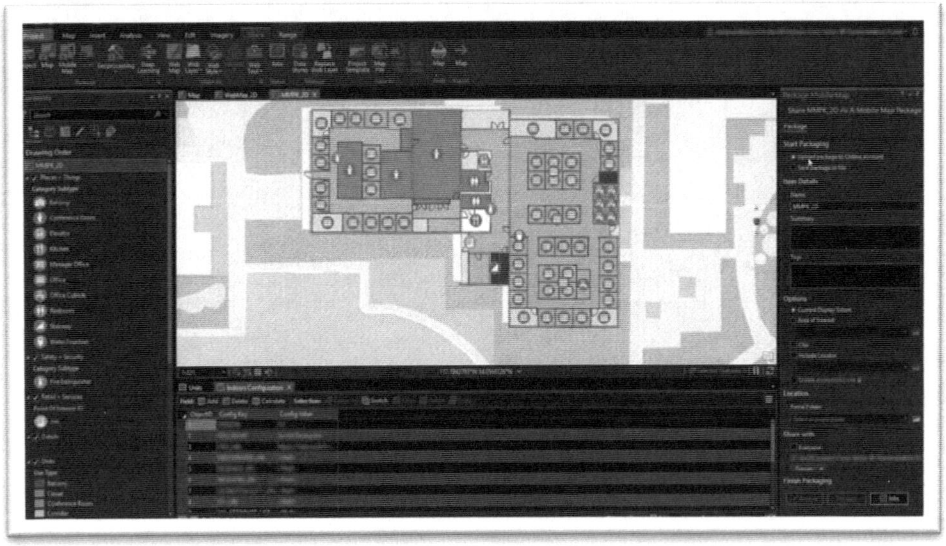

Figure 3. ArcGIS Map Design

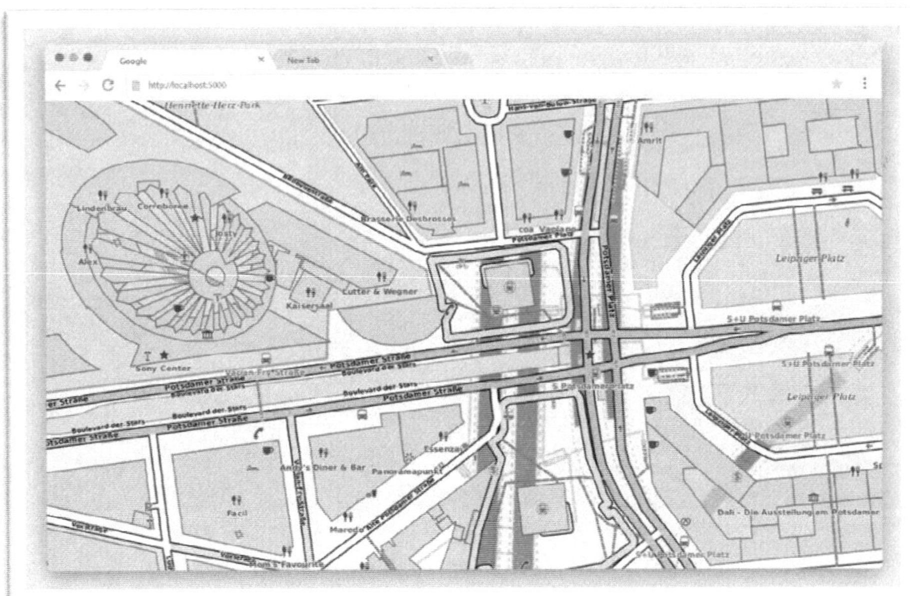

Figure 4. Map hosted on web server

There is a build.sh script which creates all the libraries and the "fatJar" files needed. After executing it, we can find a collection of jar files and scripts within the bin directory. This folder can be used as a sandbox for trying Osiris. Also the configuration files EnvConf.yml and env.properties provides the customization of the installation. There are two things to do to set an Osiris environment. First, we need to import a map, second, we will launch our Rest Services application. For both processes a MongoDB instance should be running. This is represented in Figure 5.

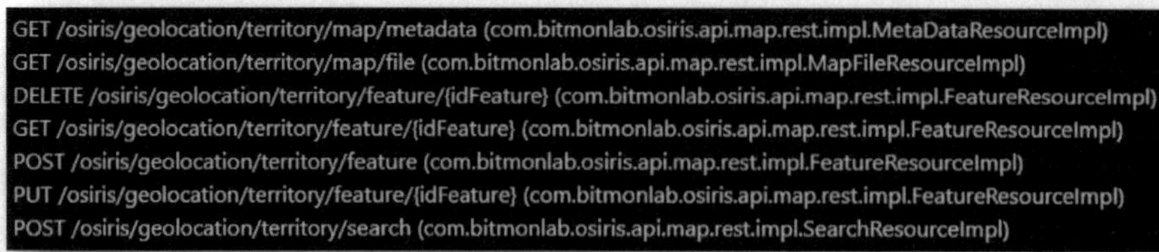

Figure 5. API Endpoints of web server

4.4 The Front-End Application

Every web server or a backend API requires a frontend application to display data. In our case, we have created an Android application that connects to the web server using the preconfigured API and displays the map data. The Android application is created using the Android Studio as represented in Figure 6. It is the official integrated development environment for Google's Android operating system, built on JetBrains' IntelliJ IDEA software and designed specifically for Android development. Figure 7. represents the android app. created with REST API server and MongoDB for indoor navigation.

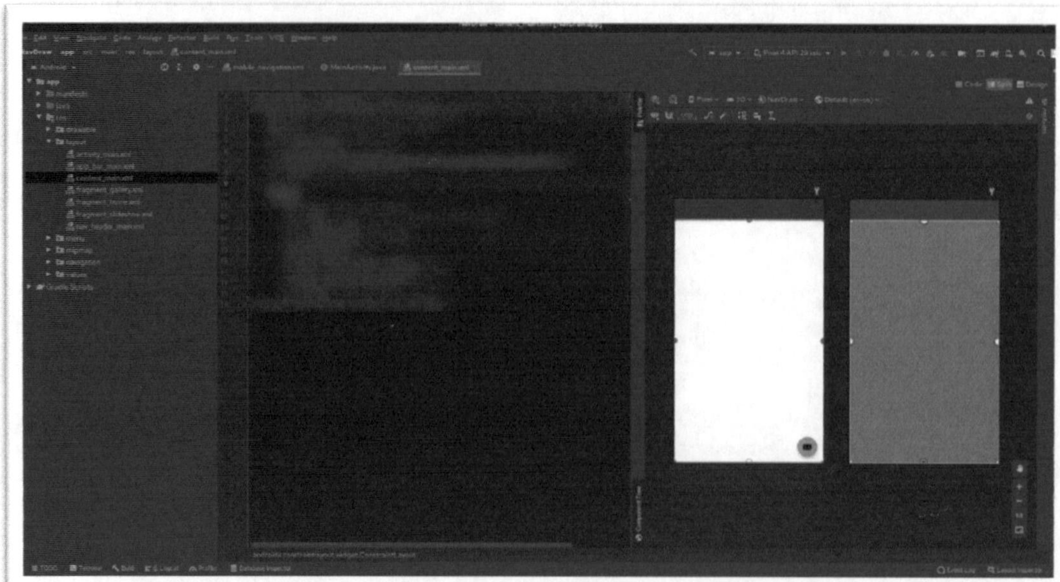

Figure 6. Android application created using android studio

Figure 7. Map Application deployed on android device

5. CONCLUSION

In this paper we focus on the task of indoor navigation particularly to provide precise user location and to deliver shortest path between user specified locales. We have created an android application with REST API server running with a MongoDB database to store the data required. Overall, a successfül result with thorough room navigation was achieved. The only time it failed was that the closest routers were not properly changed when the spot on the map shifted marginally from the current spot. Yet we strived best that could be achieved, keeping in mind the shortcomings of Android OS itself. By looking at improved methodologies, the accuracy of localization itself may be improved by researchers to achieve decimeter-level precision. This idea could be turned into a modular system, in which organizations can employ things like floor plans and indoor Wi-Fi router locations, i.e., taking advantage of their data. Perhaps it could be applied across an institution particularly the ones that are spread across multiple campuses.

We expect this technology to be implemented shortly with better algorithms, hardware, and software to make the internet a safer place. Also, if any chances of lessening the rate of access point scans, it could lower the deployment cost. Henceforth, the overall accuracy can also be improved even though the project is applied in the same manner. Moreover, there are several different indoor navigation techniques, we can use either one of those to test and find the accuracy and then implement if we are satisfied with the results.

REFERENCES

Alam, M., Moroni, D., Pieri, G., Tampucci, M., Gomes, M., Fonseca, J., ... & Leone, G. R. (2018). Real-time smart parking systems integration in distributed ITS for smart cities. *Journal of Advanced transportation, 2018*.

Apanaviciene, R., Vanagas, A., & Fokaides, P. A. (2020). Smart building integration into a smart city (SBISC): Development of a new evaluation framework. *Energies*, *13*(9), 2190.

Aydin, I., Karakose, M., & Karakose, E. (2017, April). A navigation and reservation based smart parking platform using genetic optimization for smart cities. In *2017 5th International Istanbul Smart Grid and Cities Congress and Fair (ICSG)* (pp. 120-124). IEEE.

Fangmeyer JR, J. A., Rosales, C. V., Rodríguez, D. M., & Pinero, R. F. B. (2017). Evolution of Indoor Positioning Technologies: A Survey.

Hassan, M. S., Islam, N. N., Fahim, A. M. A., Turja, T. H., & Chowdhury, S. (2020, January). Automated Parking System using Graph Algorithm. In *Proceedings of the International Conference on Computing Advancements* (pp. 1-6).

He, S., & Chan, S. H. G. (2015). Wi-Fi fingerprint-based indoor positioning: Recent advances and comparisons. *IEEE Communications Surveys & Tutorials*, *18*(1), 466-490.

Jamil, F., Iqbal, N., Ahmad, S., & Kim, D. H. (2020). Toward accurate position estimation using learning to prediction algorithm in indoor navigation. *Sensors*, *20*(16), 4410.

Kotaru, M., Joshi, K., Bharadia, D., & Katti, S. (2015, August). Spotfi: Decimeter level localization using wifi. In *Proceedings of the 2015 ACM Conference on Special Interest Group on Data Communication* (pp. 269-282).

Palamakula, S. (2015). *Trackindoors: Real-time Infrastructure-less Indoor Tracking Using Hybrid Approach* (Doctoral dissertation).

Poply, P., & Shetty, S. D. (2019, December). Urbanised Real-time Parking Detection System using Deep Learning. In *Proceedings of the 2019 3rd International Conference on Computer Science and Artificial Intelligence* (pp. 83-87).

Satan, A. (2018, May). Bluetooth-based indoor navigation mobile system. In *2018 19th international carpathian control conference (ICCC)* (pp. 332-337). IEEE.

Verma, S., Omanwar, R., Sreejith, V., & Meera, G. S. (2016, December). A smartphone based indoor navigation system. In *2016 28th international conference on microelectronics (ICM)* (pp. 345-348). IEEE.

Wang, H., & He, W. (2011, April). A reservation-based smart parking system. In *2011 IEEE Conference on Computer Communications Workshops (INFOCOM WKSHPS)* (pp. 690-695). IEEE.

SPELLING BASED RANKED CLUSTERING ALGORITHM TO CLEAN AND NORMALIZE EARLY MODERN EUROPEAN BOOK TITLES

Evan Bryer[1], Theppatorn Rhujittawiwat[1], John R. Rose[1] and Colin F. Wilder [2]
[1]*College of Engineering and Computing, University of South Carolina, USA*
[2]*Center for Digital Humanities, University of South Carolina, USA*

ABSTRACT

The goal of this paper is to modify an existing clustering algorithm with the use of the Hunspell spell checker to specialize it for the use of cleaning early modern European book title data. Duplicate and corrupted data is a constant concern for data analysis, and clustering has been identified to be a robust tool for normalizing and cleaning data such as ours. In particular, our data comprises over 5 million books published in European languages between 1500 and 1800 in the Machine-Readable Cataloging (MARC) data format from 17,983 libraries in 123 countries. However, as each library individually catalogued their records, many duplicative and inaccurate records exist in the data set. Additionally, each language evolved over the 300 year period we are studying, and as such many of the words had their spellings altered. Without cleaning and normalizing this data, it would be difficult to find coherent trends, as much of the data may be missed in the query. In previous research, we have identified the use of Prediction by Partial Matching to provide the most increase in base accuracy when applied to dirty data of similar construct to our data set. However, there are many cases in which the correct book title may not be the most common, either when only two values exist in a cluster or the dirty title exists in more records. In these cases, a language agnostic clustering algorithm would normalize the incorrect title, and lower the overall accuracy of the data set. By implementing the Hunspell spell checker into the clustering algorithm, using it to rank clusters by the number of words not found in their dictionary, we can drastically lower the cases of this occurring. Indeed, this ranking algorithm proved to increase the overall accuracy of the clustered data by as much as 25% over the unmodified Prediction by Partial Matching algorithm.

KEYWORDS

Pre-Processing, Clustering, Cleaning, Data Mining, Spellchecking

1. INTRODUCTION

Clustering can be a powerful tool for cleaning repetitive string data. Able to catch many common errors such as typos, word swaps, punctuation mistakes, it is an efficient and robust tool so long as the correct version of your string exists in your data set. However, most of these algorithms will simply normalize the most common member of the cluster onto all values in the cluster. While this is a good approach, as it can often be assumed a misspelling will occur less frequently than the correct version within highly repetitive data, this assumption may not always be true. In cases where it is in fact false, the normalization process further lowers the accuracy of the data set. Furthermore, when there are only two members of a cluster, the algorithm often does little more than guess at which is the proper value. In attempts to improve the ability for clustering to be used for data cleaning, we have implemented a ranking system for values in the cluster based on the number of misspelled words that exist in the string.

Our research team makes use of a large dataset of book catalog records for early modern Europe, approximately six million records in total. This dataset has been created and maintained by the Online Computer Library Center (OCLC). A more detailed history of this organization as well as our relationship with them can be found in our previous paper (Bryer et al, 2021). The data contained within the MARC records (in MARC 21 format) stores the metadata of a book, all of the bibliographic and publishing information without containing any of the actual data from the book. This includes many valuable fields such as book title, author, publisher, publishing location, year of publication, as well as many others. The focus here will be on book title data.

Because this metadata has been collected throughout upwards of 18,000 libraries, it is only natural that many of the records contain duplicative data. Due to the libraries in our data set originating from multiple countries throughout Europe, as well as encompassing books from 1500 to 1800, this duplicative data contains many inconsistencies that make a simple deduplication process difficult. As language progressed over time, the spellings of many words changed, as well as differing between regions of a country. Additionally, a book reprinted in a different country may make some slight changes to the spelling of a title. These factors, along with the human error of typos during digitization, makes for a messy set of data that requires extensive processing to clean. However, this repetition makes clustering a good fit for this data set.

2. RELATED WORKS

The plight for a method to ensure clean data is far from recent in the field of both Computer Science as well as Bibliography. Methods of cleaning data are numerous, as well as those which normalize data. Specifically for bibliographic data like ours, cleaning and dedupliacting records are a common concern for ensuring the information extracted from data sets is valid. Indeed, some studies have identified duplication problems in OCLC's catalog (O'Neill, 1993; Taniguchi, 2013), where our data originates.

One particularly pervasive group of researchers in the field of bibliography, and by extension the cleaning of the bibliographic data they study, is Mikko Tolonen and his colleagues. In Tolonen, Mikko, et al (Mikko et al, 2019), they used cleaning in a way similar to our goal of taking information like titles and authors and attempting to fix any errors within them. As it is not the central point of their paper, they do not go in depth about this cleaning process, unfortunately. In another paper, Tolonen, Mikko, et al. (Mikko et al, 2019) also used some innovative methods of cleaning their data. Their paper describes their usage of string distance ranking algorithms and utilizing additional information such as number of pages to rank the matches. The idea is similar to how we intend to rank our clusters, but in a less broadly applicable way. While the use of page count can be extremely valuable for book matching, as the total will likely vary little in republications, it would not be universally applicable as few of our records contain this information.

The ability of clustering to normalize data is equally valuable as its ability to clean data, particularly when studying such a large period of time. Language is ever evolving, and changed spellings for words could drastically impact the results of the queries we perform. This is an issue tackled in many papers. For example, the work of Marjanen, Jani, et al. (Jani et al., 2019) describes how they normalize special characters and spelling errors. They even go a step beyond simple clustering and employ a method to normalize synonymous words to lower the variability of titles. This would certainly improve the ability for querying such large data sets, allowing for a broader search based on the idea a title represents than the exact match for it.

Various ways of cleaning and normalizing data exist, however not many are capable of doing both with the accuracy of clustering in data sets such as ours. This is primarily due to three factors, the multilingual nature of our data set, the fact many words in the data set have multiple valid spellings, and the fact titles may use names and other words not normally understood by spell checkers. As such, there are many papers exploring the forms and usage of a clustering based approach. Some of these works use the vast amount of readily available bibliographic data to test their developments, which is a very similar application to what we seek. For example, in the work of Li, Jingxuan, and Tao Li (Jingxuan & Tao, 2010), they address existing forms of clustering algorithms and additionally create their own algorithms to test against pre-existing methods. In their paper, they use an example data set consisting of books and keywords. Their method, called Hierarchical Co-Clustering (HCC), utilizes two features: hierarchical clustering and co-clustering. Hierarchical clustering enables browsing and navigation, while co-clustering clusters different types of data simultaneously by using information about their relationship. HCC begins with singleton clusters and merges the two closest clusters until only one remains, all while using the agglomerative hierarchical clustering algorithm as the framework. By comparing the HCC algorithm to more common techniques such as K-Means and Single Linkage Hierarchical Clustering (SHLC), they can show how much more effective their method is. The work of Waluyo, Arif Mardi, Eko Prasetyo, and Arif Arizal (Arif et al., 2018) also sought to improve on the method of clustering. Their work introduces a method of clustering book titles based on the K-Means average of distance dissimilarity. This method produced excellent results for categorizing books based on shared features, but the issue they attempted to solve required far fewer clusters than title normalization. While there are a fair number of genres a book can fit into, this number is far lower than the number of unique clusters we find while looking for semantic identicality. The method can efficiently group books into categories such as law, economics, accounting, engineering, management, and information technology, as demonstrated by their tests utilizing a data set of 500 book titles from the Library of Bhayangkara Surabaya. Peter Kiraly (Péter, 2019) attempted to validate the metadata of records, ensuring that linked titles existed in records, that ISBN and ISSN fields had the correct identifiers, and that the control field was properly formatted. Some works used the petition around medoids (PAM) algorithm to improve clustering performance such as the works of De Amorim, Renato Cordeiro et al. (De Amorim et al., 2013) and Zampeieri, Marcos et al. (Zampieri & de Amorim, 2014). This technique can significantly improve the performance when the optimal parameters are known. It is relatively similar to our method of choice but it requires much computational resources and the optimal parameters. There were many great insights about the problem of duplicate MARC data within this paper, focusing mainly on classifying records as either valid or invalid.

Many researchers also use machine learning techniques to tackle this problem. Ozsarfati, Eran, et al. (Eran et al., 2019) explored a variety of machine learning algorithms to classify the genres of books based on their titles. This paper analyzes six different machine learning techniques: Naive Bayes, Convolutional Neural Network (CNN), Recurrent Neural Network (RNN), Gated Recurrent Unit (GRU), Long Short-Term Memory (LSTM), and Bi-Directional LSTM (Bi-LSTM). Their paper assessed 207,575 book titles, attempting to categorize them into 32 genres. If expanded from attempting to classify genres to extracting a larger variety of semantic information from titles, it could be possible for a similar method to be used to compare titles in a way pure string comparison could not expand to. Bleiweis (Avi, 2017) presents a model capable of combining a word vector set of a varying number of elements in order to represent a verse or a sentence, with an iterative distance metric that evaluates similarity in pairs of non-conforming verse matrices. The work in this paper investigates linguistic structure in raw texts and uses Word2Vec to explore clustering and search tasks to train the underlying word representations. Representing the text in this way improves the performance of semantic clustering as well as searching searching, an extremely valuable improvement given the time costs of these procedures.

3. METHODOLOGY

This paper builds on earlier analysis of popular clustering algorithms which sought to determine which performed the best for data analogous to ours. Prediction by Partial Matching (PPM) clustering has been shown to outperform the other algorithms and gave us a good place to start with our data cleaning. However, the glaring issues of cases where the incorrect title would be normalized onto correct titles was a cause for concern. To attempt to improve the accuracy of choosing the correct title to normalize, leaving it to the most common value in the cluster would not suffice. As such, we implemented a spell-checking system into the clustering algorithm.

PPM clustering is a method of clustering based on the PPM data compression algorithm. The PPM compression algorithm is a commonly used algorithm in RAR and 7z compressed files, and employs the use of a statistical model to predict what the next character is most likely to be. To use this to compute clusters, we calculate the distance that exists between the two compressed strings. Following the logic of OpenRefine's PPM clustering, a data management tool created by Google, we can compute this distance relatively easily. To get the distance between two strings, A and B, we need to look at how concatenating the strings affects the length of the compressed string. Because PPM compression compresses duplicated text data very effectively, the difference between compressing string A and the string A+A would be very slight, where "+" is the concatenation of the two. Of course, that means that if B was an identical string to A, the compression of A+B would be the same as A+A. The more that string A and B differ, the greater the difference in length of the compressed concatenation will be. Because of this, we can calculate the distance using $comp(A + B) + comp(B + A)/(comp(A + A) + comp(B + B))$, where comp() returns the length of the compressed string. By comparing the lengths, we get a much more time efficient algorithm than if we were to compute the distance between the two compressed strings using something such as Levenshtein Distance.

We can convert this into a score by taking this value, D, and computing 10*(D-1). This is because, if all strings are identical, it would give us a D of 1, and as the strings get less and less similar, D fractionally increases. With this score, we can now compute clusters using PPM compression by selecting a distance cutoff for values to be grouped. For this, we will analyze a distance of 1 and 2. (Chen et al., 2004)

After creating and verifying the functionality of this PPM clustering algorithm, the next step was to decide on a method of spell checking the titles to create the ranking. We decided with Hunspell, the spell checking library used by LibreOffice, OpenOffice, Mozilla Firefox, Google Chrome, as well as many other programs. Being a well trusted library with an extensive dictionary selection, it was a perfect choice for a multilingual dataset like the one we are working with. The test data sets we created included English, French, German and Latin idioms and proverbs, all of which are publicly available dictionaries provided by Hunspell.

To rank the members of the clusters, we process each of the titles in the clusters found by PPM clustering. For each word in the title, we check if it exists in Hunspell, and if not, we increase the score of that title by 1. After each title in the cluster is processed, we know that the least number of words absent in the dictionary belong to the title with the lowest score. Doing it this way opposed to simply counting the number of correct words accounts for additional words in titles, such as "a" or "the" which would artificially increase the score of titles which may have misspelled words that do not outweigh the additional words. It also allows for correctly spelled words that do not exist in the dictionaries to be inconsequential, as the score increase is identical between each of the titles.

To accurately compare the performance of the algorithm against the original PPM clustering algorithm, we created two test data sets. While the preferable way to test these data sets would be to use the data provided by OCLC, as it is the end goal for these algorithms to be used on, however they have a fatal flaw of not having a "base truth". Because we cannot resolve the correct title based on only the possibly dirty title, without vetting the data by hand, this solution is not feasible. The scale of the data makes manually cleaning even a portion of it difficult as well, as trying to clean enough records for it to be a representative sample would take far more time than reasonable. Given this, the creation of test data sets that mirror the data in as many ways as possible is necessary to properly gauge the ability of each algorithm to be used to clean data.

The first data set will be one preferable for our new algorithm, and is the same data set we used in our last paper to compare the different clustering algorithms (Bryer et al, 2021). The data set is made up of approximately 1,000 idioms and proverbs taken from English, French, German and Latin. Idioms and proverbs were a choice made to mirror both the average length of book titles, as well as the age of the titles we will be using this to clean. Because many idioms and proverbs were created using the version of languages that existed around the time of our books being published, we would not run into the issue of modern spellings that have changed skewing the test data in favor of our spell checking, as the dictionaries will be biased towards the more modern forms of the language.

We then corrupted these using the most commonly observed inaccuracies in our records as well as noted in other scholar's data (O'Neill, 1993). Specifically, we randomly corrupted letters, as well as swapping words with those adjacent to it. We created two copies of our idioms and proverbs, the first copy being "mild" corruption, and the second being "severe" corruption. In the first copy, we had a 7% chance for it to be randomly swapped with any alphanumeric character. In the severe case, for any letter, there was a 10% chance of it being changed, and for any word there was a 6% chance of it being swapped with the adjacent word.

While this mock data set worked well to compare the quality of multiple different clustering algorithms, the fact it has 3 copies of each title, with one being correct and all three being different, it is not an impartial data set to be used against our new algorithm. Because the unmodified algorithm will favor the most common value in a cluster, having three distinct titles puts it at a distinct disadvantage. This disadvantage would likely not be nearly as severe in the real use case, as generally typos and misspellings would be less common in a repetitive data set than the correct version of the value. To account for this, we needed to create a more fair test data set for this test, one that would more accurately represent the repetition found in our real data set. To do this, we randomly duplicated entries in the mock data set. Looking at the OCLC data set, we can see that approximately one third of the entries are unique titles. Because correct titles are likely to appear more often when an entry is duplicated, we randomly duplicated correct titles in our mock data set with a probability of 33%, and had corrupted duplicates at a rate of half that. Further to the benefit of the original PPM algorithm, we corrupted the duplicated titles separately, as few duplicate records in the OCLC data set would contain the same typo.

4. RESULTS

To compare the results of the improved clustering algorithm implementing spell check, we will compare it against the version of this algorithm not using spell check. In Table 1, we can observe how each performed against the first test data sets. This was examined by comparing the full strings, if the string was not identical to the correct string it was marked as a failure.

The increase of accuracy is extremely significant between the unmodified clustering algorithm and our new algorithm. Especially in the case of using a radius of two, we find that there is a bigger difference between the improved algorithm and the unmodified algorithm than there is between the unmodified algorithm and the original. This trend of significant increases does not disappear with the next test, visible in Table 2. We tested the improvement based on characters, instead of full string matching. This would reward the algorithms for improving the overall accuracy of the strings, even if the most accurate string was not the one selected. While this would not be the preferable case, it is still an important test as any improvements to the data set are significant.

Table 1. String based comparison for data set 1

String Based	Original	Unmodified PPM	Improved PPM
Radius of 1	0.422	0.473	0.545
Radius of 2	0.422	0.551	0.705

Table 2. Character based comparison for Data Set 1

Character Based	Original	Unmodified PPM	Improved PPM
Radius of 1	0.954	0.956	0.959
Radius of 2	0.954	0.965	0.976

Once again, we observe a significant increase in the accuracy, matching the increase between the original and the unmodified clustering algorithm. A visualization of these results can be seen in Figure 1. We then ran these same tests on our second test data set. Table 3 shows the results of the string matching analysis, and Table 4 shows the character based.

Table 3. String based comparison for Data Set 2

String Based	Original	Unmodified PPM	Improved PPM
Radius of 1	0.557	0.686	0.704
Radius of 2	0.557	0.810	0.836

Table 4. Character based comparison for Data Set 2

Character Based	Original	Unmodified PPM	Improved PPM
Radius of 1	0.967	0.973	0.973
Radius of 2	0.967	0.984	0.986

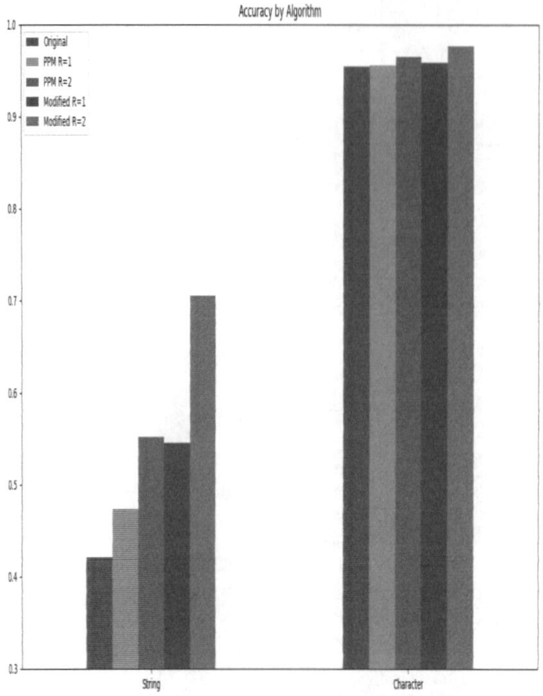

Figure 1. Visualization of Data Set 1 Accuracies

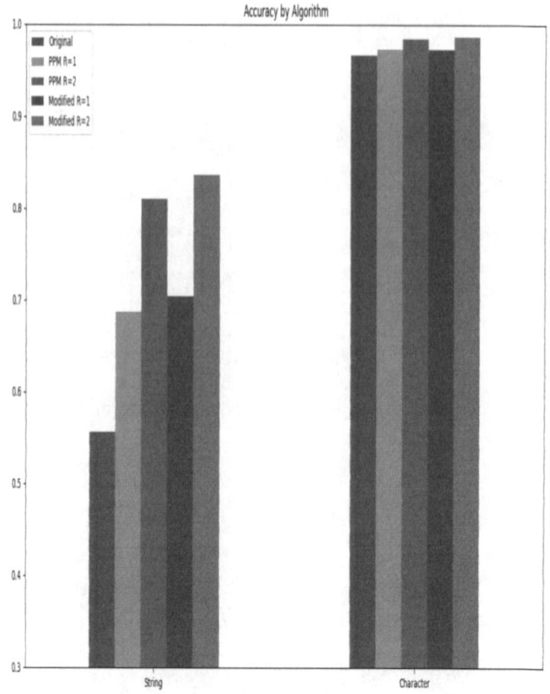

Figure 2. Visualization of Data Set 2 Accuracies

As expected, the increases between the unmodified algorithm and our original algorithm is much smaller than it was previously, as can be seen in Figure 2. However, the increase in accuracy is still significant, even when compared under more favorable conditions for the unmodified algorithm. For more in depth statistics about the performance of each, Table 5 and Table 6 show the positives and negatives, both true and false, for each data set.

Table 5. Positives and Negatives for Data Set 1

Positive/Negative	True Positive	True Negative	False Positive	False Negative
Unmodified (R=1)	478	954	320	1275
Unmodified (R=2)	833	834	440	920
Modified (R=1)	614	1226	52	1135
Modified (R=2)	1241	1120	158	508

Table 6. Positives and Negatives for Data Set 2

Positive/Negative	True Positive	True Negative	False Positive	False Negative
Unmodified (R=1)	616	1885	143	999
Unmodified (R=2)	1116	1837	191	499
Modified (R=1)	572	1994	36	1043
Modified (R=2)	1126	1924	106	489

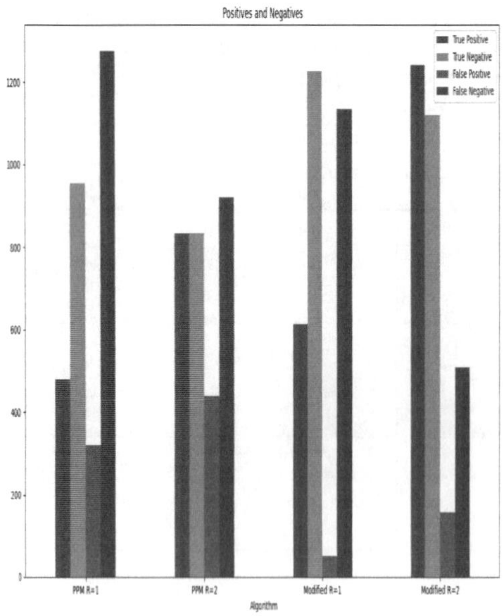

Figure 3. Visualization of True/False for Data Set 1

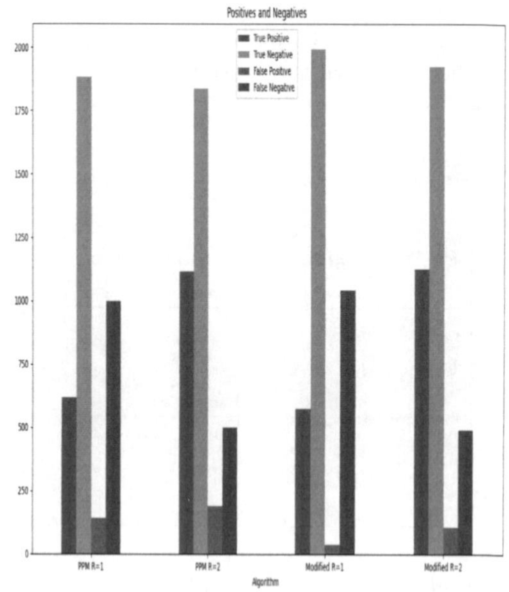

Figure 4. Visualization of True/False for Data Set 2

Using these values, we can calculate the precision, recall and F-Scores, shown in Table 7 and Table 8.

Table 7. Precision and Recall for Data Set 1

Precision and Recall	Precision	Recall	F-Score
Unmodified (R=1)	0.599	0.273	0.375
Unmodified (R=2)	0.654	0.475	0.550
Modified (R=1)	0.921	0.522	0.666
Modified (R=2)	0.887	.710	0.789

Table 8. Precision and Recall for Data Set 2

Precision and Recall	Precision	Recall	F-Score
Unmodified (R=1)	0.812	0.381	0.519
Unmodified (R=2)	0.854	0.691	0.764
Modified (R=1)	0.941	0.354	0.514
Modified (R=2)	0.914	0.697	0.790

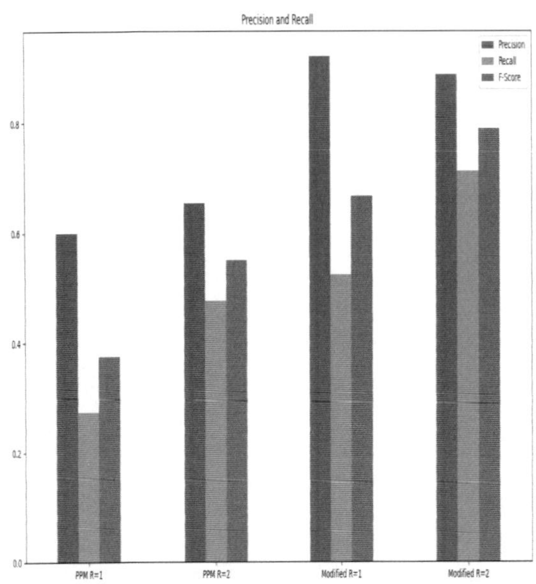

Figure 5. Visualization of Recall for Data Set 1

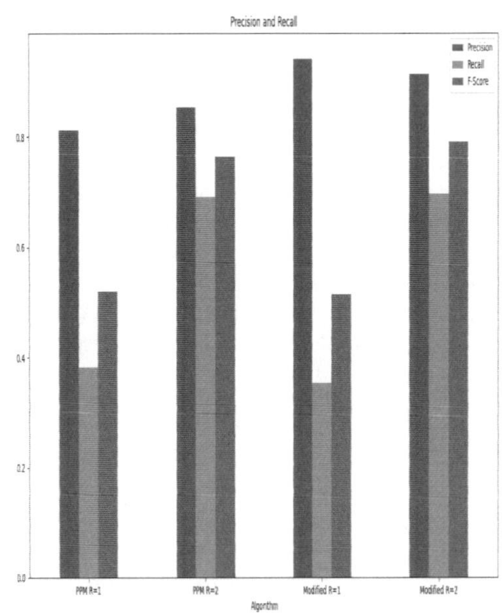

Figure 6. Visualization of Recall for Data Set 2

On the first data set, we see significant improvements in all three in our improved PPM algorithm. Interestingly, however, there is one case where the original algorithm outperformed ours, using a radius of one for data set 2. Our algorithm produced far fewer false positives, at the cost of fewer true positives and more false negatives. While the difference in F score between the two's performance in this case is minimal, it is an interesting trade off that shows the potential use case for choosing these parameters when cleaning a data set. If cleaning highly sensitive data where false positives are a worst case outcome, the updated algorithm consistently produces the fewest false positives when using a radius of one.

5. CONCLUSION

To get the most valuable information as possible out of the expansive OCLC data set, it is imperative that we normalize and clean the data as thoroughly as possible. Due to being compiled over many years, by many librarians and separately digitized, naturally there are errors of all sorts throughout. As found in our last paper, due to the duplicative nature of many of the entries in this data set, using clustering for the purpose of cleaning excelled in its ability to improve the accuracy of our data.

By implementing the Hunspell library into the best performing clustering algorithm we tested, we are able to significantly improve it over its base form for the purposes of text data cleaning. Hunspell and its ability to link dictionaries from multiple languages is especially important for our use case. Given that we must be able to account for misspelled words regardless of the language of the title, so long as it falls within the set of languages the data provides us with, being able to check every pertinent language at once greatly increases the efficiency of ranking clusters.

Because testing our improved algorithm against the original PPM clustering algorithm resulted in higher accuracy scores in both a blind test data set as well as one set up to favor the original algorithm, it is a safe interpolation that it will perform significantly better on increasing the overall accuracy of the OCLC data set than the unmodified PPM clustering algorithm. Even in cases where we must prioritize avoiding false positives for clustering over overall improved accuracy, using a radius of one in the modified algorithm produced far fewer false positives, and therefore would be a better algorithm to apply for this case.

The one drawback of this method of clustering is the increase in time taken to process and clean the data. Naturally adding a spell checking and ranking step to this process would increase the run time, and through our tests we found the increase in run time to hover around 35%. Clustering is already a relatively time intensive process, so this increase could indeed be an important factor when performing data cleaning on extremely large data sets. However for our cases, the benefits of vastly increased accuracy improvements outweighs the increased cost of time.

Methods of expanding on this research would either focus on decreasing the time cost of adding the spell checking functionality, or improving the ability for clusters to be ranked. The first method would likely rely on heuristics, such as only calculating the maximum length two strings could differ to fall within the radius for PPM clustering before the compression, to reduce the number of unnecessary compressions made. The second may implement other methods into the ranking system, not only relying on individual word spelling. This may take the form of grammar checking, or comparison against a database of book titles.

REFERENCES

A Hierarchical Book Representation of Word Embeddings for Effective Semantic Clustering and Search. *In ICAART, Volume 2*, 154–163.

Arif et al. (2018). Clasification System of Library Book Based on Similarity of the Book Title Using K-means Method (Case Study Library of Bhayangkara surabaya). *Journal of Electrical Engineering and Computer Sciences, Vol 3 Number 1*

Bryer et al. (2021). Analysis of Clustering Algorithms to Clean and Normalize Early Modern European Book Titles. *In Proceedings of the 4th International Conference on Software Engineering and Information Management (ICSIM '21).*

Chen et al. (2004). The Similarity Metric. *IEEE Transactions on Information Theory. 50*. 3250-3264.

De Amorim et al. (2013). Effective spell checking methods using clustering algorithms. *Proceedings of the International Conference Recent Advances in Natural Language Processing RANLP 2013*, 172-178.

Eran et al. (2019). Book Genre Classification Based on Titles with Comparative Machine Learning Algorithms. *In 2019 IEEE 4th International Conference on Computer and Communication Systems (ICCCS)*. IEEE, 14–20

Jani et al. (2019). A National Public Sphere? Analyzing the Language, Location, and Form of Newspapers in Finland, 1771–1917. *Journal of European Periodical Studies, Volume 4, No.1*, 54–77

Jingxuan L. & Tao L. (2010). HCC: a hierarchical co-clustering algorithm. *In Proceedings of the 33rd international ACM SIGIR conference on Research and development in information retrieval*, 861–862

Mikko et al. (2019). A quantitative approach to book-printing in Sweden and Finland, 1640–1828. *Historical Methods: A Journal of Quantitative and Interdisciplinary History Volume 52, No. 1*, 57–78

Mikko et al. (2019). Scaling Up Bibliographic Data Science. *In DHN, 450–456*

O'Neill, E. (1993). Characteristics of Duplicate Records in OCLC's Online Union Catalog. *Library Resources & Technical Services, 37,* 59-71.

Péter K. (2019). Validating 126 million MARC records. *In Proceedings of the 3rd International Conference on Digital Access to Textual Cultural Heritage*. 161–16.

Taniguchi, S. (2013). Duplicate Bibliographic Record Detection with an OCR-Converted Source of Information. Jo*urnal of information Science*, *Volume 39*. 153-168.

Zampieri, M. & de Amorim, R. (2014). Between sound and spelling: combining phonetics and clustering algorithms to improve target word recovery. *International conference on natural language processing,* 438-449.

VISUALIZATION CONCEPTS OF A DIGITAL ECOSYSTEM TO INCREASE UNDERSTANDABILITY

Frank Elberzhager, Kathleen Späth and Sven Storck
Fraunhofer Institute for Experimental Software Engineering IESE
Fraunhofer Platz 1, Kaiserslautern, Germany

ABSTRACT

A digital ecosystem contains many different services, including apps, physical objects, and a digital platform that provides these services to everyone. This complex structure is often hard to understand for people not developing these systems. Therefore, we are developing three different approaches aimed at supporting stakeholders and users in understanding and efficiently using such a digital ecosystem.

KEYWORDS

Gamification, Exploration, Information visualization, Platform, Ecosystem, Urban District

1. INTRODUCTION

The impact of the digital transformation on cities is steadily on the rise. They are being transformed into smart cities, which has implications for a variety of topics, such as smart mobility, digital public services, climate-friendly energy consumption, or smart infrastructure, which are becoming very complex, comprising technical, legal, constructive, and many other issues [Alavi18].

We are currently part of a research project where a climate-neutral smart urban district is being developed. In particular, we are responsible for creating a digital ecosystem to support citizens and other stakeholders in behaving in a climate-friendly manner. This digital ecosystem basically consists of a platform and many services [Averian18]. As this is a complex topic in itself and it is sometimes difficult to understand how such an ecosystem works, how services can be used, and what the benefits of using them are, we are currently looking for ways to make the topic easier to understand for these stakeholders. The goal is to increase their understanding of such a digital ecosystem and show them what services exist. Moreover, we want to convince them that it is beneficial to use digital services to become more climate-friendly and show them how digitalization can support this goal. For this, we want to think of new concepts besides posters or simple presentations.

2. VISION

Our vision is to create an "ecosystem map", consisting of different visual overviews that include the different stakeholders and services and that show solutions and results in different ways.

Our goal is to create different solutions that appeal to different types of people. We will focus on three: free exploration, story-driven exploration, and static information input. They all have in common that they make people curious about the urban district platform and provide the users with all the information they need.

3. SOLUTIONS

Layered Map (static information input)

The Layered Map is a static and self-explanatory representation of the complete ecosystem. It conveys a structured overview of all services and of the platform itself. Each layer represents a different topic of the project, such as data view or service view.

This solution offers the least interaction – it is pure information transfer. Because of this, there is a risk that the users might not be motivated enough to learn about the platform on their own. The challenge in the design is to give the users enough incentive to explore all areas of the platform. These incentives can be generated by an appealing graphical design and exciting content. However, a certain degree of intrinsic motivation is still required.

Virtual Reality Tour (story-driven exploration)

The Virtual Reality (VR) Tour is a more story-driven approach to explain to people the main platform and all the services used on it. The idea is to create a digital tour consisting of different 360 ° images or videos. These 360 ° files are different steps or chapters in the tour and can be visited by the users one after the other. They are packed with additional information provided via voiceovers, text, links, etc.

Although this solution is based on a story told in different steps, at some points, the users can decide on their own which chapter they want to go to next. This leads to a much less restricted exploration of the platform.

Open Area Exploration (free exploration)

The Open Area Exploration approach is a solution based on the idea of gamification. Users can move independently through the area. They are shown stations where they can learn more about the individual topics. Moving through the area is fun and creates an incentive to explore and understand the topics of the platform. The complexity of the area is conveyed to the users in a playful way.

Compared to the other approaches, Open Area Exploration is the most independent approach for the users, which also entails certain risks: Users must be driven by their own curiosity. They must become active themselves and not lose their desire to explore.

4. CONCLUSION

The three solutions presented above are an attempt to make a complex digital ecosystem easier to understand. Our goal is to create a toolset that can mitigate the complexity of the system visually. It is possible that these results will be modified over the course of the development of the implemented solution, or that research will come up with another way to solve the problem. The solutions will be verified by user tests to check which solution is the most promising one, or how they can be combined or benefit from each other.

The main obstacle is accessibility for everyone: We must build solutions that are accessible to both digital natives and digital immigrants. There are differences in visual understanding between these groups, due to their different levels of digital experience. Based on user tests, we will further develop and adapt our solutions.

ACKNOWLEDGEMENT

The research described in this paper was performed in the EnStadt:Pfaff project (grant no. 03SBE112D and 03SBE112G) of the German Federal Ministry for Economic Affairs and Energy (BMWi) and the Federal Ministry of Education and Research (BMBF). We thank Sonnhild Namingha for proofreading.

REFERENCES

Alavi, A. H. et al, 2018, Internet of Things-enabled smart cities: State-of-the-art and future trend. *Measurement*, Vol. 129, https://doi.org/10.1016/j.measurement.2018.07.067, pp. 589-606.

Averian, A., 2018, A Reference Architecture for Digital Ecosystems. In Jayip, S. *Internet of Things - Technology, Applications and Standardization*. IntechOpen, London, UK, pp. 105-119.

VISUALIZATION OF THREE-DIMENSIONAL REACHABLE SET FOR THE DUBINS CAR

Pavel Vasev, Andrey Fedotov and Valerii Patsko
Krasovskii Institute of Mathematics and Mechanics, Yekaterinburg, Russia

ABSTRACT

A mathematical model of controlled motion (called the Dubins car in the literature on optimal control) is considered. This model is widely used to describe various motions: an airplane in a horizontal plane, a car, etc. The paper deals with the problem of visualization of the three-dimensional reachable sets for the Dubins car. The developed visualization tool can be useful for research purposes, as well, for teaching a course of the optimal control.

KEYWORDS

Dubins Car, Three-Dimensional Reachable Set, Specialized Visualization System

1. INTRODUCTION AND STATEMENT OF THE PROBLEM

The mathematical "Dubins car" (the origin of this name is the article by Dubins (1957)) is a model of controlled motion, in which two phase variables x, y are the coordinates of the point geometric position of the object on the plane, the third variable φ is the angle formed by the velocity vector w.r.t. the positive direction of the x axis. The value of the linear velocity is considered constant and equal to 1. The scalar control has the meaning of the angular rotation velocity (or, equivalently, instantaneous radius of rotation) and is restricted by the constraint $u \in [u_1, u_2]$. Such a model, often called "unicycle", is widely used when considering the motions of an aircraft in a horizontal plane, as well as, when simplifying the description of the motion of ground-controlled wheeled "bogies", see Laumond (1998).

When studying various control problems associated with the Dubins car, it is useful to describe the boundary of the three-dimensional reachable sets "*at the instant*". The reachable set at the instant t_f is the set of all phase states each of them can be achieve by the system with the help of some admissible control exactly at the instant t_f. The initial instant and the initial phase state are assumed to be zero. As the admissible controls, we take piecewise constant time functions with values from the interval $[u_1, u_2]$. The boundary of the reachable set $G(t_f)$ is generated by the controls satisfying the Pontryagin Maximum Principle (PMP). Such a necessary condition allows us to perform a detailed analysis of the boundary of the three-dimensional reachable set, see Patsko *et al* (2003), Patsko, Fedotov (2018).

The paper is devoted to visualization of the reachable set $G(t_f)$ under the assumption $-1 \le u_1 < 0 < u_2 = 1$. The relations $u_2 = 1, u_1 \ge -1$ are not essential: the geometric variables and time can always be normalized in such a way that the value of the linear velocity is equal to 1 and the conditions $u_2 = 1, u_1 \ge -1$ are satisfied. The inequalities $u_1 < 0 < u_2$ mean that the controlled object can rotate in both sides. In the case of $u_1 = -1, u_2 = 1$, there is a symmetry of the "right" and "left" turns. If the relations $-1 < u_1 < 0 < u_2 = 1$ are satisfied, then the rotation is possible in both sides, but the symmetry is broken.

The normalized mathematical description of the Dubins car dynamics on the plane x, y has the form

$$\dot{x} = \cos\varphi, \qquad \dot{y} = \sin\varphi, \qquad \dot{\varphi} = u; \qquad u \in [u_1, u_2].$$

We assume that the angle φ of the velocity vector direction is counted counterclockwise from the positive direction of the x-axis and takes values in the interval $(-\infty, \infty)$. That is, we do not identify the angle φ by modulo 2π. Under identification, the structure of the reachable set becomes significantly more complex that makes it difficult to understand its changes in time.

The resulting three-dimensional reachable sets can have a very nontrivial structure. The set $G(t_f)$ for $t_f > 0$ is not convex and can be non-simply connected. Its boundary is formed by pieces of smooth surfaces that do not always fit together smoothly. In the works of Patsko *et al* (2003), Patsko, Fedotov (2018), a parametric description of such smooth pieces was obtained.

The purpose of this work is to create a convenient specialized visualization system that allows us to view the development in time of three-dimensional sets that can have different mathematical and physical interpretations. There are a number of basic requirements that need to be satisfied:

1. It should be possible to get images from different angles of view and to make various cut-offs. This is necessary, for example, to study the time changes the structure of the surfaces forming the boundary of the reachable set.

2. In particular, the visual representation is required for the surfaces that form an internal cavity (not belonging to the reachable set). Note that such a cavity can occur on a very short time interval. In this interval, the reachable set is not simply connected, and its boundary is divided into two parts: "external" and "internal" ones.

3. Besides, it is also necessary to additionally display the extreme motions of the system (with the possibility of animation in time) that satisfy the PMP and go along the boundary of the time-varying three-dimensional reachable set. Such motions can split and, thus, generate trajectory bundle (going on the boundary). There are bundles that can again gather into one motion after a while. These splitting and merging occur at certain parts of the boundary. It is desirable to have a visual adequate reproduction of such processes.

For convenience, in this paper we denote our specialized visualization system as a visualization tool. The initial stage of creating the visualization tool is described in Vasev, Fedotov (2020). The possibilities of the developed visualization tool are shown by the example of the Dubins car reachable set.

2. VISUALUZATION TECHNOLOGY

2.1 Overview of the Visualization Method

We are in the field of optimal control, and it relies on phase space phenomena. The history of visualization of phase spaces and, in particular, phase trajectories is interesting and contains a set of efficient visualization methods. We can note, for example, approaches that use Poincare sections, return maps, and common methods like feature detection and feature outlining, various multidimensional projections onto 3d space, creation of synthetic helper spaces for visualization purposes, critical subsets outlining, interconnected separate views, symbolic representation of meaningful places (Figure 1a), filtering (Figure 1b), high-level entity reconstruction (Figure 1c).

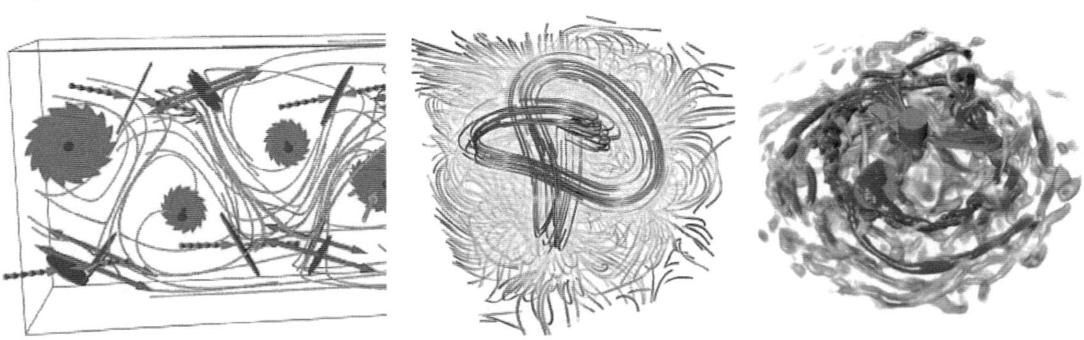

Figure 1. Examples of phase space visualizations by ETH Zurich (https://cgl.ethz.ch/research/visualization/)
Left to right: (a) inertial particle dynamics, (b) visibility optimization, (c) vortex extraction

However, as we are in optimal control field, we have a special entity as a first-class object of interest – the reachable set at the instant, described in introduction section. We paint the reachable set almost as is, as we may effectively calculate this set for Dubins car. We paint it with an animation evolving over time. We apply various cross-sections, filtering, and linear transformations to the reachable set's geometry. And then we accompany it with specific phase trajectories of extreme motions. It is discussed in section 3.

2.2 Extension to the CinemaScience Format to Display the 3D Graphics

We have developed the visualization tool for the purpose of visualizing the reachable sets according to requirements defined in introduction section. Our tool is based on the CinemaScience data format, see Rogers *et al* (2018). We have created a universal viewer for this format with the 3d graphics support and then adapted this viewer for the reachable set visualization.

In the CinemaScience format, information is stored in a *data.csv* text file. It contains a table with columns for parameters and columns for data artifacts (artifacts can be images, grids, csv files; *i.e.*, any type of data that can be written to disk). Thus this table defines a combination of parameters and artifacts. The interpretation of these combinations is free and determined by the scope of an application.

Our extension suggests that artifacts may be 3d entities, and all such entities should be rendered into common 3d space. Each 3d entity type of artifact is defined by artifact name, currently by second underscores-surrounded word. For example, *FILE_points_alfa* artifact name defines "points" entity type. The list of supported types is extensible, and the following types are currently implemented: points, lines (segments), triangles, spheres, vrml (for VRML graphic files), obj (for OBJ files).

For each parameter column, a graphical control is generated: slider for numeric parameter and combobox for string parameter. User manipulates these controls and thus specifies combination of parameters values. This determines the current combination of artifacts 3d data files to be rendered.

Specifically for the task of visualization of reachable sets, the *data.csv* file looks like this:

```
T,     FILE_vrml_rset,  FILE_treki_all, FILE_treki_currentT
1.00,  Symm-20.vrml,    treki.csv,  pts_1.00.treki.csv
1.05,  Symm-21.vrml,    treki.csv,  pts_1.05.treki.csv
1.10,  Symm-22.vrml,    treki.csv,  pts_1.10.treki.csv
 ...
4.00,  Symm-80.vrml,    treki.csv,  pts_4.00.treki.csv
```

Here, one parameter (*T*) and three artifacts are defined (*FILE_vrml_rset, FILE_treki_all, FILE_treki_currentT*). For the first artifact, *FILE_vrml_rset*, the vrml type is specified (by its name); that means loading and visualizing data in the VRML format. We use such format to store the surface of the reachable set. For the second and third artifacts, the *treki* type is specified for visualizing point trajectories.

The specially designed *treki* view type requires a csv file with the columns *N, X, Y, Fi.* Each line of this file defines a point in a 3d scene, and a set of such points form a trajectory. In the column *N*, there is a trajectory number. Then, in the graphical interface, a researcher can filter the view by the value of ***N*** and thus see only necessary trajectories.

The researcher selects the value *T* in the automatically created graphical user interface and the program calculates the corresponding values of artifact files and renders them. As a result, the overall view gets the necessary form: the surface for the selected instant, the points of the trajectories, and the points on the trajectories corresponding to this instant.

2.3 Technical Aspects

Procedures for visualization in this work consist of two parts: calculation and visualization. The first one performs the calculation and generates scene in the CinemaScience format. The visualization tool loads and displays scene interactively with the ability to apply visual filters.

In fact, the calculating and drawing parts are participants of a single visualization pipeline with calculation parameters at the input and interactive images on the screen at the output.

The described approach with the CinemaScience format allows one to program various 3d scenes, not just those shown in the paper. The list of artifacts is the list of 3d entities in scene. The applied semantics (selection of parameter values and rendering corresponding files of 3d entities into common 3d space) makes it possible to solve a wide range of visualization tasks. Other advantages of the used approach include CinemaScience's natural ability to create animated films using parameters specified in input files.

In addition, we added visual filters to our visualization tool. For the task of visualizing the reachable set (especially for the convenience of perceiving the structure of the boundary of the set), the following filters were found to be useful: half-space cross-section, cross-section series, sections edge tint. Different filters may be applied simultaneously, for example, half-space section on the X axis and section series on the Y axis.

The visualization tool is implemented using the WebGL and works in a web browser. We also made it compatible with the WebXR virtual reality standard. We observed our reachable sets in virtual reality with positive effects on perception. We have come to the conclusion that working in the visualization system requires using additional methods that could increase both the convenience of navigation in the graphic space and the convenience of managing the graphic filters.

Web technologies can be used together with virtual reality and with the addition of multi-user environment support and online connection with simulations. It brings us to the perspective of virtual test stands as described in the innovative work by Averbukh *et al* (2020).

The developed visualization tool for the reachable sets is available online at https://viewlang.ru/dubins/ as well as its source codes at https://github.com/pavelvasev/38parrots.

3. VISUALIZATION OF EXTREME MOTIONS

The description of extreme motions that go along the boundary of the time-varying reachable set has a theoretical and applied significance. For specialists in the field of optimal control, the answers to the following questions are of interest:

1. Extreme motions that satisfy the PMP go along smooth parts of the boundary, or may at some time intervals go along "edges of non-smoothness"?
2. Can extreme motions split and then merge back together into one motion?
3. Can extreme motion go into the interior of the reachable set?
4. If so, where on the boundary can this happen?

The developed tool provides ability to explore such issues. In particularly, it allows to see the location of the current phase point (x, y, φ) of the trajectory at the boundary of the reachable set $G(t)$ corresponding to a given instant. It is possible to trace at what instants the motion is on a smooth part of the boundary or on the non-smooth edge, and so on. Some trajectories are very interesting. For example, after the certain instant t^*, they cannot be continued by motions that going on the boundary of the reachable set with *any permissible control* for $t > t^*$. Such a motion goes to the interior of the reachable set. Also, there are situations when the extreme motion leading at some instant into some point on the boundary of the set $G(t_f)$ is not unique, and the splitting of the motions does not necessary occur at the initial instant. Thus, we are dealing with a bundle of extreme motions that exit at the instant t_0 from the same phase point and arrive also to the same phase point at the instant t_f.

At the address http://sector3.imm.uran.ru/confers/CGS2020/index_eng.html there are animation materials showing a three-dimensional reachable set, as well as some extreme trajectories.

In Figure 2, a frame is shown from a motion video of a trajectory bundle going on the boundary of the reachable set, which changes in time in the three-dimensional phase space x, y, φ. The bundle comes out from the origin at the initial instant and consists of motions that coincide at some initial time interval. The splitting effect is demonstrated by the six motions that are going on the boundary of the set $G(t_f)$ and connect at the end of a given time interval. The red dots show the phase trajectories (they coincide in the initial time interval) in the three-dimensional space. The yellow balls correspond to the current position of the motions at the time of the freeze frame. For the corresponding instant, the three-dimensional reachable set is also shown. The boundary of the reachable set is divided into color-highlighted parts generated by different types (in this case, 6 types) of extreme PMP controls leading to the boundary, see Patsko *et al* (2003).

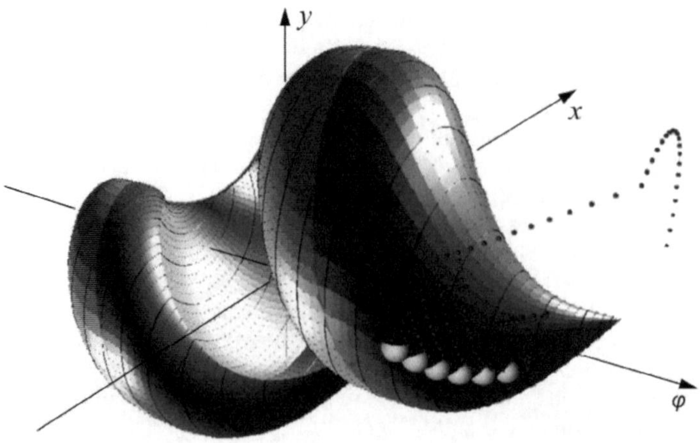

Figure 2. A frame from a video with the motion of a trajectory bundle going on the boundary of the time-evolving reachable set

4. CONCLUSION

The paper is devoted to visualization of the three-dimensional reachable set "at the instant" for the Dubins car model of the controlled object. The created visualization tool makes it possible to explore the features of the structure of the reachable set and the extreme motions that go on its boundary. The tool provides various visual filters for a better perception of the complex structure of the reachable set. The user's interface allows one to create animation movies on the basis of some scripting language. The suggested approach of scientific visualization is suitable for a big variety of visualization tasks besides the presented one.

ACKNOWLEDGEMENT

The authors are thankful to the reviewers for their contribution to the paper.
The work was performed as a part of research conducted in the Ural Mathematical Center.

REFERENCES

Averbukh, V.L. et al, 2020. The tasks of designing and developing virtual test stands. *In Global Smart Industry Conference (GloSIC)*, Chelyabinsk, Russia, pp. 49-54. doi: 10.1109/GloSIC50886.2020.9267835.

Dubins, L.E., 1957. On curves of minimal length with a constraint on average curvature and with prescribed initial and terminal positions and tangents. *In American Journal of Mathematics,* Vol. 79, No. 3, pp. 497-516.

Laumond, J.-P. (ed.), 1998. *Robot Motion Planning and Control. In Lecture Notes in Control and Information Sciences,* Vol. 229. Springer-Verlag, Berlin Heidelberg.

Patsko, V.S. et al, 2003. Three-dimensional reachability set for a nonlinear control system. *In Journal of Computer and Systems Sciences International,* Vol. 42, No. 3, pp. 320-328.

Patsko, V.S., Fedotov, A.A., 2018. Investigation of reachable set at instant for the Dubins' car. *In Proceedings of the 58th Israel Annual Conference on Aerospace Sciences*, Tel-Aviv & Haifa, pp. 1655-1669.

Rogers, D. et al, 2018. Cinema Database Specification Dietrich Release v1.2. *In Tech. Rep. LA-UR-17-25072.* https://github.com/cinemascience/cinema/blob/master/specs/dietrich/01/cinema_specD_v012.pdf

Vasev, P.A., Fedotov, A.A., 2020. Visualization of motions going along the boundary of the three-dimensional reachable set for the Dubins car. *In Materials of III International Seminar dedicated to the 75th anniversary of Academician A. I. Subbotin: Control Theory and Theory of Generalized Solutions of Hamilton–Jacobi Equations*. Ekaterinburg, Russia, pp. 122-126.

REAL-TIME OPEN FIELD CATTLE MONITORING BY DRONE: A 3D VISUALIZATION APPROACH

Fei Yang, Ningbo Zhu, Shuonan Pei and Irene Cheng
University of Alberta, Computing Science Department, Multimedia Program
2-32 Athabasca Hall, University of Alberta, Edmonton, Alberta, T6G 2E8, Canada

ABSTRACT

Monitoring a large herd across an open field is challenging in the agricultural industry but is essential for the welfare of cattle. With the advancement of Unmanned Aerial Vehicle (UAV) technology, drones are now commonly used for surveillance. In this work, we apply UAV technology and drone-captured videos to monitor cattle in open pastures. We use cow headcount as a use case. Although cattle headcount in a confined indoor environment has been studied extensively, our contribution lies in developing a framework that can localize the cows in the video and track their movements on a 3D canvas in real-time. By using a 3D visualization approach, we expect to resolve many of the occlusion issues by guiding the drone operator to navigate the drone to discover important information. We use a pre-trained Mask R-CNN classification model to detect and track cows in the video. We then use Matplotlib 3D to create the 3D canvas and display the relative cow positions. Our real-time 3D cow visualization framework allows tracking herds remotely, saving time and labor for on-site manual herding, as well as providing better global monitoring of the herd. The complete implementation can be found in our publicly available GitHub link upon request.

KEYWORDS

Object Detection, Image Processing, Drone Video Analysis, 3D Visualization, Remote Monitoring, Livestock Management

1. INTRODUCTION

Governments maintain cattle welfare standards, which the agriculture sector has to follow. Keeping the headcount of livestock is a part of the process but it is a challenging task when herds are scattered in open fields. It is labor intensive and time consuming when on-site manual cattle-herding is performed. It can be expensive, as it may require farmers to slog through pasture, bush, wind, and snow in order to monitor and search them. To keep track of headcount too close to the cattle, i.e., cows in this work, often creates accidents especially when the cows are under stress. Every year, many people are hurt by cattle, mostly when cattle kick or crush them, since cattle have a weight advantage over human and cattle can move surprisingly fast. Agitated cattle are of a particular risk, and it takes training to handle them safely. Furthermore, manual headcount usually takes multiple trials to get it right because cows move, hide behind each other, or stand behind obstacles, e.g., a big hay bale or a tree. Counting is difficult even when the cattle are lying down.

According to the livestock statistics from the Government of Alberta, there were over 4.9 million units of cattle and 1.6 million pigs in 2020. These are staggering numbers. Hence, drone technology is becoming popular to provide smart agriculture, as it can find different applications here, including perform headcount of livestock across large open grazing areas. As the technology evolves, the costs of drones have come down and the accessibility and utility of drones have improved. Yinka and Ajayi (2019) introduced the different types of Unmanned Aerial Vehicles (UAVs) and the applications of UAVs in crop farming and in livestock. They also discussed some of the open challenges to the application of UAVs in Agriculture. Maddikunta et al. (2021) explored and presented the adaptation and usage of UAVs, and identified the key requirements of UAVs in smart agriculture, such as the accuracy of results, network availability, and data storage. Xu et al. (2020) presented a system that combined a quadcopter and artificial intelligence image processing for automated livestock detection. They applied the Mask R-CNN algorithm and demonstrated its effectiveness in livestock monitoring task. Barbedo and Koenigkan (2018) found that there were a limited number of UAV applications used to monitor and count cattle. They analyzed the reasons for this apparent lack of progress and discussed both the technical challenges and the difficulties in finding target users. Hsieh et al. (2017) created a large drone view dataset, CARPK, and introduced a method to generate feasible region proposals, which will be helpful for the drone-based vehicle counting method using the deep learning method. Van Gemert et al. (2014) proposed combining UAVs with automatic object recognition techniques to solve the manual animal surveying problem. Reinecke and Prinsloo (2017) expounded the benefit of drone monitoring on agriculture. A drone can effectively capture detailed pictures and videos to help farmers observe crops remotely and cultivate them better, and scare away the birds (Hill, 2000). Based on all these studies, it can be seen that there is a huge potential for the applications of drones in agriculture. From a livestock perspective, drones are being used to perform headcount and animal monitoring. Cow counting with drones saves time and is more accurate, because an aerial maneuver can provide a clearer multi-view perspective of the scene without cows blocking each other along the line of sight.

In some countries, farmers are already using a live stream drone, but they still count animals in the stream video manually. Al-Thani et al. (2020) assembled and installed a drone by themselves attempting to count and monitor sheep on a farm. They compared offline processing, online pre-processing, and online processing findings and concluded that online processing had the highest accuracy. Real-time processing also helps making just-in-time decisions. Shao et al. (2020) and Rivas et al. (2018) utilized convolutional neural networks on UAV image detection. Hodgson et al. (2018) considered drones as suitable devices to detect and count objects. Despite the above studies, counting the number of cows using drones is still a challenging problem when the herd is too large scattered in open pastures. To address this problem, we designed a machine learning based framework that can automatically count the number of cows via a live stream drone. Based on the evaluation in our pre-trained model feasibility study, we found that the Mask R-CNN (He et al., 2017) model had the best performance. Note that head counting is not sufficient for cattle welfare. It is important to localize individual cows and understand if a cow displays healthy postures and is socially accommodated in the herd. To check the location of each cow, our framework plots its relative position in a 3D canvas, which can be navigated in a 360° viewport so that the viewer can monitor the health state of the entire herd.

2. METHOD AND IMPLEMENTATION

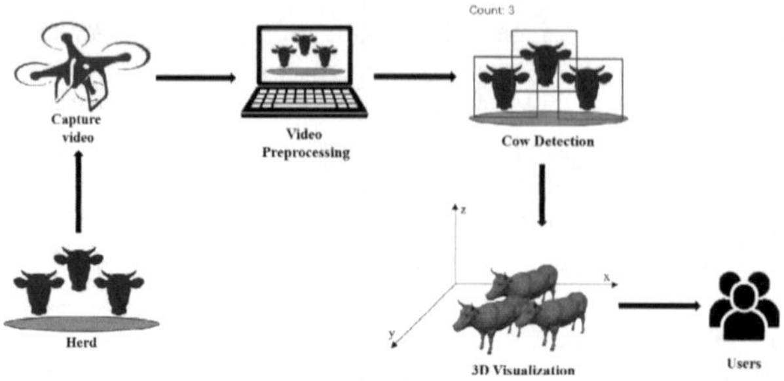

Figure 1. Proposed system processing pipeline

In this section, we will introduce our proposed cow counting and 3D visualization system. Figure 1 illustrates the processing pipeline. We first capture videos of the pasture using a drone, and then detect and count the cows. The pipeline is composed of different stages as explained in the subsections below.

2.1 Data Fetching

Due to the constraint imposed by the machine learning model, only one image is allowed for every input. Therefore, we had to divide the captured video into a sequence of frames, detect cows and record their positions in each frame. In other words, for each frame of the video, we generated a headcount and a list of cow positions.

2.2 Cow Detection

We detected cows using two pre-trained models and compared their accuracy performance. The first one was YOLO-v3 (Redmon & Farhadi, 2018). We installed MXNet (Chen et al., 2015) of the GluonCV Toolkit package. Following the model's input structure, we prepared each image into three grids, 8*8, 16*16, and 32*32. We found that YOLO (You Only Look Once) does not have the highest accuracy, but it is a good compromise between accuracy and speed. YOLO-v3 was an enhanced version, based on a combination of YOLO-v1 (Redmon et al., 2016) and YOLO-v2 (Redmon & Farhadi, 2017). It improves the detection accuracy, while maintaining the speed advantage of other YOLO models, especially when detecting small objects. The YOLO-v3 model divides the image into multiple regions of different sizes. It then classifies each object bounding box based on the calculated probability. YOLO-v3 implements the Darknet-53 model structure, which has 53 convolution layers. Each convolution layer is followed by a batch normalization layer and a leaky ReLU layer as the activation function. The detected result is not ideal, as the speed of the model is too slow, requiring around 10 seconds per frame, which cannot support a real-time application. The accuracy is also not sufficiently high, especially when the cows in the image stack on each other, causing double counting.

For the above reasons, we tested another pre-trained Mask R-CNN model. We installed the Detection 2 (Wu et al., 2019) package, which is made available by Facebook and import R50-FPN-3x. This model can only be tested on the Google Colab on Mac or Linux systems. Mask R-CNN performs an instance segmentation, which not only needs to localize the objects correctly, but also needs to segment the detected objects accurately. Therefore, instance segmentation combines both object detection and semantic segmentation. Mask R-CNN is an improved Faster R-CNN (FCN) (Ren et al., 2015). It semantically segments each proposal candidate box. There are three steps in the Instance Segmentation Mask R-CNN framework: (1) target detection – draw a bounding box around the target object to mark what is detected; (2) target classification – for each target, find the corresponding class to determine whether it is a person, a car, or other categories; and (3) pixel-level target segmentation. For each target, it is necessary to separate the foreground and background. The output of the model is the bounding box position, classified label, and label probability. We count the number of the bounding boxes in each frame as the number of cows.

2.3 Cow's 3D Visualization

We compared two publicly available free software tools: Blender and Matplotlib 3D, to visualize cows and their movements in a 3D canvas. Blender cannot update the 3D scene frame by frame; it only shows the final scene at the end. Therefore, we selected Matplotlib 3D. Based on the position of each bounding box in the video frame, we placed a cow model in the 3D canvas. We used the x-coordinate and y-coordinate of the bounding box in the image to represent the horizontal position of the cow, and the distance between the cow and the camera in the 3D canvas. The runtime of Matplotlib 3D visualization is around 2 frames per second.

3. EXPERIMENTAL RESULTS

The runtime and accuracy of the two cow detection models are shown in Table 1. Compared with Mask R-CNN, YOLO-v3 is too slow. It cannot meet the requirements of real-time applications. The final accuracy of the YOLOv3 model is 14/15 after scanning every video frame, and 15/15 is the accuracy of Mask R-CNN. Since both the herd and the drone are moving, detection error can easily happen when the scanning device changes direction, which can blur the entire frame. As shown in Figure 2, Mask R-CNN can clearly detect every cow in the herd, even if only a small part of the cow is exposed. However, YOLO-v3's result is not accurate. YOLO-v3 cannot distinguish each cow in a group when they are of the same color crowding together. Therefore, we used the detection result of Mask R-CNN for 3D visualization.

Table 1. Comparison of YOLO-v3 and Mask R-CNN

Method	Runtime	Detected Value/True Value
YOLO-v3	10s per frame	14/15
Mask R-CNN	2.18s per frame	15/15

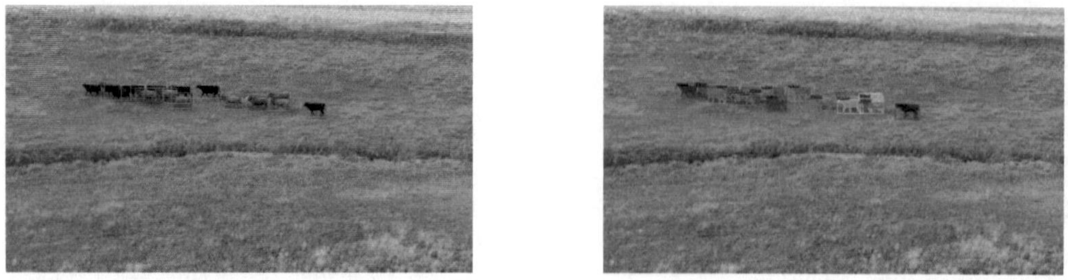

(a) (b)

Figure 2. An example comparing the detection results of frame50 using (a) YOLO-v3 and (b) Mask R-CNN

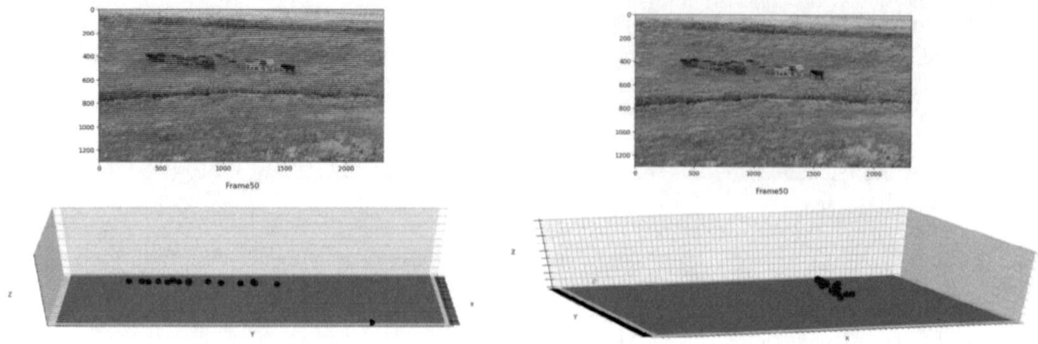

(a) (b)

Figure 3. 3D Visualization of frame50 using Matplotlib 3D

Figure 3 is an example of the 3D visualization output. The current video frame and its detection result are shown at the top, and the number detected is shown at the upper left corner of the frame. The frame number is displayed below the frame. The bottom half of Figure 3 shows the corresponding 3D visualization of the herd in the current frame. Each detected cow is simulated as a 3D point and their positions are updated based on the current frame. Figure 3 (a) and (b) represent the different viewing angles of the same frame. The viewer can switch the viewing perspective to monitor herds and control the flight route of the drone accordingly.

Our 3D visualization framework combined with the UAV, i.e., drone, technology can monitor herds scattering across open fields in real-time. The cow counting result and the 3D visualization show that our system is more effective and accurate than a manual counting process.

4. CONCLUSION

The ability to accurately and quickly perform cattle headcount and monitor their movements in open fields is a time-saver for busy ranchers with big herds. The process has important financial implications. In this paper, we review state-of-the-art methods and develop a real-time cow counting and 3D visualization framework. The processing pipeline starts from taking videos from the drone, localizing the targets, counting the number of cows using object detection, to 3D visualization of the relative position of each cow. We analyzed and compared different object detection models and selected the best performed one to achieve our goal. Monitoring and counting cattle using drones is a challenging problem because it involves a dynamic scene and a moving scanning device. There are many factors that can impact accurate cattle detection and counting, e.g., lack of contrast, cow movements, large cow clusters, and hidden calves. In future work, we will collect more videos for model training. The speed of 3D rendering can also be approved by using more powerful GPU.

REFERENCES

Al-Thani, N., Albuainain, A., Alnaimi, F., & Zorba, N. (2020, June). Drones for Sheep Livestock Monitoring. In 2020 IEEE 20th Mediterranean Electrotechnical Conference (MELECON) (pp. 672-676). IEEE.

Barbedo, J. G. A., & Koenigkan, L. V. (2018). Perspectives on the use of unmanned aerial systems to monitor cattle. Outlook on agriculture, 47(3), 214-222.

Chen, T., Li, M., Li, Y., Lin, M., Wang, N., Wang, M., Xiao, T., Xu, B., Zhang, C., & Zhang, Z. (2015). Mxnet: A flexible and efficient machine learning library for heterogeneous distributed systems. arXiv preprint arXiv:1512.01274.

He, K., Gkioxari, G., Dollár, P., & Girshick, R. (2017). Mask r-cnn. In Proceedings of the IEEE international conference on computer vision (pp. 2961-2969).

Hill, C. M. (2000). Conflict of interest between people and baboons: crop raiding in Uganda. International journal of primatology, 21(2), 299-315.

Hsieh, M. R., Lin, Y. L., & Hsu, W. H. (2017). Drone-based object counting by spatially regularized regional proposal network. In Proceedings of the IEEE international conference on computer vision (pp. 4145-4153).

Hodgson, J. C., Mott, R., Baylis, S. M., Pham, T. T., Wotherspoon, S., Kilpatrick, A. D., ... & Koh, L. P. (2018). Drones count wildlife more accurately and precisely than humans. Methods in Ecology and Evolution, 9(5), 1160-1167.

Maddikunta, P. K. R., Hakak, S., Alazab, M., Bhattacharya, S., Gadekallu, T. R., Khan, W. Z., & Pham, Q. V. (2021). Unmanned aerial vehicles in smart agriculture: Applications, requirements, and challenges. IEEE Sensors Journal.

Redmon, J., Divvala, S., Girshick, R., & Farhadi, A. (2016). You only look once: Unified, real-time object detection. In Proceedings of the IEEE conference on computer vision and pattern recognition (pp. 779-788).

Redmon, J., & Farhadi, A. (2017). YOLO9000: better, faster, stronger. In Proceedings of the IEEE conference on computer vision and pattern recognition (pp. 7263-7271).

Redmon, J., & Farhadi, A. (2018). Yolov3: An incremental improvement. arXiv preprint arXiv:1804.02767.

Reinecke, M., & Prinsloo, T. (2017, July). The influence of drone monitoring on crop health and harvest size. In 2017 1st International conference on next generation computing applications (NextComp) (pp. 5-10). IEEE.

Ren, S., He, K., Girshick, R., & Sun, J. (2015). Faster r-cnn: Towards real-time object detection with region proposal networks. Advances in neural information processing systems, 28, 91-99.

Rivas, A., Chamoso, P., González-Briones, A., & Corchado, J. M. (2018). Detection of cattle using drones and convolutional neural networks. Sensors, 18(7), 2048.

Shao, W., Kawakami, R., Yoshihashi, R., You, S., Kawase, H., & Naemura, T. (2020). Cattle detection and counting in UAV images based on convolutional neural networks. International Journal of Remote Sensing, 41(1), 31-52.

van Gemert, J. C., Verschoor, C. R., Mettes, P., Epema, K., Koh, L. P., & Wich, S. (2014, September). Nature conservation drones for automatic localization and counting of animals. In European Conference on Computer Vision (pp. 255-270). Springer, Cham.

Wu, Y., Girshick, R., Lo, W.-Y., Massa, F., & Kirillov, A. (2019). Detectron2. GitHub. https://github.com/facebookresearch/detectron2.

Xu, B., Wang, W., Falzon, G., Kwan, P., Guo, L., Sun, Z., & Li, C. (2020). Livestock classification and counting in quadcopter aerial images using Mask R-CNN. International Journal of Remote Sensing, 41(21), 8121-8142.

Yinka-Banjo, C., & Ajayi, O. (2019). Sky-farmers: applications of unmanned aerial vehicles (UAV) in agriculture. In Autonomous Vehicles. IntechOpen.

PHYSICALLY BASED MATERIAL SYNTHESIS

Tassilo Scharnagl and Dieter Meiller
Ostbayerische Technische Hochschule Amberg-Weiden (OTH - Technical University of Applied Sciences)
Kaiser-Wilhelm-Ring 23, 92224 Amberg, Germany

ABSTRACT

This paper demonstrates an experimental approach of synthesizing features from real-world materials for use as a virtual physically based rendering material for computer generated imagery via photo scanning and photogrammetry.

KEYWORDS

PBMS, PBR, PBR Material, PBR Texture, Texture Maps

1. INTRODUCTION

Creating physically based rendering (PBR) textures from real-world surfaces is a time-efficient way to create high detail virtual materials. However, normal photographic processes only capture a limited number of features - such as color and height data. To increase the amount of information present within the textures, a new process can be implemented, capable of efficiently extracting true color, roughness, metallic, normal and height data (Baranoski 2001). This methodology is called "Physically Based Material Synthesis" or shortened "PBMS".

2. EXISTING METHODOLOGIES

Material from single panorama The main advantage of this process is the time required to create a PBR material, but due to the lack of the captured data, a realistic depiction cannot be guaranteed.

Material from photogrammetry By capturing a large set of images, the real-world surface can be reconstructed to a virtual 3D-model by triangulation, thus the height data can be sufficiently extracted. However, most other features need to be approximated and are thereby subject to inaccuracy.

Material from multi-angle capture For this process the angle of the incident light needs to be adjusted for each capture to enable a reconstruction of the surface. This process grants sufficient information about color, normal and height data, which can be reconstructed through differences in shadows and reflections (Salvi 2017).

3. DEVELOPED METHODOLOGIES

3.1 Capture Methodologies

HDR capture To establish a high dynamic range, an exposure stacked panorama was captured (see figure 1).

Flash captures In order to obtain more information about the roughness and structure of a surface, a powerful flash is used to provide a powerful, approximate point-source light. Two different panoramas are being captured in this way. One panorama with hard shadows and sharp reflections without any filters, referred to as "HFP" (hard flash panorama, figure 2). The other with soft shadows and reflections by softening the light source with a diffuse filter, referred to as "SFP" (soft flash panorama, figure 3).

Cross-polarized capture For the extraction of metallic features, a particular feature is needed. Metals have unique reflection characteristics compared to dielectric materials. An example of this can be shown in a metal's ability to reflect polarized light without changing its polarity. By using cross-polarization (see figure 4), metallic features of a material can be detected because most of the emitted polarized light will be reflected without changes in polarity, which can then be blocked by the second polarization filter (compare figures 6 & 7). Due to the ability to detect metallic features and roughly diffuse/specular reflections, this approach is crucial (Müller 1996, Wolff 1989).

Photogrammetry capture For the reconstruction of the height differences, photogrammetry is being used. In addition to the already created panorama images, more photographs at different angles and positions are being captured to further supplement the reconstruction (see figure 5).

Figure 1. HDR

Figure 2. Hard-flash

Figure 3. Soft-flash

Figure 4. Cross-pol

Figure 5. Photogram

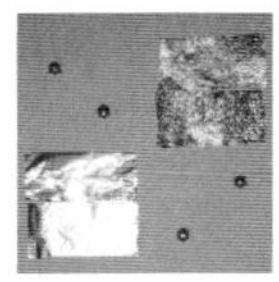
Figure 6. Un-Pol

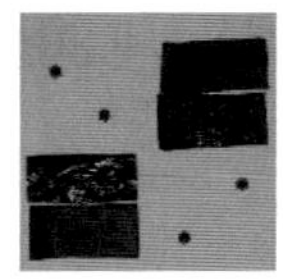
Figure 7. Cross-pol

3.2 Panoramas and Photogrammetry

Stitching process Due to the staged panorama capturing process, all photographed images of the panoramas needed to be stitched simultaneously without being merged into one panorama.

Photogrammetry process For generating the depth information *Meshroom* (AliceVision 2021), which is based on AliceVision Photogrammetric Computer Vision Framework (AliceVision 2021), was used as the reconstruction software.

Alignment & tiling The panoramas were automatically aligned and manually adjusted if any errors occurred. The photogrammetry image was manually aligned with the other panoramas and any larger surface curvatures were removed. The full image set was cropped to a 1:1 aspect ratio and made tilable.

3.3 Image Matrix Computations

The image matrices A and B are three dimensional, with a range from zero to one. The factor x has a range from zero to one and is used to adjust the overall amount.

Matrix addition, subtraction & multiplication:

$$ADD: \boldsymbol{C} = \boldsymbol{A} + \boldsymbol{B} * \boldsymbol{x}$$

$$SUB: \boldsymbol{C} = \boldsymbol{A} - \boldsymbol{B} * \boldsymbol{x}$$

$$MULT: \boldsymbol{C} = \boldsymbol{A} * (\boldsymbol{1} - \boldsymbol{x}) + \boldsymbol{A} \circ \boldsymbol{B} * \boldsymbol{x}$$

Matrix lighten:

$$\forall \boldsymbol{i} \in \{\boldsymbol{0}, \dots, \boldsymbol{n} - \boldsymbol{1}\}, \forall \boldsymbol{j} \in \{\boldsymbol{0}, \dots, \boldsymbol{m} - \boldsymbol{1}\}, \boldsymbol{C_{ij}} = \begin{cases} \overrightarrow{\boldsymbol{A_{ij}}} \ \boldsymbol{if} \ ||\overrightarrow{\boldsymbol{A_{ij}}}|| > ||\overrightarrow{\boldsymbol{B_{ij}}}|| \\ \overrightarrow{\boldsymbol{B_{ij}}}, \quad \boldsymbol{otherwise} \end{cases}$$

$$\boldsymbol{D} = \boldsymbol{A} * (\boldsymbol{1} - \boldsymbol{x}) + \boldsymbol{C} * \boldsymbol{x}$$

Matrix overlay:

$$\forall \boldsymbol{i} \in \{\boldsymbol{0}, \dots, \boldsymbol{n} - \boldsymbol{1}\}, \forall \boldsymbol{j} \in \{\boldsymbol{0}, \dots, \boldsymbol{m} - \boldsymbol{1}\}, \boldsymbol{C_{ij}} = \begin{cases} \left(\hat{e} * \left|\left|\overrightarrow{\boldsymbol{A_{ij}}}\right|\right|\right) \boldsymbol{if} \left|\left|\overrightarrow{\boldsymbol{A_{ij}}}\right|\right| < \frac{\sqrt{3}}{2} \\ \left(\hat{e} * \frac{\sqrt{3}}{2}\right), \quad \boldsymbol{otherwise} \end{cases}$$

$$\boldsymbol{D} = \boldsymbol{A} * (\boldsymbol{1} - \boldsymbol{x}) + \boldsymbol{2} * \boldsymbol{A} \circ \boldsymbol{B} \circ \boldsymbol{C}$$

3.4 Texture Map Synthesis

The main algorithm consists of five major component groups, one for each texture map. All component groups were interlinked due to information dependencies between each some map.

Albedo Synthesis The albedo synthesis removes any shadows, occlusion and reflections. The output showed alignment artefacts because the all-panorama captures were done sequentially, thus any misalignments had to be corrected (see figures 8 & 13).

Normal Synthesis For synthesizing the normal information of the material, a high frequency image is required, generated from the existing color images. The process is also supplemented by the photogrammetry data (see figures 9 & 14).

Roughness Synthesis To synthesize the roughness component of the material the different reflective characteristics of the SFP, HPF, HDR and cross-polarized panorama were used to extract the desired data (see figures 10 & 15).

Metallic Synthesis The metallic map is used by most synthesis processes and requires a high degree of accuracy because any errors would carry over. For this synthesis, the HFP, SFP and HDR panorama were used create an image with a high density of luminance data. The resulting image is then used to extract the metallic features through computations with the cross-polarized panorama (see figures 11 & 16).

Height Synthesis To generate the height map, the photogrammetry image was used and supplemented with parts of the Normal Synthesis in order to increase the overall information density (see figures 12 & 17).

Figure 8. Albedo

Figure 9. Normal

Figure 10. Roughness

Figure 11. Metallic

Figure 12. Height

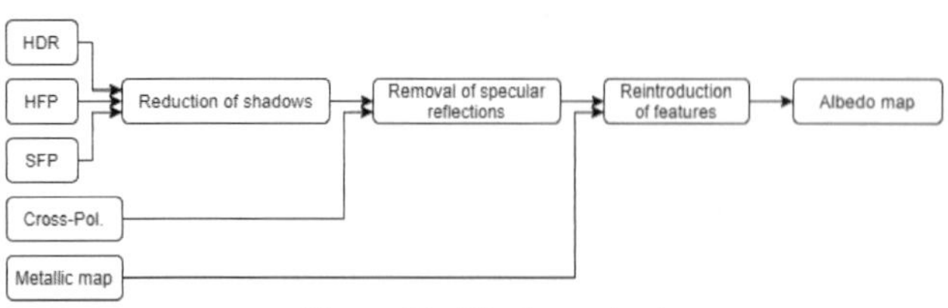

Figure 13. Albedo synthesis

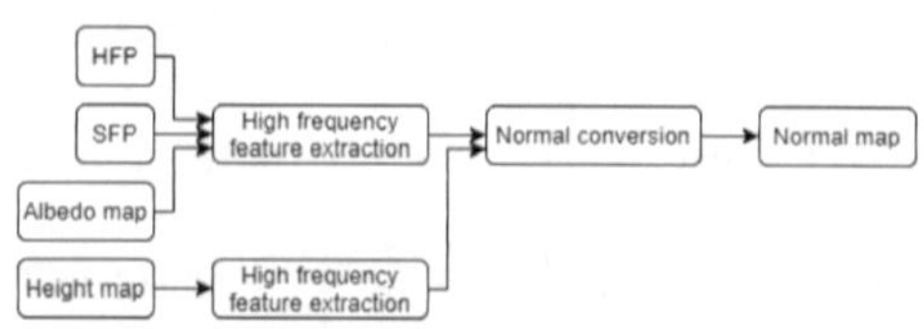

Figure 14. Normal synthesis

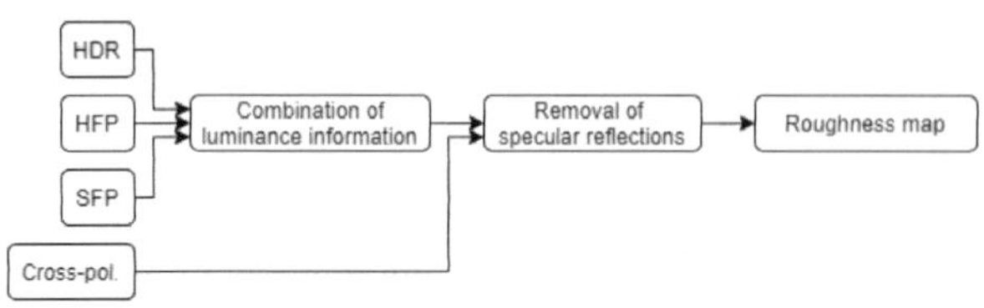

Figure 15. Roughness synthesis

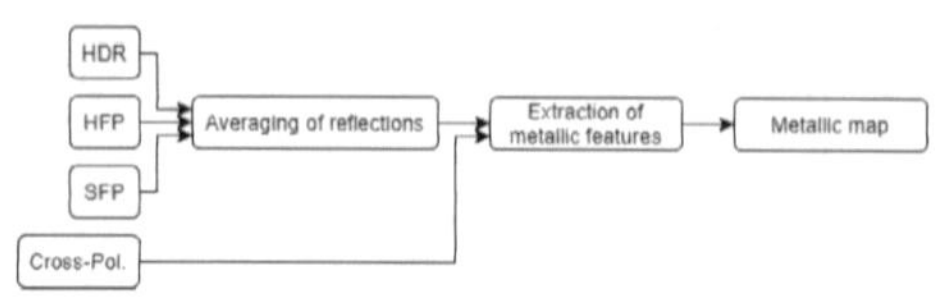

Figure 16. Metallic synthesis

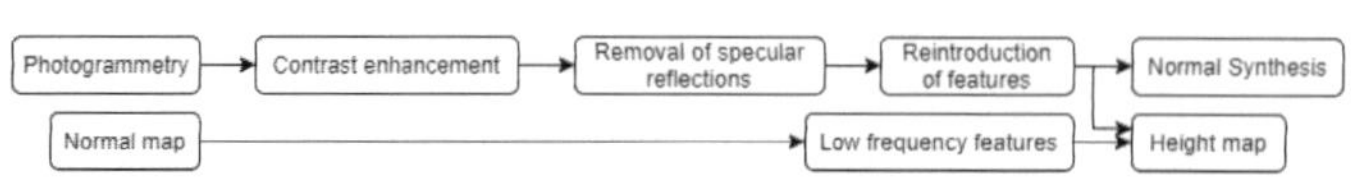

Figure 17. Height synthesis

3.5 Comparison of B2M & PBMS

An existing methodology, "bitmap to material" or "B2M" was chosen and supplemented with height data from the photogrammetry. The B2M process had to be manually adjusted for best results, unlike PBMS.

Gravel material The most apparent differences between both workflows are the distribution of roughness and the metallic features. Due to the nature of gravel, small mineral deposits create metal-like reflections, which gives the PBMS material a greater sense of realism look when compared to the B2M material (compare figures 18 - 21).

Soil material Due to the high volume of data, a better color representation can be noticed, this caused by the used HDR in the PBMS workflow. However, in its current state the B2M workflow has the better normal map and small surface details, this will be a point to explore in future research (compare figures 22 - 25).

Figure 18.
Gravel-B2M

Figure 19.
Gravel-PBMS

Figure 20.
Gravel-B2M

Figure 21.
Gravel-PBMS

Figure 22.
Soil-B2M

Figure 23.
Soil-PBMS

Figure 24.
Soil-B2M

Figure 25.
Soil-PBMS

3.6 Problems and Future Research

Metallic inaccuracies As can be seen in the metallic map parts of organic matter seem to have metallic features, this might be due to the Brewster's angle (Batchelor 2012).

Alignment issues Due to the sequential capture of the used panoramas, very slight misalignments occur between all panoramas, thus corrections need to be made during the stitching process. In order to counteract all of the aforementioned issues, further panorama captures should be taken simultaneously.

Stereogrammetry Based on the excessive need of computing power by photogrammetry, stereogrammetry could substitute or supplement this method.

Other wavelengths The PBMS methodology has been solely relying on the visible spectrum of light. However, near-IR and UV-A support different reflective, refractive and transmissive properties.

REFERENCES

AliceVision Association, 2021. URL: *https://alicevision.org/ (visited on 04/01/2021).*

Baranoski, G., Rokne, J. & Xu, G, 2001. Virtual spectrophotometric measurements for biologically and physically based rendering. *The Visual Computer*, Volume 17, issue 8, pp. 506–518.

Batchelor B.G., 2012. Light and Optics, *Machine Vision Handbook*. Springer, London, UK, pp. 157-258.

Müller V., 1996. „ Elimination of specular surface-reflectance using polarized and unpolarized light". In: Computer Vision --- ECCV '96. Springer, Berlin Heidelberg, Germany, pp. 625-635.

Salvi A., 2017. *Your Smartphone Is a Material Scanner*, Substance by Adobe. URL: *https://store.substance3d.com/blog/your-smartphone-material-scanner (visited on 23/12/2020)*

Wolff L. B., 1989, "Using polarization to separate reflection components," *CVPR '89: IEEE Computer Society Conference on Computer Vision and Pattern Recognition*, San Diego, CA, USA, pp. 363-369.

DATA-ENABLED CRYPTOCURRENCY MARKET ANALYSIS AND VISUALIZATION PLATFORM

Ningbo Zhu, Fei Yang, Mingzhi Zhu, Xinyao Sun and Irene Cheng
University of Alberta, Computing Science Department, Multimedia Program
2-32 Athabasca Hall, University of Alberta, Edmonton, Alberta, T6G 2E8, Canada

ABSTRACT

The cryptocurrency industry has evolved rapidly in recent years, and it is increasingly popular as a convenient tool to complement the traditional stock and futures exchanges. Accurate market research enables traders to make more informed decisions and benefit from their investments. Our objective is to introduce a web platform for aggregating various types of cryptocurrency data, both on- and off-chain. Its novelty lies in offering a visual representation of market data analysis, which is driven by multi-modal data fusion and representation techniques, as well as artificial intelligence. We propose a full-stack framework that consists of a front-end web application for user interaction and visualization, and a backend server for data fetching, preprocessing, and analysis. In our implementation, we used data from the cryptocurrency market, on-chain statistics, and textual data from social media, to create a deep-learning-based market trend model. For market prediction, our data analysis module processed high-frequency vocabulary extracted from social media, sentiment analysis of social media content, historical price trend, and historical hash rates. Investors and market analysts can benefit from our platform by directly observing the dynamic of multi-modal cryptocurrency data and easily exploring market trends, generated by our market prediction model delivered by a front-end application. The complete implementation can be found in our publicly available GitHub link upon request.

KEYWORDS

Cryptocurrency, Price Prediction, Data Visualization, Neural Language Processing, Sentiment Analysis, Machine Learning

1. INTRODUCTION

The values of cryptocurrencies soared in recent years as a result of recent super-exponential rise in their market capitalization. There are now over 1,500 cryptocurrencies that are regularly exchanged. Cryptocurrencies can be purchased using fiat currency in a variety of online markets. The daily transaction amount has surpassed $35 billion. With the prices of cryptocurrencies (e.g. Bitcoin) rapidly rising, the lack of an efficient tool for effective data analysis is a big challenge in this research and market domain.

The development of a self-organized market for virtual currency and/or commodity, whose worth is largely determined by social consensus has attracted the attention of the scientific community. Mohapatra et al. (2019) conducted real-time cryptocurrency market prediction using Twitter sentiment. They used decision-tree based algorithms for prediction. Between the real and expected Bitcoin prices, their model's overall Root-Mean-Square Error (RMSE) is $10. Rodolfo Saldanha (2020) used two separate versions of Recurrent Neural Networks (RNNs) to forecast Amazon's potential stock values based on historical data, which achieved perfect performance. His data preprocessing and training model development serve as our reference for developing a benchmark for our project. Saad et al. (2021) predicted the Bitcoin (BTC) and Ethereum (ETH) prices using a multivariate regression model and Long Short-Term Memory (LSTM) network (Hochreiter & Schmidhuber, 1997). They used the price, mining complexity, hash rate, and user count, as features. Their model had a Mean Absolute Error (MAE) of 0.0162 on BTC and 0.0563 on ETH. Jay et al. (2020) applied stochastic Multi-Layer Perception (MLP) and LSTM networks by randomizing the activation functions at runtime. The stochastic module had incorporated market responses to improve the expected outcome. Phaladisailoed et al. (2018) compared the effectiveness of many machine learning techniques to forecast Bitcoin prices. They created the models based on Bitcoin prices using the Scikit-learn library, Theil-Sen, and Huber regression models, and LSTM and Gated Recurrent Unit (GRU) deep learning models.

Despite the above efforts, current methods do not provide an intuitive picture to the investors. Their numerical results lack a clear development trend of cryptocurrency, to show the historical price changes and the predicted price trends. To address this issue, we develop a web interface for visualizing cryptocurrency-related data using the latest state-of-the-art intelligent data processing and analysis methodologies.

2. PROPOSED PLATFORM

The visualization of historical market trends can reflect the social confidence (investor sentiment) in a cryptocurrency. The long-term pricing pattern provides insight into prospective market movements. Our objective is to analyze the price patterns and provide visualization for the last seven years of the Bitcoin market. Apart from the historical patterns, reliable price predictions are important, based on which investors decide to commit their transactions. In this work, we present three different machine-learning based forecasting frameworks for cryptocurrency. Because cryptocurrency is a decentralized currency, we also examine the relationship between the cryptocurrency's price shift rate and social network-based sentiment data. A careful analysis of social media data often leads to the discovery of high-frequency vocabularies, associated with popular social interests (conversations), which can reflect a trigger of significant market fluctuations. For this reason, our platform focuses on the description and visualization of high-frequency terms, and conducts a hybrid analysis, incorporating both quantitative and textual sentiment information to better explore the market sentiment.

Our platform is composed of three main components: (1) Data Fetching and Preprocessing, (2) Price Prediction, and (3) Data Visualization. Figure 1 shows the architecture of our proposed platform.

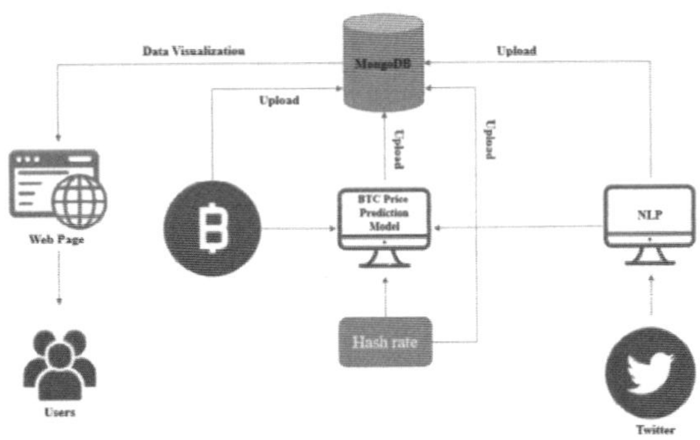

Figure 1. Platform Architecture

2.1 Data Fetching and Preprocessing

We use Bitcoin to demonstrate the performance of our platform because it is the most widely used and representative cryptocurrency. We obtained the daily exchange market data from January 1, 2014, to December 31, 2021 via Coindesk (Coindesk, 2021) as off-chain data, and the Bitcoin hash rates for the same period from Quandl (Quandl, 2021) as on-chain data. Our backend server obtained social media information by crawling Twitter tweets using Twint (Poldi, 2020). Models based on neural networks have delivered impressive results, including Natural Language Processing (NLP) applications. Thus, we used an NLP based analytics library NLTK (Bird et al., 2009) to formalize tweets into keywords, enable machines to comprehend simple sentences. To achieve Bitcoin price prediction, we extracted a one-hot vector of high-frequency vocabularies over time, that may have a relationship with the pace at which the Bitcoin price increases. We incorporated them into the training model as a function. We observed that a significant cluster of positive or negative sentiments appearing in social media can indicate a potential change in the cryptocurrency price. We fed the sentences into a sentiment analysis model called vaderSentiment (Hutto & Gilbert, 2014), which computed the sentiment strengths of the sentences. We set seven days as a training batch for the model. After each batch, we shifted one day and collected the next batch. The same procedure was applied on other features. Normalization was the next stage of preprocessing. Each seven-day combination of the input data was normalized using the Min-max method. The hash rate was normalized similar to the price. Additionally, we shuffled the normalized sliced data to ensure the robustness of the trained model.

2.2 Price Prediction

For price prediction, we compared three different machine-learning models in this work: LSTM, bi-LSTM, and GRU. Additionally, we evaluated different feature combinations to forecast the trends of Bitcoin price. Recurrent Neural Networks (RNNs) are a subclass of artificial neural networks capable of solving problems such as prediction, machine translation, and emotion classification, by making repeated use of sequential data. However, RNNs have limited short-term memory and are incapable of training very long input sequences. As the training of long sequence data progresses, the vanishing gradient problem becomes obvious. The gradient is used to update the neural network's weights. If the gradient is too small, each update's weight has a more negligible effect on subsequent training, and the model stops learning or learns very slowly.

LSTM aims to address this issue by storing and restoring long-term data without consuming excessive memory. LSTM has three gates, while GRU has just two. As a result, GRU has fewer parameters and is thus simpler to converge. The bi-LSTM (Reimers & Gurevych, 2017) model contains one more collection of LSTM layers than the LSTM model. It consists of a forward and a backward LSTM. Bi-LSTMs significantly increase the amount of information extracted and enhance the network content availability. Root Mean Square Error (RMSE) was used as the loss function in training and validation for the weight backpropagation in each epoch. The training and validation losses were plotted to determine if the model converged well.

After completing model training, we used the trained model to analyze the historical price data from January 2014 to December 2020 in order to determine the Predicted Rate in Equation (1). We then obtained the predicted price, which was passed to the Visualization Module of our web application to assist users making cryptocurrency purchase decisions.

$$\text{Predicted Price} = \text{Analyzed Historical Price } (1+\text{Predicted Rate}) \qquad (1)$$

2.3 Data Visualization

Figure 2. Price Prediction with Recharts

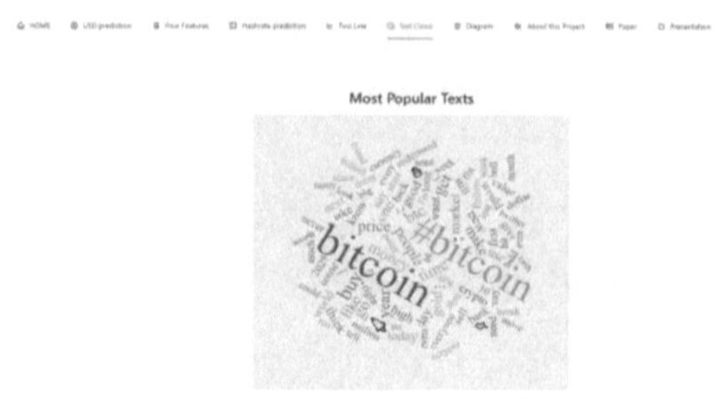

Figure 3. Word count with World-cloud

Our front-end web application is constructed using the React-Router-Dom, Sass, and AntD (Ant-Design, 2015) frameworks. Charts are used to visualize all numerical data using the Recharts library.

The line chart page in Figure 2 allows the users to select a date range to visualize the data and let them select any of the three models to see the trend predication. We also provide tabs for users to view details on four additional pages, each of which has its own set of trend features. By comparing different maps, investors can make informed investment decisions.

Since tweets are used as input in our prediction model, users might be curious about the types of keywords listed and their frequency of occurrence. For users to understand the social sentiment, we provide a React-Word Cloud tab as illustrated in Figure 3. Users can check the cryptocurrency keywords most discussed on Twitter through this tab.

3. RESULTS AND DISCUSSION

Tables 1 and 2 summarize the results of the three models for Bitcoin price predication. In Table.1, "Sign Correct" denotes the proportion of correctness when predicting whether the change in price rate is positive or negative. "Error< 0.05" indicates that the difference between the expected and ground-truth rates is less than 5%. In other words, the predicted outcome is considered accurate if it has the same sign as the ground-truth and the difference is less than 5%. To keep investor decisions in the loop, our system also lists predictions with "Sign Correct" or "Error < 0.05" so that users can make their judgements. Note that GRU has the best prediction output. When p (price) is used as an input feature, it has 72.35 % accuracy on the "Sign Correct" and "Error < 0.05" criteria. In general, it also outperforms the other models when using other features or combination of features. Table.2 shows the evaluation of the training, validation, and test prediction results of the three models. We use RMSE and Mean-Square Error (MSE) (Sammut & Webb, 2011) to evaluate the results.

Table 1. Prediction results of LSTM, bi-LSTM, and GRU (p: Price, hr: Hash rate, t-sen: Twitter Sentiment Intensity, t-key: Twitter Keywords)

		LSTM			bi-LSTM			GRU		
Features	Processing	Sign Correct	Error< 0.05	Sign Correct & Error < 0.05	Sign Correct	Error< 0.05	Sign Correct & Error < 0.05	Sign Correct	Error< 0.05	Sign Correct & Error < 0.05
p	Train	0.7830	0.9675	0.7560	0.8197	0.9828	0.8056	0.7793	0.9510	0.7382
	Validation	0.7083	0.8627	0.6127	0.7353	0.8603	0.6446	0.7819	0.9118	0.7132
	Test	0.7725	0.9235	0.7098	0.7706	0.9235	0.7000	0.7863	0.9255	0.7235
hr	Train	0.5383	0.8676	0.4746	0.5303	0.8719	0.4641	0.5267	0.8657	0.4629
	Validation	0.4975	0.8284	0.4093	0.4779	0.8284	0.3995	0.4951	0.8284	0.4093
	Test	0.5412	0.8549	0.4588	0.5510	0.8549	0.4725	0.5412	0.8549	0.4588
p + hr	Train	0.7474	0.9761	0.7284	0.7836	0.9859	0.7713	0.7284	0.9626	0.7032
	Validation	0.7034	0.8725	0.6029	0.6838	0.8431	0.5760	0.6961	0.8750	0.6078
	Test	0.7196	0.9039	0.6431	0.7235	0.8941	0.6431	0.7392	0.9098	0.6706
p + hr + t-sen + t-key	Train	0.5310	0.8688	0.4697	0.5395	0.8700	0.4776	0.5671	0.8749	0.4954
	Validation	0.5049	0.8309	0.4314	0.4632	0.8309	0.3922	0.5294	0.8260	0.4485
	Test	0.5353	0.8549	0.4529	0.5235	0.8608	0.4529	0.5373	0.8510	0.4706

Table 2. MSE and RMSE of BTC Prediction Result of LSTM, bi-LSTM, GRU

Features	Model	RMSE		MSE	
		price	price increasing rate	price	price increasing rate
p	LSTM	479.24666	0.02966	229677.36324	0.00088
	bi-LSTM	472.48233	0.02954	223239.55571	0.00087
	GRU	469.90102	0.02878	220806.96473	0.00083
hr	LSTM	354.78032	0.04035	125869.07334	0.00163
	bi-LSTM	354.50125	0.04033	125671.13781	0.00163
	GRU	354.65508	0.04034	125780.22648	0.00163
p + hr	LSTM	472.55968	0.03327	223312.64773	0.00111
	bi-LSTM	509.86317	0.03433	259960.45556	0.00118
	GRU	482.64162	0.03332	232942.93189	0.00111
p + hr + t-sen + t-key	LSTM	357.16888	0.04028	127569.61041	0.00162
	bi-LSTM	357.72260	0.04034	127965.46017	0.00163
	GRU	359.60044	0.04038	129312.47500	0.00163

4. CONCLUSION

We propose a full-stack platform for cryptocurrency market data analysis and visualization. Using Bitcoin as a use case, we examine a complete data processing pipeline, from data aggregation to historical data analysis, future trend prediction and output visualization embedded in a user friendly web interface. We use a set of intelligent data analysis techniques, including machine learning and neural language processing, to assist users to understand market trends and make informed decisions. By incorporating social sentiment in data analysis, the experimental results demonstrate a promising outcome. Our front-end web application, which involves investors in the loop, allows users to visualize both on-chain and off-chain data, as well as social media and data analysis rationale, e.g., high-frequency keywords in social media. In future work, we will extend the framework to include additional cryptocurrencies beyond Bitcoin.

ACKNOWLEDGEMENT

The technical advice of Hengming Zhang from WhiteMatrix LTD. (Nanjing, Jiangsu, China) is gratefully acknowledged.

REFERENCES

Ant-Design. (2015). ant-design/ant-design. GitHub. https://github.com/ant-design/ant-design/.

Bitcoin Price Index - CoinDesk 20. CoinDesk. (2021, June 24). https://www.coindesk.com/price/bitcoin.

Bird, S., Klein, E., & Loper, E. (2009). Natural language processing with Python: analyzing text with the natural language toolkit. " O'Reilly Media, Inc.".

Hutto, C., & Gilbert, E. (2014, May). Vader: A parsimonious rule-based model for sentiment analysis of social media text. In Proceedings of the International AAAI Conference on Web and Social Media (Vol. 8, No. 1).

Hochreiter, S., & Schmidhuber, J. (1997). Long short-term memory. Neural computation, 9(8), 1735-1780.

Jay, P., Kalariya, V., Parmar, P., Tanwar, S., Kumar, N., & Alazab, M. (2020). Stochastic neural networks for cryptocurrency price prediction. IEEE Access, 8, 82804-82818.

Mohapatra, S., Ahmed, N., & Alencar, P. (2019, December). KryptoOracle: A Real-Time Cryptocurrency Price Prediction Platform Using Twitter Sentiments. In 2019 IEEE International Conference on Big Data (Big Data) (pp. 5544-5551). IEEE.

Phaladisailoed, T., & Numnonda, T. (2018, July). Machine learning models comparison for bitcoin price prediction. In 2018 10th International Conference on Information Technology and Electrical Engineering (ICITEE) (pp. 506-511). IEEE.

Quandl. quandl.com. (2021). https://www.quandl.com/data/BCHAIN/HRATE-Bitcoin-Hash-Rate.

Reimers, N., & Gurevych, I. (2017). Optimal hyperparameters for deep lstm-networks for sequence labeling tasks. arXiv preprint arXiv:1707.06799.

Saad, M., Choi, J., Nyang, D., Kim, J., & Mohaisen, A. (2019). Toward characterizing blockchain-based cryptocurrencies for highly accurate predictions. IEEE Systems Journal, 14(1), 321-332.

Saldanha, R. (2020, June 3). Stock Price Prediction with PyTorch. Medium. https://medium.com/swlh/stock-price-prediction-with-pytorch-37f52ae84632.

Sammut, C., & Webb, G. I. (Eds.). (2011). Encyclopedia of machine learning. Springer Science & Business Media.

Poldi, F. (2020). Twint-twitter intelligence tool. URL: https://github. com/twintproject/twint (visited on 01/02/2020).

ON THE ROAD TOWARDS A SMART URBAN DISTRICT SUPPORTED BY A MOCK PLATFORM

Frank Elberzhager, Patrick Mennig and Phil Stüpfert
Fraunhofer Institute for Experimental Software Engineering IESE
Fraunhofer Platz 1, Kaiserslautern, Germany

ABSTRACT

The world is becoming more and more connected, which is also true for smart cities. The digital transformation is making rapid progress, and part of this are digital ecosystems, consisting of a platform and digital services that support several stakeholders with digital services. In the context of smart cities, we are currently developing a climate-neutral smart urban district and use digital solutions to address topics such as mobility, energy, smart home, and communication among the citizens involved. However, new ideas for services are challenging to invent, develop, and test in our situation, as this particular urban district is currently under construction. This is why we have developed a mock platform, which makes it much easier to evaluate new ideas fast, as qualities of a productive environment such as security or performance are not as highly relevant as an easy-to-use environment. We present details of our mock platform and our experiences in applying it to date. Such a solution is also beneficial for other practitioners and researchers in other smart cities and smart urban districts who are developing a digital ecosystem with new digital services.

KEYWORDS

Digital Ecosystem, Smart Urban District, Platform, Mock Platform, Digital Services

1. INTRODUCTION

Nowadays, we live in a highly connected world. Connected cars, homes, and factories, smart and mobile devices, and even combinations of these are only some examples. In this context, topics such as the Internet of Things (IoT), digital ecosystems, or cyber-physical systems have become established. With respect to smart cities, many of these topics are highly relevant. Doku and Rawat provide an overview of smart city applications (e.g., smart transportation, smart energy, smart infrastructure), and refine them into many more smart services [Doku19]. Wang et al. [Wang21] provide a literature survey in the area of energy management solutions in the IoT showing that many topics are currently under research, and some are already being evaluated. With respect to our own research agenda with a focus on digital ecosystems, several open issues exist, such as: How to design, develop, deploy, and operate a digital ecosystem? What concrete technology to use? Which stakeholders to involve? How to build a platform that other parties can use?

On the way towards smart cities, one intermediate step is to address such topics in a smaller part, such as a local urban district. We are currently part of a big research project that strives towards realizing a climate-neutral urban district. In this project, several different players are involved, such as the local city government, research partners, and companies. A former industrial complex about 18 ha in size is being revitalized and rebuilt for this. Many sub-topics are currently being worked on, such as energy, mobility, smart home, or social-technical topics. We are responsible for creating a digital ecosystem for this urban district that supports several different stakeholders in behaving in a more climate-friendly manner. One focus is on the citizens who will live and work in this urban district, and who we want to support in the first phase. Examples of digital solutions in this digital ecosystem are a game to make citizens aware of existing climate-neutral mobile services, an app to enhance communication about climate-relevant topics in such a district, and advice on how to save energy with a digital pet. A major challenge with respect to our urban district is the fact that it is currently under construction. This means that only a very limited number of stakeholders are already known, and we have to find ways to (1) anticipate and gather requirements of future citizens and (2) further stakeholders that will use our digital ecosystem. Furthermore, we need to find ways to deploy, apply, and evaluate our digital solutions. We have performed different kinds of project-internal and external workshops, done a literature research, and used other techniques to gather such requirements. In this publication, we focus on the second aspect, i.e., we provide one solution for coming up with and testing digital services with concrete users.

The central part of our digital ecosystem is a platform with several basic services (such as a central login or user administration) and higher-level services such as those mentioned above. As this is a productive environment, qualities such as performance or security are of high relevance. Consequently, running services need a certain level of quality in order to be allowed to run, which also results in some deployment effort. As, among other things, these conditions are obstacles in terms of having an efficient environment for a fast evaluation of new ideas and early versions of new digital services, we had to find a different way. Therefore, we developed a so-called mock platform. This is a simpler version of the real urban district platform that does not care about, for example, privacy issues, but is similar enough to the real platform to give us a realistic evaluation environment.

In this publication, we provide some details on our current mock platform and its technical details (Section 2). Then we show examples of how we are already using the mock platform and share some initial experiences (Section 3). Finally, we conclude our paper and give an outlook on future ideas (Section 4).

2. MOCK PLATFORM

2.1 General Idea and Benefit

Our main goal is to create a way to connect different (also external) applications through one platform. However, this should be as simple as possible when developing new applications, which is why we have specifically neglected requirements such as privacy, security or safety. For this reason, we also chose a very simple and lean communication protocol. In order to address the above-mentioned problems with respect to our need for fast evaluation of new ideas for digital services in our smart urban district ecosystem, we developed a mock platform. On the one hand, this mock simulates a real platform with basic functionality, on the other hand, makes it much easier for us to deploy and test new digital services on the other hand.

One major challenge when connecting an application to the platform is the correct semantic and syntactic communication. For this, we decided to us asynchronous communication, which also enables us to facilitate connections between different digital services. We use the publish-subscribe pattern, which makes it possible to publish messages easily via an interface without the sender having to know the exact recipient or their exact address. Basically, any application can receive all messages. In order for a potential recipient to receive the correct messages, the sender publishes a message on a specific topic. A recipient can now subscribe to this topic and will then receive only the messages published on this topic.

2.2 Insights from Architecture and Technology

The core of the mock platform is an MQTT broker, serves as a central asynchronous communication interface according to the publish-subscribe-pattern (see Figure 1). The MQTT protocol is very common, especially in the IoT domain. In addition, we offer various basic functionalities in the form of services, that are required again and again, especially in the platform context but also generally in prototype creation. For example, on our mock platform, a user service offers the possibility to create users who receive a unique global ID in the ecosystem. In addition, there is the storage service, which serves as a central storage location and enables storage of configurations of applications, which can then be loaded when an application is started. There are a number of other services like calendar service that are intended to shorten the development time.

The messages via the MQTT broker always have an event character. This means that messages can be sent by a sender whenever something has happened in its own application. For example, every time a user registers, the user-service publishes this information on the MQTT broker.

To make messages not only easy to receive technically, but easier to process in addition, we have introduced so-called shared-topics. These summarize some groups of data containing a similar information. It is defined precisely on which topic this information must be sent and what form the message must have. For example, we have defined the smart home shared topic for the smart home domain. This includes messages containing information about sensor values, such as a room's current temperature or the opening status of a window. It is exactly prescribed how the topic is structured, so that one can read from it which room's data it is about. The message itself must also follow a precise schema which is defined for every shared topic. For example, the message must be formatted as a JSON string (see Figure 1, left part).

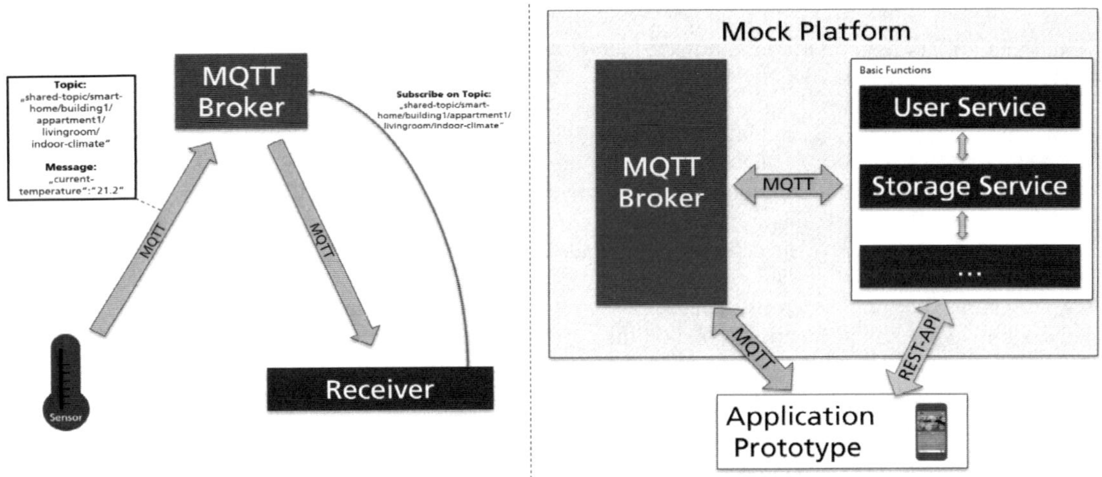

Figure 1. Example communication via MQTT and high-level architecture of the mock platform and communication

With this precise specification, a sender always knows how to publish information from a shared topic. In addition, a receiver who has previously subscribed to a shared topic can always be sure that they can process this message. However, the communication path via the MQTT broker should not be used in all cases. For synchronous requests, where it is important for the sender to know who the receiver is and whether the receiver has received and correctly processed the information, this path is unsuitable, since the MQTT protocol does not forward receipt confirmations from the receivers back to the initial source. For example, it may be important to an application that an object has been successfully stored on the storage-service. Since this is not possible with the asynchronous communication of the MQTT broker, we use a synchronous communication in these cases, which takes place directly between application and service. This is realized with a Rest-API, which is provided by a service.

To enable a developer to connect an application to the mock platform as quickly as possible, we provide software development kits (SDKs) in common programming languages (Java, Java-Script, Type-Script, Python), which provide easy-to-use methods that handle the correct communication with the MQTT broker. Furthermore, we provide event builder methods for all shared topics, which generate valid events including the correct topics. All this makes it possible to realize communication without much effort. For the MQTT broker we use Amazon-MQ, which provides a native MQTT interface. The services are deployed on servers in Docker containers for cost reasons, so it is easy to exchange and update the services.

3. USING THE MOCK PLATFORM – INITIAL EXPERIENCES

Within our organization, we have used the mock platform to develop prototypes of interconnected applications. It has allowed us to test the vision of such a networked smart city application within a short period of time by reducing the development efforts, mostly for the user interface, and still providing us with a means to test the interconnectedness of applications. Using pre-defined shared topics is simple due to the event broker architecture, which in turn helps to realize distributed but interconnected applications.

One example of such an application is the *smart home simulator*. Part of our ongoing research efforts for the climate-neutral smart urban district is concerned with the potential use of smart home technology, i.e., sensors and actuators that help to reduce the energy consumption of residential homes and business premises. The *smart home simulator* is a web-based 3D visualization of an apartment with several smart home sensors and actuators, such as controllable light bulbs, or window sensors that register open and close events. Even though the general concept of such smart home appliances could be demonstrated in any building, the *smart home simulator* and the mock platform can be used to simulate the actual "smart homes" as they are being planned in this concrete smart urban district to help investors and future residents understand the impact of this technology. Physical smart home sensors and actuators can be connected to the mock platform and can publish their state through shared topics. The *smart home simulator* visualizes these states in its 3D user interface. Users can interact with the simulated smart home and trigger actuators. Through the connection with the mock platform, other applications can respond to status changes by listening to shared topics, and novel smart home solutions can be prototyped rapidly, either with or without actually using physical smart home appliances.

The update events that can be issued through the *smart home simulator* are used within another prototype application that harnesses the simple interconnectivity through the mock platform's event-based architecture. The *environmental hints* application provides users with feedback on the environmental impact of and possible alternatives for their daily life activities (e.g., the effects of heating their homes above a certain temperature on energy consumption and related costs). The better these hints fit the actual activities of a given user, the better the perceived value of such hints, leading to a higher chance that the user will change climate-relevant habits. In order to match the correct hints with the users who actually performed certain activities, the activities need to be registered by the digital smart city platform. The mock platform gives the ability to prototype such activities through fake events issued by the *smart home simulato*r, a prototype *calendar* application, and *public transport information*, and to assign them to user personas in the *user service*. The hints are generated in the *environmental hints-giver service*, which is connected to the mock platform, analyzes various shared topics for relevant user actions, and assigns hints to specific user accounts based on the events that other applications emit for that particular user account. Test users interact with the *smart home simulator*, e.g., by increasing the temperature in the living room and then indicating they are leaving the house, which results in a certain hint given in the *environmental hints* application. This gives us real feedback on the perceived value of such hints.

4. CONCLUSION AND OUTLOOK

We are developing a digital ecosystem for a smart urban district in order to support climate-neutral behavior. As this urban district is currently under construction, we face the challenge of how to develop digital solutions for the future citizens and other stakeholders working and living in that area. The future digital ecosystems will basically consist of a platform and several basic and enhanced digital services such as smart home or mobility services. However, in order to be able to develop new ideas and deploy them as services in the environment, we decided to first develop a so-called mock platform, as this suits our needs much better, especially with respect to speed (i.e., fast deployment and evaluation). The mock platform is already being used by project members, but has also been applied in events such as hackathons where the intention is the same: try out new ideas fast. The mock platform simulates our smart urban district environment and reflects the future area well.

In the future, we will develop this mock platform further, e.g., with more support during the deployment and evaluation phases, and increase its usability. In addition, more digital service prototypes should be developed and evaluated to prepare for the real digital smart urban district.

ACKNOWLEDGEMENT

The research described in this paper was performed in the EnStadt:Pfaff project (grant no. 03SBE112D and 03SBE112G) of the German Federal Ministry for Economic Affairs and Energy (BMWi) and the Federal Ministry of Education and Research (BMBF). We thank Sonnhild Namingha for proofreading.

REFERENCES

Doku, R., Rawat, B. R. 2019, *Chapter 8 - Big Data in Cybersecurity for Smart City Applications*, Editor(s): Danda B. Rawat, Kayhan Zrar Ghafoor, Smart Cities Cybersecurity and Privacy, Elsevier, Pages 103-112

Wang, D., Zhong, D., 2021, Alireza Souri, *Energy management solutions in the Internet of Things applications: Technical analysis and new research directions*, Cognitive Systems Research, Volume 67, Pages 33-49

SMART AND SUSTAINABLE URBAN MOBILITY: HOW CONNECTIVITY MAY SUPPORT BIKE-SHARING OPERATORS' BUSINESSES

Arash Rezazadeh[1], Elisabete Sá[2], Joaquim Silva[2], Ana Carvalho[3], Maher Georges Elmashhara[3] and Ricardo Pessoa[4]

[1]NIPE, School of Economics and Management, University of Minho
Universidade do Minho, Escola de Economia e Gestão, Campus de Gualtar, 4710-057 Braga, Portugal
[2]Interdisciplinary Centre of Social Sciences (CICS.NOVA.UMinho),
School of Economics and Management University of Minho, Portugal
[3]NIPE, School of Economics and Management, University of Minho, Portugal
[4]Bosch Car Multimédia Portugal, S.A., PO Box 2458, 4701-970, Braga, Portugal

ABSTRACT

Smart urban mobility, particularly cycling, is seen as playing an important role, not only in making cities smarter but also more sustainable. One of the most important characteristics of smart cycling is connectivity, which allows the generation of considerable amounts of mobility data that, in turn, may support the decision-making of the different members of the specific two-wheeler urban mobility (2WUM) ecosystem, encapsulated within the larger smart city ecosystem. One particular member of the 2WUM ecosystem that can benefit from such information are bike-sharing operators. Their number has grown dramatically over the last few years, but they also face important challenges that can threaten business sustainability in the long run. Based on an in-depth qualitative study with six bike-sharing operators, following the jobs-to-be-done framework, this paper explores how smart products and services based on mobility information can contribute to improve the bike-sharing operators' jobs, mitigate their pains and help to reach their expected gains.

KEYWORDS

Connected Urban Mobility, Bike-Sharing Operators, Jobs-to-Be-Done Framework

1. INTRODUCTION

Smart cities involve the innovative and intelligent delivery of urban services based on ICT-based solutions with the view to improve urban sustainability and quality of life (Pereira et al., 2018). The mobility aspect of smart cities relates to the enhancement of sustainability in mobility systems, as well as the reduction of citizens' transportation problems (Pereira et al., 2018). Compared to other smart transportation modes, such as intelligent cars, two-wheeler urban mobility (2WUM) has received little attention, despite its important role as a sustainable mode of transport in the context of smart cities and the Internet of Things (Behrendt, 2016).

Connected 2WUM is acknowledged as a promising trend involving an ecosystem of different parties that interact with each other by generating and sharing data (Hensher et al., 2020). Bike sharing operators are one of the members of this ecosystem that leverage the potential of the sharing economy for the Internet of Things (Kamargianni and Matyas, 2017). These operators provide key social, environmental, and economic benefits by encouraging citizens to use green transportation modes that minimise carbon emissions and energy consumption while enhancing their health (Zhang and Mi, 2018). Bike sharing operators are recognised as a smart city innovation (Townsend, 2013) and the participation of these operators in connected mobility services is key to improve city smartness (Cerutti et al., 2019).

The business of bike sharing has been growing remarkably around the world (Boufidis et al., 2020). Increased attention from both academics and practitioners has been paid to this industry (Ma et al., 2020). Less, however, has been done to explore how these operators can benefit from the data that can be generated from smart information systems applied to urban mobility. Therefore, the research question in this research is what are the jobs-to-be-done, gains and pains of bike-sharing operators, and how can connectivity-enabled solutions address them? The main purpose is to identify potential solutions based on the connectivity premise of smart cities that could allow them to perform their jobs better.

2. METHOD

A qualitative research design was adopted, using in-depth interviews (the interview guide is available from the authors upon request), framed by the jobs-to-be-done model (Ulwick, 2016), with representatives from bike sharing operators acting around the world. The interview guide included questions to (1) understand their internal mechanisms and operations and (2) identify their most challenging pains, and key expected gains from the business, with the purpose of identifying how information derived from a 2WUM connected system would allow them to accomplish their jobs more effectively and efficiently, and propose a set of smart products and services.

The purposeful sampling method was employed to identify and select the most reliable, well-established, and widely-used bike sharing system operators around the world. The Bike-Sharing World Map (bikesharemap.com) was used to identify the operators and contact them. Six interviews were conducted with their respective representatives. Table 1 presents the profile of the participants, revealing the heterogeneity of the sample in terms of size, model, and country of operation. This was specifically sought so that the proposed solutions are independent from specific policy and regulation concerns.

Table 1. Bike-sharing operators' sample profile

Interview	Position of the interviewee	Operational mode	Headquarters	System infrastructure	Number of users subscribed
1	Operations' manager	dockless	USA	about 120,000 scooters and 5000 bikes	more than 150,000
2	Business Development Manager	docked	Canada	more than 90,000 bikes and 7,000 stations	more than 1 million
3	International Business Development Manager	docked	Germany	more than 30,000 bikes and 3,000 stations	more than 1 million
4	Head of the company	docked and dockless	Austria	1,500 bikes and 120 stations	about 50,0000
5	Business developer	dockless	Slovakia	1,100 bikes	more than 10,000
6	Deputy Managing Director	dockless	Belgium	5,000 bikes and 360 stations	114,000

3. RESULTS

Based on the content analysis of the interviews, we concluded that bike-sharing operators have three key jobs-to-be-done: customer management, operational management, and financial management. Customer management covers the tasks of reaching new customers and maintaining existing ones. Operational management is related to several, sometimes, cost-ineffective logistic factors; while the financial management job regards the often difficult balance of costs and revenues to achieve profitability. Based on the needs diagnosis, we suggest different information-based smart products and services aligned with the connectivity principle of smart mobility for smarter cities that can address bike-sharing operators' jobs-to-be-done, lessens their pains and allows them to obtain expected gains. Four main solutions are proposed (Figure 1): i) smart devices used in the bicycle to acquire mobility data; ii) a data analytics system that converts mobility data from the whole system, into relevant information for each individual player; iii) a two-wheeler digital platform that connects bike-sharing operators and users and delivers the information provided by the previous solutions and the users themselves; iv) hyper-local marketing solutions, enabled by the whole system. By following a fully connected approach, where each player can draw value from the connection with other smart city players, this constitutes a major advancement on the solutions referred to in previous literature (e.g., Moon-Miklaucic et al., 2019; Say et al., 2018; Shen et al, 2018) and currently used by interviewees in their single-purpose apps, which support only bidirectional connectivity relationships.

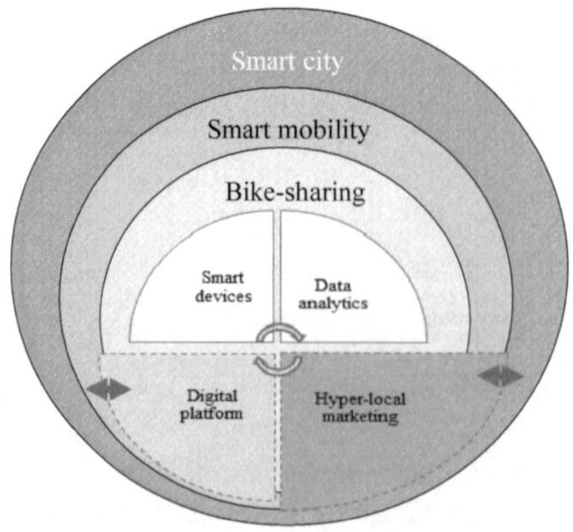

Figure 1. Information-based smart products and services for bike-sharing operators

3.1 Customer Management Jobs

The customer management job entails tasks to reach new users while maintaining existing ones. Participants highlighted as pains the delays and inconvenience associated with the registration of new users in physical kiosks, and to users misbehaving when disregarding riding and parking rules. Table 2 presents the solutions that address these tasks, mitigate the pains and enhance their gains by, among others, attracting and involving new customers, facilitating online registrations, profiling and segmenting customers through data analytics and integrating alerts.

Table 2. Connected products and services for bike-sharing operators' customer management jobs

Jobs-to-be-done		Tasks	Making Bike-sharing operators' jobs better, easier and more profitable with **information-based smart products and services**
Customer management	New customers	Acquiring new customers	- advertising and promotions on the two-wheeler *digital platform.* - integration with complementary mobility modes present in the mobility ecosystem connected to the *digital platform.* - *hyper-local marketing* (alerts about the nearest bike-sharing operator).
		Interacting with new customers	- registration and payment previously made on the *digital platform* and valid for all integrated bike-sharing operators (seamless). - communication with new customers through the *digital platform* for all integrated bike-sharing operators (e.g., service and security rule).
	Existing customers	CRM and communication with current customers	- differentiated prices based on the estimates of demand provided by the *data analytics* system (e.g., depending on weather conditions, events on a given location, etc.). - discounts based on rewards for achievements of users registered on the *digital platform* (e.g., km/miles, appropriate behaviour). - cross-benefits with partners from the mobility ecosystem integrated in the *digital platform* (e.g., price benefits in integrated tickets for different transport modes). - communication with existing customers through the *digital platform* (e.g., service and security rules, etc.).
		Dealing with misbehaviour	- *smart devices* may alert both the users about unsafe behaviour and the operator about misbehaviour. - customers with recurrent misbehaviour can be ranked and may be blocked within the *digital platform* (for all or for those that set some standards). - price could be personalised according to the user's behaviour across all integrated bike-sharing operators based on *data analytics.*

3.2 Operational Management Jobs

Tasks related to the operational management job include the design of stations, decisions about the operation model, and repair and maintenance tasks. Regarding the design of stations, interviewees emphasised decisions about size and location, the flexibility to add more racks as needed and the costly task of rebalancing the stations so bicycles are always available. Also important is deciding on docked or dockless model, regular vs. electric bicycles, and the lock/unlock system used. Finally, operators also need to deal with repair and maintenance, theft and vandalism, and disposal of bikes, which are considered particular pains. Table 3 offers suggestions on how information-based smart products and services would support these operations.

Table 3. Connected products and services for bike-sharing operators' operations management jobs

Jobs-to-be-done		Tasks	Making Bike-sharing operators' jobs better, easier and more profitable with **information-based smart products and services**
Operational management	Design of stations	Location of stations	- *data analytics* services to predict where and how many stations are the optimal offer to the users.
		Rebalancing stations	- *data analytics* to optimally determine when and where vehicles will be needed.
	Operation Model	Docked/ Dockless Regular or e-Bikes	- *data analytics* to determine when and where each model will be more profitable.
		Unlocking/ locking	- personal code generated in the *digital* platform, valid for all integrated bike-sharing operators.
	Maintenance	Repair and maintenance	- information from the *digital platform* acquired both automatically through *smart devices* in the bicycle or provided by users or based on *data analytics* estimates, informing or predicting when maintenance is required.
		Vandalism - theft	- anti-theft system from *smart devices.*
		Disposal	- sale of end-of-life vehicles to the *digital platform'* community.

3.3 Financial Management

Bike sharing operators' financial concerns include securing suitable revenues while containing operational costs. Our interviewees indicate that generating and sustaining multiple sources of revenue such as sponsorships, public funding, advertisement, and users' donations is important to complement user fees or membership plans. Considerable costs, on the other hand, stem from inefficiencies in operations management such as ineffective station rebalancing or bicycle maintenance. The suggested information-based smart products and services in Table 4 may mitigate these pains and diversify revenue streams.

Table 4. Connected products and services for bike-sharing operators' financial management jobs

Jobs-to-be-done		Tasks	Making Bike-sharing operators' jobs better, easier and more profitable with **information-based smart products and services**
Financial management	Revenues and pricing strategies	Multiple revenue streams	- sponsorship from members registered in the *digital platform.* - cross advertising with partners integrated in the *digital platform.* - shared gains from *hyper-local marketing.* - sale of end-of-life vehicles to *digital platform* community.
	Contain costs	High operational costs	- optimization of operations through *data analytics.* - partnerships with repair shops and insurance companies associated with the *digital platform.*

4. CONCLUSION

The purpose of this research was to explore bike-sharing operators' most relevant jobs-to-be-done, pains and expected gains to determine whether smart products and services based on mobility information, aligned with the smart cities' connectivity premise, would contribute to improve their business. Our research adds to the literature by focusing on a mobility mode that, despite contributing both to smarter and more sustainable mobility in cities, has been less considered. Concerning practical implications, our findings draw the attention of bike-sharing operators to connectivity-enabled solutions that can help them with three important aspects of their business, namely customer management, operational management, and financial management. A number of IT and equipment related business opportunities also arise.

The study opens opportunities for future studies. For example, taking the business model perspective (see, for example, Gao and Li, 2020), future studies can investigate business models for smart products and services based on mobility information. Also, although our study focuses on bike-sharing operators, other members of the 2WUM may be relevant targets for such solutions and business models.

ACKNOWLEDGEMENT

This work is supported by: European Structural and Investment Funds in the FEDER component, through the Operational Competitiveness and Internationalization Programme (COMPETE 2020) [Project nº 039334; Funding Reference: POCI-01-0247-FEDER-039334].

REFERENCES

Behrendt, F., 2016. Why cycling matters for smart cities. Internet of bicycles for intelligent transport. *Journal of transport geography*, Vol. 56, pp. 157-164.

Boufidis, N., Nikiforiadis, A., Chrysostomou, K., Aifadopoulou, G., 2020. Development of a station-level demand prediction and visualization tool to support bike-sharing systems operators. *Transportation Research Procedia*, Vol. 47, pp. 51-58.

Cerutti, P.S., Martins, R.D., Macke, J., Sarate, J.A.R., 2019. Green, but not as green as that: an analysis of a Brazilian bike-sharing system. *Journal of cleaner production*, Vol. 217, pp. 185–193.

Gao, P., Li, J., 2020. Understanding sustainable business model: A framework and a case study of the bike-sharing industry. *Journal of cleaner production,* Vol. 267, pp. 1-11.

Hawkins, A., 2020. *Uber is scrapping tens of thousands of Jump bikes during a nationwide bike shortage*. Retrieved from: https://www.theverge.com/2020/5/27/21271927/uber-jump-bike-scooter-scrap-photos-video-lime-junkyard.

Hensher, D.A., Mulley, C., Ho, C., Wong, Y., Smith, G., Nelson, J.D., 2020. *Understanding Mobility as a Service (MaaS): Past, present and future*. Elsevier, Amsterdam.

Kamargianni, M., Matyas, M., 2017. The business ecosystem of mobility-as-a-service. *96th Transportation Research Board (TRB) Annual Meeting*. Washington DC, USA, pp. 1-14.

Ma, X., Yuan, Y., Van Oort, N., Hoogendoorn, S., 2020. Bike-sharing systems' impact on modal shift: A case study in Delft, the Netherlands. *Journal of cleaner production*, Vol. 259, pp. 1-13.

Moon-Miklaucic, C., Bray-Sharpin, A. N. N. A., De La Lanza, I., Khan, A., Re, L. L., & Maassen, A. (2019). The evolution of bike sharing: 10 questions on the emergence of new technologies, opportunities, and risks. Working paper, pp. 1-44.

Pereira, G.V., Parycek, P., Falco, E., Kleinhans, R., 2018. Smart governance in the context of smart cities: A literature review. *Information Polity*, Vol. 23, No. 2, pp. 143-162.

Say, A. L., Guo, R., & Chen, C. (2018). Disruption or new order?: The emergence of the unicorn bike-sharing entrepreneurship in China. In *2018 Portland International Conference on Management of Engineering and Technology* (PICMET) (pp. 1-9).

Shen, S., Wei, Z. Q., Sun, L. J., Su, Y. Q., Wang, R. C., & Jiang, H. M. (2018). The shared bicycle and its network—internet of shared bicycle (IOSB): A review and survey. *Sensors*, 18(8), 2581.

Townsend, A.M., 2013. *Smart cities: Big data, civic hackers, and the quest for a new utopia*. W.W. Norton, New York.

Ulwick, A.W., 2016. *Jobs to be done: theory to practice*. Idea Bite Press, New York.

Zhang, Y., Mi, Z., 2018. Environmental benefits of bike sharing: A big data-based analysis. *Applied Energy*, Vol. 220, pp. 296-301.

M-LEARNING - A MULTI AGENT APPROACH

Terje Solsvik Kristensen and Joachim Coetzee Kjærvik
Western Norway University of Applied Sciences,
Department of Computing, Mathematics and Physics, Bergen, Norway

ABSTRACT

In this paper we have developed a framework for learning by mobile based on JADE and JESS as software components. Such a software integration makes it possible to exhibit ACL communication properties from JADE and rule-based reasoning capability from JESS. Software agents are implemented following the guidelines of the theoretical concept of Zone of Proximal Development (ZPD), as a means of supporting and promoting opportunities for effective learning.

KEYWORDS

M-Learning, MAS, JADE, JESS, Intelligent Tutoring, Zone of Proximal Development (ZDP)

1. INTRODUCTION

Education is a domain to which agent technology has frequently being applied. This area has been gaining more attention for instance research on artificial intelligence applied to computer assisted learning [Ayala, Yano, 1998], [Jennings, Sycara, Wooldridge, 1998], [Hay, Kichin, 2004], [Novak, Canãs, 2006/2008]. In classroom learning one is mostly based on behavioral learning theories where the learner is the object of assessment. The teacher initiates the learning process and the learner responds. Another learning approach, constructivism, focuses on the learner's abilities to develop her own mental models and learning concepts [Kichin, 2000], [Kinney, Georgeff, Rao, 1996]. This approach has more and more become accepted to be a more relevant method to promote learning, even at the university level.

Agents often have a repertoire of available *actions* that can manipulate their environment. This set of possible actions is what constitutes an agent's *actuators*. For agents to be able to operate independently and represent our best interests, we delegate high-level objectives, by means of some *deliberation logic*. This logic is what constitutes an agent's decision-making capability. An agent's decision-making strategy is dictated by the information it has available in its Knowledge Base (KB) and its high-level objectives.

2. AGENT ARCHITECTURES

The implementation of an agent can be done in a number of ways. An agent is typically characterized by its internal architecture or agent model. Wooldridge [2000] defines agent architectures as "the key problem facing an agent is that of deciding which of its actions it should perform in order to best satisfy its design objectives. Agent architectures are software architectures for decision-making systems that are embedded in an environment".

2.1 Belief-Desire-Intention

When describing complex systems, using abstractions, often makes it easier to explain and grasp technical concepts. Shoham [1997] describes agents using mentalistic states of beliefs, desires (choices), and intentions (commitments):

"An agent is an entity whose state is viewed as consisting of mental components such as beliefs, capabilities, choices, and commitments".

Talking about agents as if they have mental state to describe and predict their behaviour is a way of letting abstracting concepts be closer to human experiences. Singh [1998] describes the mental states of an agent as beliefs, characterizing what an agent imagines its world state to be, the goals that describe what states the agent would prefer and desires that describes the agent's preferences. The BDI model [Kinney, Hay, Adams, 2000] is an abstraction that lets us predict and explain how agents behave. The assumption is that by attributing agents with beliefs and desires, we expect them to act rationally in order to try to accomplish their desires, given their beliefs. By using this model, we may express reasonably briefly the behaviour of a system, without going into too low-level details e.g., at the physical or the design level.

2.2 Type-Message Agents

Charles Petrie [1996] discusses one specific class of agents so-called typed-message agents. The main difference between typed-message agents and other classes of agents is their ability to communicate using shared message protocols.

This class of agent is defined in terms of agent communities that mainly exhibits three properties: acomplishing tasks in a system requires a community of agents to exchange messages. The communication is based on using a shared message protocol where some of the message semantics are independent of the application and type. The semantics of the message protocol require a transport protocol.

2.3 Deductive Reasoning Agents

When building artificially intelligent systems, symbolic AI has traditionally been a commonly used technique. A system that exhibits intelligent behaviour, according to symbolic AI, is a system that should have a symbolic representation of its environment in which it operates and a symbolic representation of its desired behaviour, syntactically manipulating the representation.

In deductive reasoning agents' symbolic representations are logical formulae and the act of manipulation equates to logical deduction. Agents based on such an architecture typically embed a knowledge base KB, containing formulae in First-Order Predicate Logic (FOPL) [Russel, Norvig, 2000] that are used to represent properties of an agent's environment.

An agent's KB is the actual information it has available of its environment, and can be thought of how we humans have beliefs. For instance, a person might believe that valve 221 is open, whereas an agent might have the predicate Open (valve 221) in its KB. However, it is important to note that just like humans, agents can be wrong. Deduction rules are essentially rules of logical inference that agents use to derive new information. By taking perceptual information as input, an agent will use its deduction rules to attempt to derive optimal actions, given the situation.

3. AGENT COMMUNICATION LANGUAGES

In order to communicate the agents should use some form of agent communication language (ACL). The language ACL is responsible for defining the types of messages that agents are able to exchange in the system. In addition, the semantics of these messages have to be shared and known before runtime. In other words, the shared message protocols discussed in typed-message agents, are what constitute an ACL. By using these protocols and having messages with defined semantics, agents are able to understand and converse with each other in a common language. The actual communication using an ACL is handled by lower-level protocols such as for instance Simple Mail Transfer Protocol and Transmission Control Protocol (TCP)/Internet Protocol (IP).

3.1 Speech Acts

In a general scenario, an agent would be unable to force another agent to perform some action or write information onto its internal state. What agents do, performed as actions or *Communicative actions (CA)* – is an attempt to influence other agents [Austin, 1962]. A simple example would for instance be stating the fact

"It is raining in Bergen". Under normal circumstances, stating such a CA would be an attempt to modifying your beliefs. However, by simply stating or uttering the fact alone would usually not be enough to convince you to change your beliefs - you have control over your own beliefs (desires and intentions). Upon stating this fact it can be thought of as an attempt to change someone's internal state. In addition, since the utterance is an action in itself - it is performed with some purpose or intent. Thus, the assumption is to make someone believe that it is raining.

This concept is drawn from Speech Act Theory which has heavily influenced the development of many of today's ACLs. In his book, Searle [1969] describes Speech Act Theory as,

"Speech act theory treats communication as actions. It is predicated on the assumption that speech actions are performed by agents just like other actions, in the furtherance of intentions."

4. THE FIPA COMMUNICATION LANGUAGE

FIPA's Agent Communication Language (ACL) is based on speech act theory, whereby messages are actions or communicative acts that are intended to perform some action. The FIPA ACL specification is composed of a set of message types and the description of their effects on the mental attitudes (BDI) of the sender and receiver agents. This ACL defines an outer language for its messages, whereby each ACL message contains a message parameter – the *performative*. The performative denotes a message's type of communicative act, which in turn defines the actual intended meaning of a message. The FIPA Communicative Act Library (CAL) also defines an inner, or content language that is used to describe the content of a message. This includes how the content is expressed, how the expression is encoded in the message, and how a receiving agent should interpret the expression. This allows agents to "understand" each other, such that they ascribe a shared meaning of the content. It is important to note however, that FIPA ACL does not dictate any specific language for the content of a message.

4.1 Semantics of the FIPA ACL specification

A Semantic Language (SL) is the formal language used to define FIPA ACL's semantics. This language makes it possible to represent beliefs (B), desires (D), uncertain beliefs (U), and intentions of agents (I) (persistent goals (PG)), as well as actions the agents can perform. The semantics of each communicative act is specified as a set of SL-formulae that describes the communicative act's *Feasibility Precondition* (FP) and its *Rational Effect* (RE). The FP denotes a constraint that a sender agent must satisfy to be considered conforming to the specification. The RE of an action denotes the intent of a message, meaning what an agent wants to achieve by sending the message (perlocutionary act). It is important to note however, in a MAS consisting of autonomous agents, the RE of a message is not guaranteed. This means that conformance to the standard does not require the receiver of a message to respect the RE part of the ACL semantic - only the FP part.

5. LEARNING BY MOBILE PHONE

There is a lot of excitement about mobile technology today. Mobile devices are being used in an increasingly wide variety of ways. With the ubiquity of smart devices and the processing power they provide a phone no longer is just a phone. The phones have essentially become computing devices in their own right. We use them for banking, sending emails, consuming media and learning.

Learning by a mobile or m-learning we may call it, is the term referring to learning using mobile devices, and can be defined as learning mediated through mobile technologies. m-learning can be thought of as the natural evolution of e-learning [Kristensen et al., 2006-2013] whereby learning material is delivered on mobile platforms rather than on computers. Learning anytime anywhere or "ubiquitous learning" is just one of the many reasons why mobile learning has spurred on a lot of interest. By using mobile devices, one is not physically constrained to any specific location. In addition, mobile devices have at a steady rate grown in terms of processing power and memory capability. This trend is partly due to the continual reduction in cost of computing capability and the devices are becoming more powerful and more reasonable in price. By having more power available, we are able to do interesting things that a couple of years ago may have been unfeasible. Thus, bringing "heavy" paradigms such as agent technology to mobile platforms is more viable now than ever.

5.1 Learner Modelling

Learner modelling is a concept drawn from artificial intelligence. It is the key concept concerning the application of artificial intelligence in educational software. Learner models are important within computer-based systems intended to promote learning because they provide the means to support individually adapted instruction. The task of 'learner modelling' or 'cognitive diagnosis' (that is, the task of building a learner model) is the process of inferring the learner's knowledge by analyzing his or her behaviour."

A learner model is in other words, a system's derived representation of a learner's abilities. This representation is based on the information a system is able to obtain from its learner. Learner models are typically used in decision-making systems in an attempt to promote 'effective learning'. By using these models, autonomous agents could for instance be able to adapt to a learner's individual needs. This would make it possible to differentiate the material that is presented to each learner, and the agent could attempt to derive optimal tasks to be working on, based on the information it has available.

In the individualization approach of learner modelling, the effectiveness of a system is quantified based on its ability to dynamically adapt to each individual learner's needs. In order for this adaptation to work, it relies on a "student model" or a learner model. In the group adaptation approach a system will adapt to groups of learners. This necessitates a representation of groups rather than individual learners – a group model.

There are a number of different ways to implement learner models, one concrete instance of this technique used in an agent-based context, was presented in the paper by Ayala and Yano [1998]. Here the learner model is implemented in terms of the theoretical concept of Zone of Proximal Development, presented by the Russian psychologist L. Vygotsky [1995].

5.2 Zone of Proximal Development

The concept of Zone of Proximal Development (ZPD) is based on "the premise" of two development levels in a learner's learning process. *The Actual Development Level* (ADL), comprising of those knowledge elements (belonging to some domain) that have been internalized by the learner as a result of a completed development cycle. *The Potential Development Level* (PDL), comprising of those knowledge elements that the learner constructs in collaboration with other learners or with the assistance of a more knowledgeable others (MKO). Vygotsky defines the ZPD as "the distance between the actual developmental level as determined by independent problem solving and the level of potential development as determined through problem solving under adult guidance or in collaboration with more capable peers."

Figure 1. Zone of Proximal Development

The basic idea of this theory is that learning enhances a learner's developmental level. In order to learn we must be presented with tasks that are just slightly beyond our current reach of abilities. In other words, solving the tasks that are too complex or too simple, does according to this theory, not promote learning. The tasks that are just slightly beyond a learner's present abilities exist in the ZPD. These are tasks that a learner is almost able to solve independently, but require some degree of guidance. After having received help on a particular task, the idea is that learners will eventually be able to do it themselves – bridging the gap between the ADL and the PDL. By presenting tasks that fall within a learner's ZPD, we attempt to promote *effective learning* (https://www.researchgate.net/publication/258519369_Effective_Learning_in_Classrooms). One important thing to note with this theory, is that every learner will have his own ZPD.

5.3 Agents in a Mobile Learning Environment

Based on the definition and description of ZPD, it can be derived that there is a dynamic aspect to learning using this approach. Using this model, a system attempts to promote effective learning by attempting to adapt and identify the optimal tasks each individual user should be working on. The ZPD is in no way static, it constantly shifts. As a user develops new abilities, the ZPD will progressively move further or become wider in scope.

A mobile learning environment based on this theory will have certain computational requirements that demand *flexibility*, *autonomy*, and social *behaviour*. These are all aspects that agent technology may provide. This adaptive learning approach will involve an agent using a learner model to determine which tasks would be most beneficial for a given user in a given situation. The decision-making or reasoning would be based on what a user has been able to internalize in his knowledge domain.

6. JADE AND JESS

In JADE the software agent abstraction is implemented as a Java thread, one thread per agent. Each running instance of JADE runtime is called a *container* [Shenghuan, Kungas, Matshin, 2006], [Naser, 2008]. By using FIPA ACL to represent messages, the agents are able to interact using the asynchronous message passing mechanism providing by JADE [Bellifemini, Caire, Geenwood, 2007]. In order to endow agents with the capability to reason, it is possible to integrate external software with the Behaviour class. One software suite that is compatible with JADE is JESS [Friedman-Hill, 2000]. JESS is an expert system shell that supports a rule-based symbolic language, similar to CLIPS. JESS is described as from the official homepage given by (http://jade.atilab.com/support/faq/). JESS is small, light and one of the fastest rule engines available. JESS also provides a scripting environment. The rule engine that JESS implements is based on an enhanced version of the *Rete algorithm* [Forgy, 1982] for processing rules.

By integrating JESS with JADE it is possible to implement declarative decision-making modules. These modules enable agents to reason with respect to the declarative language. The agents are therefore rule-based JADE-agents that are capable of doing automated reasoning, making them more "intelligent". The Rete.run() method allows us to run the inference engine and will make the engine fire all rules that apply to facts in the current working memory. The engine returns once there are no more rules to fire.

7. CONCLUSION AND FURTHER WORK

In this paper we have laid the foundation of a framework of a system for learning by the mobile phone. The implementation is based on two separate software components JADE and JESS. This software integration has resulted in an architecture that exhibits ACL communication properties derived from JADE, and rule-based reasoning capability derived from JESS. A learner model has additionally been implemented in an attempt to facilitate learning optimization or 'effectively learning'

Vygotsky's theoretical concept of ZPD serves as the foundation of the agents' behaviour. By using the ZPD as a guideline, the agents attempt to promote learning by deriving optimal tasks and proposing them for their users. However, this requires that the agents are able to collect information about the user and inferring a representation of their abilities. The concept of Learner Modelling supports such a process. The learner model is used in the agent's decision-making process and enables the agents to propose tasks that are specific to each individual user's ability level.

REFERENCES

Austin, J. L. (1962). How to Do Things with Words. Oxford University.

Ayala, G., & Yano, Y. (1998). A collaborative learning environment based on intelligent agents. *Expert Systems with Applications*, 14(1):129–137.

Bellifemine, F., Caire, G., & Greenwood, D. (2007). Developing multi-agent systems with JADE. Wiley.

Forgy, C. L. (1982). Rete: A fast algorithm for the many pattern/many object pattern match problem. *Artificial intelligence*, 19(1): 17–37.

Friedman-Hill, E. (2003). *JESS in Action*. Manning Greenwich, CT.

Hay, D., & Kinchin, I. M. (2000). Using Concept Mapping to Measure Learning Quality. Education & Training, 167-182.

Jennings, H. V., Sycara K., & Wooldridge, M. (1998). Roadmap of agent research and development. Autonomous agents *and M*ulti-agent systems, 1(1):7–38.

Kinchin, I. M. (2000). Using Concept Maps to Reveal Understanding: A Two-Tier Analysis, In School Science Review 81:296, 41-46.

Kinchin, I. M., Hay, D., & Adams, A. (2000). How a qualitative approach to concept map analysis can be used to aid learning by illustrating patterns of conceptual development, in Educational Research,

Kinney, D., Georgeff, M., & Rao, A. (1996). A methodology and modelling techniques for systems of BDI agents. In van de Velde, W. and J.W. Perram, Editors. Agents Breaking Away. Proceedings of the Seventh European Workshop on Modelling Autonomous Agents in Multi-Agent World, 56-71. Springer, Berlin, Germany.

Kristensen, T. (2011). The Dynamic Content Management System. IEEE Explorer Digital library, 1-8.

Kristensen, T., & Johansen, J. (2006). Simulation of Attentional Networks in the Brain – an Agent based Approach. Proceedings of European Simulation and Modelling Conference, ESM'2006. Toulouse, France.

Kristensen, T., Dyngeland, M., & Bech, Ø. (20013). Towards a Multi-Agent E-learning Platform. Journal of Computer Engineering and Informatics. Volume 1, 64-81, Hong Kong,

Kristensen, T., Hinna,K., Hole, F.O., Lamo, Y. (2007). Different E-learning paradigms - a Survey. In Proceeding of MIT-LINC (MIT Learning International Network Consortium 4.th International Conference: Technology-Enabled Education: A Catalyst for positive Change), Amman, Jordan.

Kristensen, T., Lamo, Y., & Mughal, K. (2006). E-learning Systems in the Bergen Region, Norway - an Overview. Proceedings of the IRMA International Conference, Washington DC USA.

Kristensen, T., Lamo, Y., Mughal, K., Tekle, K. M., & Bottu, A.K. (2007). Towards a dynamic, content based e-learning platform. In V. Uskov, editor, Computers and Advanced Technology in Education. ACTA Press, 107–114, Beijing, China.

Naser, S.A. (2008). Agent Based Intelligent Tutoring System for Parameter Passing in Java Programming. Journal of Theoretical and Applied Information Technology.

Novak, J., & Canãs, A. (2006/2008). The theory underlying Concept Maps and how to construct them, Technical report, IHMC Maps Tools, Florida Institute for Human and Machine Cognition, USA.

Petrie, C.J. (1996). Agent-based engineering, the web, and intelligence. *IEEE expert*, 11(6):24–29.

Russel, S., & Norvig, P. (2003). Artificial Intelligence. A modern approach. Prentice Hall, Second edition.

Searle, J. (1969). An Essay in the Philosophy of Language. Cambridge University Press, 203.

Shenghuau, L., Kungas, P., & Matskin, M. (2006). Agent-Based Web Service Composition with JADE and JXTA. International Conference on Semantic Web and Web- services.

Shoham, Y. (1997). An overview of agent-oriented programming. Software agents.

Singh, M.P. (1998). Agent communication languages: Rethinking the principles. *Computer*, 31(12): 40–47.

Vygotsky, L. (1980). Mind in society: The development of higher psychological processes. Harvard university press.

Wooldridge, M., Jennings, N. R., & Kinney, D. (2000). The Gaia Methodology for Agent-Oriented Analysis and Design. Journal of Autonomous Agents and Multi-Agent Systems.

EXTRACTION OF TOURIST ATTENTION POINTS FROM LOW-RATED REVIEWS AND CLASSIFICATION BY VIEWPOINT

Junichi Fukumoto and Kazuki Ito
College of Information Science and Engineering, Ritsumeikan University
1-1-1 Noji-higashi, Kusatsu, Shiga 525-8577 Japan

ABSTRACT

There are various Internet sites for tourists and a lot of positive and negative word-of-mouses are posted from tourists. Negative information can be used as attention points for sightseeing to prevent the same mistakes for their first visit. The purpose of this research is to extract such negative information from word-of-mouth as tourist attention points and classify them for easy-to-understand. In the experiments, we successfully extracted attention points from actual tourist reviews and classified them based on target of the points.

KEYWORDS

Tourism Information, Attention Points, Low-Rated Reviews, Classification, Dependency Relation

1. INTRODUCTION

There are various Internet sites for tourists and a lot of word-of-mouses are posted. When people plan to visit some sightseeing spot at the first time, they refer posted word-of-mouses of these sites to get useful information and select tourist destinations. Internet posted information were used to improve sightseeing satisfaction and recommend appropriate place to visit and stay (Dincer, 2017) (Han, 2020) (Ogawa 2014). There are various positive and negative opinions such as recommendation of a location, dissatisfied experience, stories of failed experiences, and so on. Important point is that negative information can be used as “attention points for sightseeing” to prevent the same mistakes. There are some approaches that negative information is used to for product improvement (Kurihara, 2014) (Ohmori, 2012). In tourism information, for example, if you read the review "There is no toilet in the castle and it is a little unsuitable for children because of the stairs", you can use a toilet before you go into the castle. Now a huge amount of reviews has been posted, there are many reviews that include tourist attention points. However, it is difficult and time-consuming to read all such reviews to find tourist attention points from negative reviews.

The purpose of this research is to extract such negative information from the huge amount of word-of-mouth as tourist attention points and present it to user in an easy-to-understand manner. We will focus on 1 to 3-star low-rated reviews that contain a lot of contributors’ dissatisfaction and complain based on our preliminary survey of reviews. We will extract attention points from sentences that include negative expressions and classify the extracted tourist caution points based on the negative evaluation viewpoint.

In the following chapters, we will show our proposed method: extraction method of attention point and classification method of the extracted attention points. In the experiment, sample extraction of attention points and classification using tourist reviews of Wakamatsu castle and discuss the extraction results and some problems in our current method.

2. PROPOSED METHOD

2.1 Extraction of Attention Points from Negative Reviews

From the tourist site "Jalan net", we obtained 3814 reviews of 1 to 3 stars related to the castle by web scraping. To select negative reviews effectively, we used sentiment analysis module of Watson NLU tool and classified the reviews into positive, neutral, and negative ones. As a result, we obtained 1260 negative reviews. To extract attention points for tourists, we used negative expressions and dependency structure of negative review sentences.

Firstly, all the documents of negative reviews are divided into sentences using Japanese sentence separator such as a punctuation mark. Next, sentences will be morphologically analyzed using Japanese morphological analyzer MeCab with dictionally NEologd and syntactically analyzed with Japanese syntax analyzer CaboCha. We will extract attention points using dependency relation of syntax structure in the following patterns.

Pattern 1: extract phrases depending to a negative expression and phrases to the dependent phrases
Pattern 2: extract dependent phrases of a negative expression and phrases to the dependent phrases
Pattern 3: if there is a negative expression sentence, the next sentence will be extracted.

In the pattern 1 and 2, related elements with negative expression are extracted using dependency structure, however, adverb phrases will not be extracted. Pattern 3 is a case that some unpleasant situation will be described, and only negative impression will be added after the situation. This type of description is often used in blogs. We prepared Japanese negative expressions shown in Table 1. English translations are shown in brackets.

Table 1. A list of Japanese negative expressions

残念(unfortunate), 小さい(small), 大変(hard), 狭い(narrow), がっかり(disappointed), 暑い(hot), 断念(give up), キツイ(hard), 諦め(give up), しんどい(hard), 苦労(hardship), 足りない(not enough), 後悔(regret), 悪い(bad), 邪魔(disturbing), 厳しい(severe), 退屈(boring), 重い(heavy), 嫌悪(disgust), 微妙(negative mood), 汚い(dirty), 不便(inconvenient), 怖い(scare), 興ざめ(disappointed), 辛い(hard), うるさい(noisy), 疲労(fatigue), 危ない(dangerous), 不満(dissatisfied), 難しい(difficult), 注意(attention), 遠い(far), こじんまり(small), 退屈(boring), 苦労(hard), 混雑(crowded)

2.2 Classification of Attention Points

There are many kinds of attention points extracted from negative reviews. We will classify attention points based on viewpoints in the description. This classification will help these points easy to check. It will be effective to classify by very related words to a negative expression of attention points. To choose this related word, we use dependency analysis of description of attention points.

In case of extraction pattern 1, shown in the above, noun or proper noun of dependent phrase to a negative expression will be a classification clue. If there is no noun in this dependent phrase, a dependent phrase to the first dependent phrase will be checked to extract noun or proper noun, repetitively, and the extracted noun or proper noun will be the classification clue. All the classification clue words will be extracted in pattern 1 type sentences because there are no such related words in pattern 2 and 3 type attention points. To classify pattern 2 and 3 type attention points, we will use classification clues. The pattern 2 and 3 attention points will be classified by the words they contain in the list. In the extracted classification clues, we set a stop word list of Japanese one letter words such as "中 (middle)", "上 (upper)", "事 (thing)" to exclude meaningless clues.

Figure 1 shows an example of dependency analysis of extracted attention point although the word order of Japanese is different from its English translation. Word level translations are shown in the below of words with brackets, and full translation is at the bottom of this figure. In this example, the phrase "大変です (hard)" is a negative expression. The phrase "行くのが (go to)" modifies the negative expression but this is not noun. The phrase "天守閣が (the castle tower)" modifies the phrase "行くのが (go to)" and this is noun, then this phrase will be a classification clue.

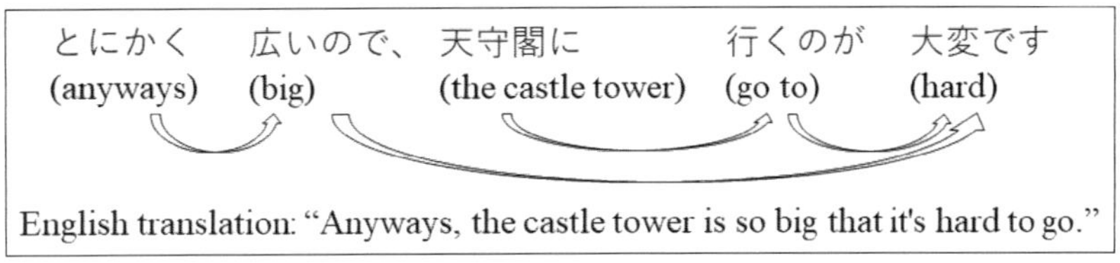

Figure 1. Example of dependency analysis of attention point

3. EXPERIMENTS

We used 259 reviews of Wakamatsu Castle for the experiment. A part of results of extraction of attention points is shown in Table 2. English translations are shown in brackets.

Table 2. Example of extraction of attention point

Negative expressions	Attention points
悪い (bad)	ライトアップしてましたが天気が悪かった (It was light up, but the weather was bad.)
難しい (difficult)	登りは階段なので足が不自由な方は難しい (Climbing is with staircase, so it is difficult for people with disabilities.)
大変 (hard)	子供も段差が大変 (The steps are also hard for children.)
悪い (bad)	全体的にみれば悪い場所ではないので商売っ気が少々強すぎる気がして、私には合わない場所でした (Overall, it's not a bad place, so I felt that the business was a little too strong, so it was a place that didn't suit me.)
汚い (dirty)	トイレが汚く (The toilet is dirty.)
残念 (disappoint)	こちらで残念だったのは入場券を購入する際に何も言わないと茶室の入場券付のチケットがくる事、その茶室に行くとまた別料金で抹茶和菓子が如何か聞かれる事、城の出口に向かうと売店を通るようになる事が興ざめ (What was disappointing here was that if you didn't say anything when purchasing the admission ticket, you would get a ticket with an admission ticket for the tea room, and when you went to the tea room, you would be asked what kind of matcha Japanese sweets would be for an extra charge. When you go to the exit, you will be able to go through the shop.)

For extraction of classification clues, we applied our method for the extracted attention points. Among the extracted classification clues, 10 single letter clues are excluded using stop word rule. We will show sample results of classification of attention points with clue word "階段 (stairs)", "トイレ (toilet)" and "天守閣 (castle tower)" in the following.

clue word: “階段 (stairs)”

登りは階段なので足が不自由な方は難しい (Climbing is a staircase, so it is difficult for people with disabilities)
階段は小さい子は抱っこしなきゃいけないし、狭いしきつい (The stairs are narrow and tight, small children must hug.)
階段しかないので、抱っこして上まであがるのが大変 (Since there are only stairs, it is difficult to hold children and climb up.)
ご年配の方には階段を昇るは大変 (It is difficult for elderly people to climb the stairs.)
階段が多くて当日は筋肉痛も有ったので辛かった (It was painful because there were many stairs and I had muscle pain on the day.)
2回目の鶴ヶ城！修学旅行生で混んで居るけど学べましたまた桜の時期に行きたいです。年配の人には階段キツイ (The second time of Tsuruga Castle! It's crowded with school students, but I learned it. I want to go again at the cherry blossom season. Stairs are hard for older people.)

clue word: “トイレ (toilet)”

トイレが汚くて (The toilet is dirty.)
お城の中を見ていて、子供がトイレに行きたくなり、中になく外まで行かないとないので大変です (It's hard because I'm looking inside the castle and my child wants to go to the bathroom, so I must go outside.)
お城の中にトイレが無いので幼年には少し不向きそれだけのために階段の上り下り歩いて入口まで戻るのは辛い (Since there is no toilet in the castle, it is a little unsuitable for childhood because it is difficult to walk up and down the stairs and return to the entrance.)

clue word “天守閣: (castle tower)”

ただ連休中だったので天守閣の回りは人で溢れて一周回るのが一苦労 (However, since it was a consecutive holiday, it was difficult to go around the castle tower because it was full of people.)
時間があれば、若松城周辺の公園等はじめ見所がたくさんあり楽しみがあります、強いて言えば、天守閣の窓が、普通の窓であるのが残念 (If you have time, there are lots of things to see, such as the parks around Aizuwakamatsu Castle, and you can have fun.)
最上階天守閣は・・・思ったより狭い (The castle tower on the top floor is ... narrower than I expected.)
だけど、お城の中は年表やら何藩がどうだとかのボードばかりで、当時の物の展示が少なく、天守閣からの眺めは良かったですが、それ以外は残念 (However, in the castle, there are only boards such as the chronological table and what kind of clan it is, there are few exhibits of things at that time, and the view from the castle tower was good, but other than that, it is disappointing.)
天守閣への入場が大変 (Admission to the castle tower is difficult.)
天守閣も工事中で外の景色が見れず残念 (It's a pity that the castle tower is also under construction and I couldn't see the outside scenery.)
期待をして行ったが、天守閣の修理中で（中は入れる）外観および天守閣から風景を見ることができず残念 (I was expecting it, but I am sorry that the castle tower is being repaired (the inside is inside) and I couldn’t see the scenery from the castle tower.)
残念ながら…屋根の瓦のふきかえ工事にあたってしまいお城が見れませんでしたが、逆に工事の方がめずらしいので天守閣などに使う瓦に名前が刻める寄付的なコトもあり…記念にどうでしょう？ (Unfortunately, ... I couldn't see the castle because the roof tiles were repairing, but on the contrary, the construction is rare opportunity, so there is a donation to engrave the name on the tiles used for the castle tower, etc. ... how about a memorial?)
雨天で天守閣からの眺めは厚い雲で覆われて山々がと見えず、残念 (Unfortunately, the view from the castle tower was covered with thick clouds and I couldn’t see the mountains due to rain.)

4. DISCUSSIONS

As for extraction of attention points, there are many cases that sentences with negative expressions co-occurred with attention points in 1 to 3 stars negative reviews. If a sentence is only negative expression, extracting adjacent sentence also works well to take an attention point. In case that here are some sentences which use negation with a negative expression, attention points will be positive ones. When an attention point appears with a negative expression, it will be extracted, but other attention points will not. Moreover, a long sentence including negative expression has several attention points and some positive points. It is impossible to extract all attention points and a positive point might be extracted by mistake. It is also necessary to make the extracted negative point more compact.

As for choosing classification clues, we choose noun or proper noun related to a negative expression using syntax analysis result. This strategy works well because such nouns are very related to negative expression, then it was appropriate for classification clue. In addition, classification using clue words helped to make it easier to understand the points that user dissatisfied at. To exclude meaningless clue words, we used to stop word list of Japanese single character words, but there is some case that some important words were deleted. It is necessary to improve the rule, for example, use of word frequency of review documents and so on.

5. CONCLUSION

In this paper, we focused on low-rated reviews and extracted tourist attention points from sentences that include negative expressions using dependency relation. The extracted tourist attention points are classified using clue words related to negative expression. Extraction of tourist attention points and classification of these points were enough level to help tourist understand. However, it is necessary to improve stop word information and handling of negation sentences. It is also required to apply more reviews of other domain such as other sightseeing spots and product evaluation.

ACKNOWLEDGEMENT

The authors would like to express their sincere thanks to the anonymous referees for the useful comments.

REFERENCES

Dinçer, M. D. and Alrawadieh, Z., 2017, Negative Word of Mouse in the Hotel Industry: A Content Analysis of Online Reviews on Luxury Hotels in Jordan, Journal of Hospitality Marketing & Management, Vol. 26, No. 8, pp. 785-804.

Han, K. and Kitayama, D., 2020, An Association Method of Tourist Spots Using User Reviews for Advancing Explainability, *IPSJ Transactions on database*, Vol.13, No. 1, pp.1-7.

Kurihara, K. and Shimada, K., 2014, Trouble Information Extraction from Twitter based on Bootstrap Method, *Proc. of the 21th annual meeting of the ANLP*, Japan, pp. 341-344. (in Japanese)

Ohmori, N. and Mori, T., 2012, Automatic Extraction of Words Representing Industrial Products and Their Parts: Classification Methods According to "Word Tangibility", *The IEICE transactions on information and systems 95(3)*, pp. 697-706. (in Japanese)

Ogawa, K, Sugimoto, Y., et.al., 2014, Basic design of a sightseeing recommendation system using Characteristic Words, *IPSJ SIG on DPS*, 2014-DPS-159 (14), pp.1-6. (in Japanese)

UNMANNED VEHICLES SYSTEM UTILIZING WASTE TRACKING DATA TO TACKLE PLASTIC MARINE LITTERING ON TOURIST ISLANDS

George Plakas, Stavros T. Ponis, Eleni Aretoulaki and Theodoros Nikolaos Maroutas
School of Mechanical Engineering, National Technical University Athens
Heroon Polytechniou 9, Zografos 15780, Athens, Greece

ABSTRACT

Marine pollution is undoubtedly a global, serious and rapidly increasing problem, as millions of tons of waste end up in the marine environment annually, causing multiple negative environmental, economic, health and aesthetic impacts, which are even more damaging for islands that base their economy on the tourism industry. The majority of marine pollution comes from anthropogenic and land-based activities and therefore it remains a critical issue to be tackled, especially in the case of plastic waste, which should be prevented from infiltrating the marine environment. Researchers have made many proposals and used a plethora of innovative technologies to deal with the phenomenon, one of the most promising of which is unmanned vehicles technology. Both aerial and surface unmanned vehicles offer feasible solutions in monitoring the evolution of the problem, although there is still room for improvement in achieving more efficient monitoring. In this paper, a solution utilizing data collected from a tracking plastic litter project is proposed, designed to monitor specific areas that accumulate large amounts of waste and inform the appropriate authorities, who will subsequently recruit volunteers to clean them up in time, before the plastics enter the marine environment.

KEYWORDS

Plastic Marine Littering, Unmanned Aerial Vehicles (UAV), Unmanned Surface Vehicles (USV), Internet of Things (IoT), Low-Power Wide-Area Networks (LPWAN), Citizen Engagement

1. INTRODUCTION

The number of review papers in the field of marine plastic pollution has been growing exponentially since 2015 (Aretoulaki et al., 2020). This extraordinary raise in published review papers means there are already significant efforts and findings towards tackling the problem and reducing marine littering. European Union's objectives for sustainable development until 2030 and Paris Agreement to combat climate change and its effects, play an important role in the explosion of scientific interest in this environmental field.

The increasing demand has led to over 300 million tons of new plastics produced in 2015 (Beckman, 2018). The large amounts annually produced, along with the recalcitrant nature of the material and the waste mismanagement, are responsible for the progressive accumulation of plastics in the marine environment, a problem with serious environmental and socioeconomic effects (Aretoulaki et al., 2020). Plastics ending up in the marine environment have increased from 8 million tons in 2010 to more than 9 million tons in 2015 and are predicted to reach over 16 million tons by 2025 (Jambeck et al., 2015). Land-based sources are responsible for 80% of marine plastic pollution (Andrady, 2011) and 100% of freshwater plastic pollution (Schwarz et al., 2019) and consequently, it would be proved to be very efficient to tackle the phenomenon at its point of origin, namely the terrestrial environment.

During the past few years, innovative technologies utilizing Unmanned Aerial Vehicles (UAVs) with imaging sensors have been tested in order to effectively monitor the coasts (Deidun et al., 2018; Gonçalves et al., 2020). The urgent nature of the issue has led to the development of a multitude of proposals that complement UAVs, by utilizing machine learning to analyze acquired images with extensive use of image databases (Martin et al., 2021) or developing gamification techniques in order to increase citizen engagement (Stengos et al., 2019). The collection of comprehensive preliminary data is able to further support such efforts. Finding and visualizing the paths of plastic litter before it ends up in the marine environment, in order to locate areas of high accumulation of plastic waste and entry points in the sea along the islands' coasts, could significantly enhance the results of monitoring programs based on unmanned vehicles. Nonetheless, the authorities are not able to cope with plastic marine pollution in a cost-effective way, without the substantial involvement of citizens (Ponis, 2020).

2. TRACKPLAST PROJECT

The TRACKPLAST project is an innovative IoT technology system utilizing flexibility, range and cost effectiveness provided by Low Power Wide Area Networks (LPWANs) and sets its efforts in the determination of streams of plastic waste from land sources until they reach the shore and before entering the sea. More specifically, the project involves the development of a system aspiring to visualize the paths followed by plastic litter on specific islands, on their journey to the marine environment. The project develops an integrated methodology of plastic marine littering management through the use of a customized object identification, tracking and data capturing technology. This technology system is based on the basic principles of IoT technology and more specifically, utilizes wireless sensors operating on a LoRa Network. For the purposes of the project, LoRa end-nodes are integrated on PET water bottles produced with a custom-made mold (Plakas et al., 2020), making a unique commercial product, exclusively for the purpose of the project.

The project's large-scale pilot will take place during tourist season, on a Greek island, which attracts a large number of domestic and foreign tourists. During this period, the bottles' manufacturer will dispatch the LoRa-enhanced plastic water bottles to the island's retailers, in order for them to be sold to locals and tourists. The end-nodes, which will be attached to every bottle, will be sending a signal every 4 hours, stating the bottle ID number and at the same time, the timestamp of the signal will also be produced and uploaded to the cloud platform by the LoRa gateways. The developed plastic waste tracking system is supported by an advanced cloud platform, which is responsible for data collection, processing and reporting to the project's stakeholders. Main priority of the platform is the successful operation of a geolocation solver, which will provide the position of every LoRa-enhanced bottle having sent a signal and enable the visualization of the paths followed by the bottles to their final destination, either landfill, recycling center or sea. Among others, the project will draw useful conclusions about the waste and recycling habits of consumers that will buy one of the project's water bottles during the pilot phase. A schematic of the project's architecture is presented in Figure 1.

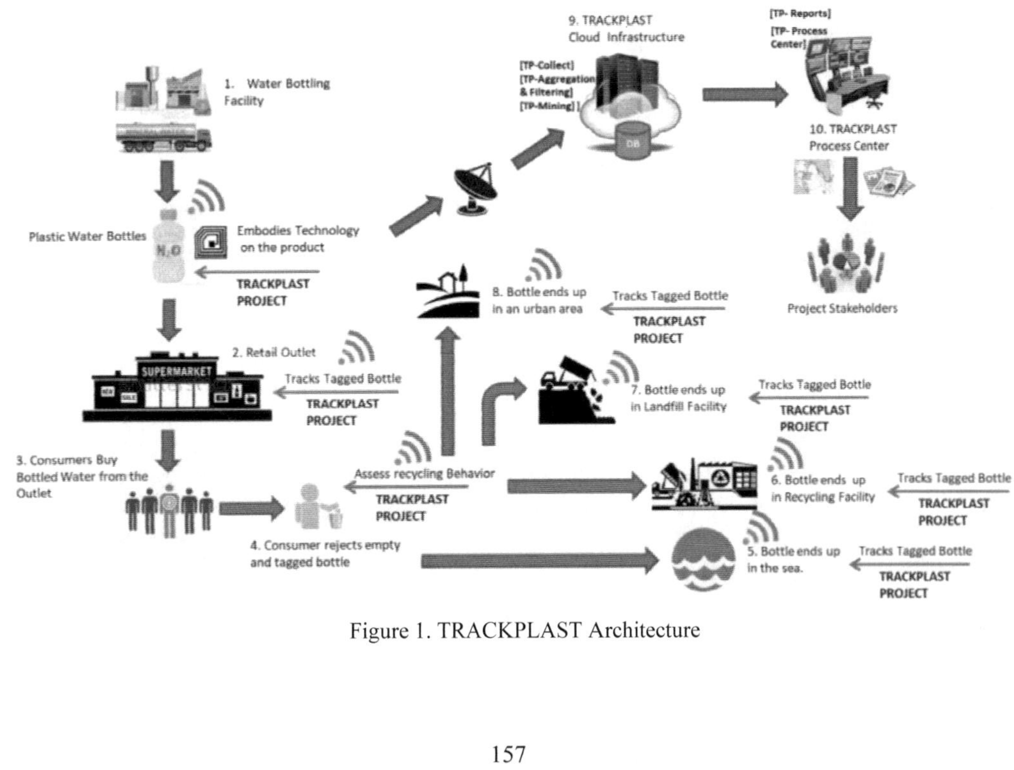

Figure 1. TRACKPLAST Architecture

3. PROPOSED SOLUTION

The project's ultimate objective is to propose effective monitoring solutions and a roadmap including preventive measures for preventing or diverting plastic waste from reaching the sea, thus reducing marine littering. The success of the project's proposal is based on the data collected from the LoRa-enhanced bottles. The project's research team aims to analyze the geolocation data provided by the LoRa network, in order to determine vulnerable areas –in terms of plastic littering- all over the island. At this point, although the pilot has not yet started and there is no actual tracking data, the research team has already set its first goals on how to exploit the project's outcome. The expected results from the project's implementation will provide two pieces of information that if used properly, will be very helpful in providing successful solutions.

The first result expected from the data visualizations will be the revelation of the island's terrestrial areas, where progressive accumulation of large quantities of plastic is taking place. If a large number of signals is sent from a specific area, without an obvious reason (e.g., landfill), then this area has to be examined more closely and possibly monitored for some period of time. The second very important expected result from the project's pilot will be the identification of the main points where plastic litter enters the sea across the island's shoreline. To define these entry points, a mix of information will be used, such as, areas of high accumulation across shoreline, last signal's location per end-node and signals located inside the sea.

The proposed technology solution involves the development of a system that utilizes Unmanned Aerial Vehicles (UAVs) and Unmanned Surface Vehicles (USVs) to exploit these very important findings, in order to protect the environment in a more efficient and cost effective way, by specifically monitoring the most vulnerable areas of the island, either they are located inlands, on the shoreline, or in the sea. Unmanned vehicles participate during the pilot phase of the project to enhance the LoRa network and provide environmental information and images through their sensors, but their key role is to be played after the pilot has ended and the LoRa network is no longer active. For the purposes of the proposed solution, two configurable unmanned vehicles have been chosen, equipped with powerful optical sensors, dual optical payloads and environmental sensors. The Atlas 4/8 is an Unmanned Aerial Vehicle (UAV), designed to be utilized in the fields of surveillance, environmental monitoring and research projects, while NIRIIS is an electric powered Unmanned Surface Vehicle (USV) also designed for applications, including surveillance as well as experimental and research applications (ALTUS LSA, n.d.). Both vehicles are shown in Figure 2:

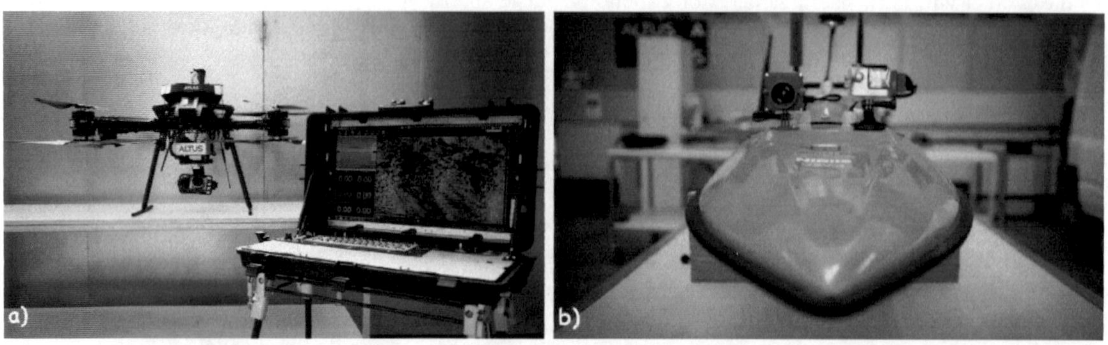

Figure 2. Unmanned Vehicles: a) ATLAS 4/8 (UAV); b) NIRIIS (USV) (ALTUS LSA, n.d.)

The development of the monitoring system consists of a set of integrated modules interacting with each other to achieve the best possible result in cleaning up waste and tackling marine littering. The solution's Cloud Platform contains the data and visualizations provided by the results of the large-scale pilot. Based on the platform's preliminary data, the Control Room navigates the unmanned vehicles to the areas of interest to collect images on a daily basis, during daytime. UAVs, supported by a mobile land-based station (van), are used for monitoring the areas with high accumulation of plastics, found from the pilot data and the authors firmly believe that large quantities of more waste and garbage will be found there as well. On the other hand, USVs are navigated to specific sea areas near the marine entry points, defined by the pilot's outcome, to capture images of plastic marine litter on the sea surface as well as under water. Data from the imaging sensors captured by both types of unmanned vehicles are sent to the Cloud Platform for aggregation and processing. The results are evaluated by the Control Room, which decides the locations to be monitored next, based not only on the pilot's preliminary data, but also the day-to-day imaging results from the monitoring program.

The Control Room is actually a key component of the solution's final product, as it controls unmanned vehicles, evaluates data received from the Cloud Platform and most importantly is responsible for the effective planning of the cleanup activities, which are of course the ultimate objective of the project. First, the Control Room reports the results to the proposed solution's stakeholders and informs the appropriate system users, i.e. local authorities and environmental NGOs, about land or underwater areas, where waste is piled up and actions are needed to be taken immediately. Alongside, the Control Room is responsible for scheduling timely cleanup activities and notifying -through a dedicated mobile application- the island's volunteers, in order to achieve maximum efficiency. Locals and tourists are able to participate in these cleanups organized across the island, while volunteer cleanups under the sea are also planned for divers and fishing boats that wish to be summoned to offer their expertise. A schematic of the proposed solution is presented in Figure 3.

Traditionally, monitoring and cleanup activities related to plastic waste, require a large number of human resources and a lot of time to keep plastics outside the marine environment. The proposed solution aspires to support both of these activities, with a specialized and comprehensive program utilizing all available resources in the best possible way and achieve much more positive results. Especially for the volunteers, an efficiently organized schedule is essential, since they should feel that the time they provide is meaningful and makes a difference, in order to be kept engaged with such activities.

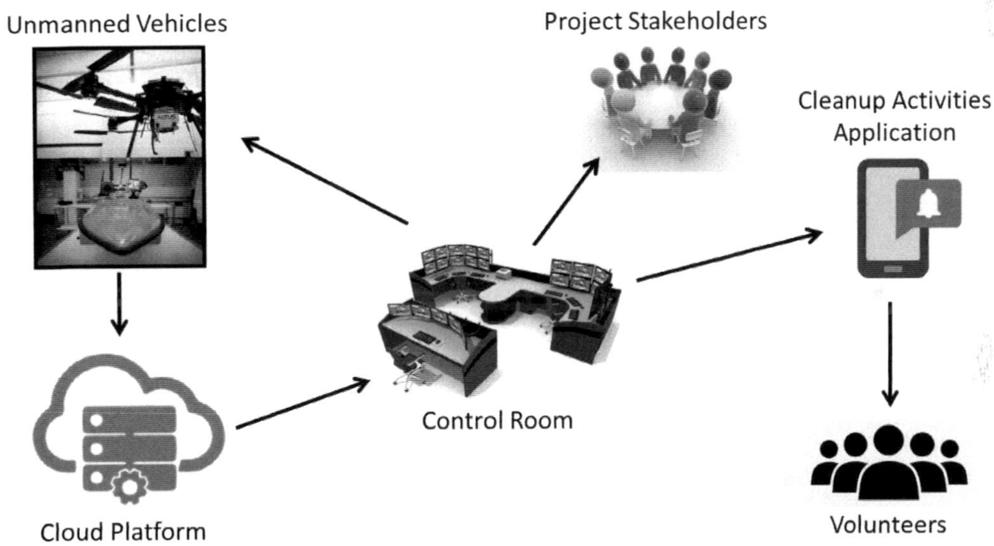

Figure 3. The proposed technology solution

The authors are currently in the phase of deploying the technical components of the TRACKPLAST system (LoRa Gateways), integrating LoRa nodes to the produced water bottles and finalizing the specifications and scenario details for the large-scale pilot program. Parameters such as model accuracy, information reporting latency, range limitations and system scalability are some of the project's technical results that will be demonstrated in the authors' future works. At the same time, the authors are already working to integrate the proposed solution by enabling the communication of the cloud platform with the unmanned vehicles.

4. CONCLUSION

This paper aims to contribute to the plastic marine littering problem, which has been rapidly increasing during the last decades and significant measures and efforts have to take place for its mitigation. The technology solution presented in this paper proposes the usage of an integrated technological system utilizing the power of UAVs and USVs, in combination with IoT technologies and LPWANs, in order to develop an ideal turnkey solution for tourist islands that are willing to tackle marine littering. The proposed system has the capacity of monitoring an island's terrestrial areas, beaches and seabed for accumulated waste and timely scheduling its cleanup activities, therefore, protecting valuable natural resources, boosting circular economy and promoting the sustainable development of tourist islands. The proper use of resources provided by local authorities on the one hand, and the well-timed involvement of volunteers on the other, are crucial keys to the success of the proposed solution. Data analysis from the concluded pilot of the TRACKPLAST project will provide even more solutions to be proposed, both in terms of monitoring and cleaning up plastic waste, as well as improving citizen recycling behavior and participation in environmental actions.

ACKNOWLEDGEMENT

This research has been co-financed by the European Regional Development Fund of the European Union and Greek national funds through the Operational Program Competitiveness, Entrepreneurship and Innovation, under the call RESEARCH – CREATE – INNOVATE (project code: T1EDK-05095).

REFERENCES

ALTUS LSA. (n.d.) www.altus-lsa.com/unmanned-systems. A Rich Unmanned Systems Portfolio. Accessed May 20, 2021

Andrady, A. L. (2011). Microplastics in the marine environment. Marine pollution bulletin, 62(8), 1596-1605.

Aretoulaki, E., Ponis, S., Plakas, G., & Agalianos, K. (2020). A systematic meta-review analysis of review papers in the marine plastic pollution literature. Marine Pollution Bulletin, 161, 111690.

Deidun, A., Gauci, A., Lagorio, S., & Galgani, F. (2018). Optimising beached litter monitoring protocols through aerial imagery. Marine pollution bulletin, 131, 212-217.

Gonçalves, G., Andriolo, U., Pinto, L., & Bessa, F. (2020). Mapping marine litter using UAS on a beach-dune system: A multidisciplinary approach. Science of The Total Environment, 706, 135742.

Jambeck, J. R., Geyer, R., Wilcox, C., Siegler, T. R., Perryman, M., Andrady, A., ... & Law, K. L. (2015). Plastic waste inputs from land into the ocean. Science, 347(6223), 768-771.

Martin, C., Zhang, Q., Zhai, D., Zhang, X., & Duarte, C. M. (2021). Enabling a large-scale assessment of litter along Saudi Arabian red sea shores by combining drones and machine learning. Environmental Pollution, 277, 116730.

Plakas, G., Ponis, S. T., Agalianos, K., & Aretoulaki, E. (2020). Reverse Logistics of End-of-Life Plastics Using Industrial IoT and LPWAN Technologies–A Proposed Solution for the Bottled Water Industry. Procedia Manufacturing, 51, 1680-1687.

Ponis, S. T. (2020). A Proposed Technology IoT Based Ecosystem for Tackling the Marine Beach Litter Problem. In Proceedings of SAI Intelligent Systems Conference (pp. 673-678). Springer, Cham.

Schwarz, A. E., Ligthart, T. N., Boukris, E., & van Harmelen, T. (2019). Sources, transport, and accumulation of different types of plastic litter in aquatic environments: A review study. Marine Pollution Bulletin, 143, 92-100.

Stengos, G., Ponis, S.T., Plakas, G., Yamas, A. (2019). A Proposed Technology Solution for Preventing Marine Littering Based on UAVS and IoT Cloud-Based Data Analytics. In Proceedings of the International Conference Connected Smart Cities 2019, Porto, Portugal, 17–19 July 2019, pp. 391–394.

REPORT ON ESTIMATING RICE FIELD QUALITY USING ARTIFICIAL INTELLIGENCE

Yahjeb Bouha Khatraty[1,2], Nedra Mellouli Nauwynck[1], Mamadou Tourad Diallo[2] and Mohamedade Farouk Nanne[2]

[1]*University of Paris 8 - Vincennes - Saint-Denis Doctoral School Cognition, Language, Interaction, Paris, France*
[2]*University of Nouakchott Al-Aasriya, Faculty of Science and Technology, Doctoral School of Computer Science, Nouakchott, Mauritania*

ABSTRACT

The use of artificial intelligence has made life easier for farmers, as analysis of agricultural data allows farmers to make informed decisions, supported by large data sets and processed by machine learning algorithms. In this paper, we present the literature on rice quality assessment according to the different criteria and factors used to predict the quality or yield of rice. Thus, we provided a list of machine learning and deep learning models that had high accuracy in predicting rice yield and quality. In addition, due to the lack of literature of a real-time rice field monitoring system, we proposed a real-time rice field condition monitoring system that collects weather and soil condition data and sends them to the web server. The farmer can see the status of its remotely field and can automate certain tasks such as irrigation based on the collected data values.

KEYWORDS

Machine Learning, Internet of Things, Intelligent rice paddies, Grain Yield Prediction

1. INTRODUCTION

Today, water scarcity is a serious problem, with fresh, clean water accounting for only 0.003% of the world's total available water, and the increase in the world's population highlights the need to tackle this problem[1].

Agriculture is the highest consumer of water[1]. Therefore, improving water management in agriculture is essential to preserve the source of life on Earth. Since rice consumes more water than any other crops, so to improve water management, it is necessary to reduce water consumption in rice fields while maintaining rice quality (Bouman 2007; Khush 2005).

To maintain good rice quality, it is essential to know the features and factors that affect it. These features change from the perspective of the farmer, the consumer and the trader. In addition, there are many factors that affect it, such as climatic factors, geographical factors and those related to soil and water supply (Dawn 2001; Pheakdey, Xuan, and Khanh 2017; Wang et al. 2019).

This paper provides a review of the literature on rice quality estimation. Section 2 contains related work. Our Proposed approach is introduced in Section 3. Section 4 concludes and gives perspectives in this research aera.

[1]*https://www.theworldcounts.com/challenges/planetearth/freshwater/are-we-running-out-of-water/story*

2. RELATED WORK

Table 1. The models and parameters used in the literature to estimate rice quality and yield and their results

Objective	Parameter used	Data type	Model used	Result	Ref
Detection and classification of rice leaf diseases	Color image	Image	**Naive Bayes algorithm**	Accuracy reached 90%	(Islam et al. 2018)
	Color, texture and shape		**Support Vector Machine SVM**	Accuracy reached 73,33%	(Prajapati, Shah, and Dabhi 2017)
				Accuracy reached 97,2%	(Yao et al. 2009)
				Accuracy reached 91,37%	(Shrivastava et a 2019)
			k-Nearest Neighbor KNN	Accuracy reached 87,02%	(Joshi and Jadha 2016)
			Decision tree, logistic regression, KNN and Naive Bayes Classifier	Accuracy was 94.9% for training and 97.9% for testing	(Ahmed et al. 2019)
Estimation of the number of spikelets in a panicle	45 characteristics of the spikelets and grain such as length, width and surface c the spikelets		**Area Method, Faster R-CNN, Cascade R-CNN and SSD**	**- Cascade R-CNN** (R^2 is 0.99, MAPE (Mean Absolute Percentage Error) < 1.42%) **- Faster R-CNN** R^2 = 0.99 and MAPE 1. 68%)	(Yu et al. 2020)
Classification of indica and japonica rice			**Resnet-50, Faster R-CNN, Cascade R-CNN, SSD and SVM**	**Resnet** attained the highest accuracy of 0.96	
Measuring the correlation between rice yield and phenological, climatic and geographical data	The dates of sowing, transplanting, maturity, Temperature, humidity precipitation, longitude, latitude, altitude ...	Phenological, climatic and geographical data	**Random Forest RF, MLR (Multiple Linear Regression), BP(Back Propagation) neural network and SVM**	R^2 was 0.24 for **BP**, 0.33 for **SVM** and 0.31 for **RF**	(Guo et al., n.d.)
Estimation of rice dry biomass	Polarisation (VH,VV or VHVV)	Satellite data (Sentinel1A)	**Random Forest RF, Gradient Boosting Decision Tree (GBDT), SVM and KNN**	**RF** (R^2 = 0,73 and RMSE = 462,4 g/ m2) and k-NN (R^2 = 0,70 and RMSE = 484,1 g/ m2)	(Mansaray, Zhang, and Kanu 2020)

Related work can be divided into two categories. The first category highlights the evaluation models of the rice quality fields. The second category focus on the estimation of rice yield during the paddy growing stages, or after rice production. For the first category, the parameters used for estimating quality are the characteristics of the rice leaves such as color, shape and texture to determine whether the leaf is diseased or healthy, as has been done in these articles (Ahmed et al. 2019; bank 2020; Islam et al. 2018; Joshi and Jadhav 2016; Prajapati, Shah, and Dabhi 2017; Shrivastava et al. 2019; Yao et al. 2009).

But the most common diseases in the major rice-producing countries (we can cite China, India, Indonesia and Bangladesh) are only four, such as Rice Blast, Rice Bacterial Blight, Rice Brown Spot and Rice Sheath Blight (Ahmed et al. 2019; bank 2020; Islam et al. 2018; Joshi and Jadhav 2016; Prajapati, Shah, and Dabhi 2017; Shrivastava et al. 2019; Yao et al. 2009). Each of these diseases has different symptoms from the others. Hence manual early detection of these diseases is very difficult and imprecise. Therefore, it is mandatory to use smart technologies that enable accurate and rapid disease detection and hence to overcome the limitations of human perception and treat plants as soon as possible.

For the second category, the parameters used to predict rice yield differ according to the prediction phase. Several parameters were used to predict rice yield during growth and post-production. Panicle length was used in (Huang et al. 2013) to estimate rice yield. However, (Mansaray, Zhang, and Kanu 2020) was based on climatic parameters, phenological variables and geographical criteria to predict rice yield. calculated the relationship between dry rice biomass and Sentinel-1A data. Whereas (Kumar et al. 2020) used grain color and the length of time the grain retains heat to predict rice yield. (Yu et al. 2020) extracted the phenotype of rice clusters (length, width, area, circumference, number of spikes, grains, etc.) to calculate the number of spikelets in a panicle and classify the different types of rice.

The use of machine learning and deep learning to improve the quality and accuracy of crops is becoming a management task known as precision farming (Triantafyllou et al. 2019). Measurements and analysis carried out with machine learning models enable better management of agricultural resources while reducing environmental impact and waste. In Table 1, we list some of the models used in the literature estimating rice yield as quality and their impacts.

We noticed that the studies already carried out were based on only one type of rice quality parameters without considering other parameters and external factors such as climate, geographical location, soil condition, demographics and water supply. As presented in Table 1, while studies have relied on physical parameters such as color, texture, shape of rice leaves to detect and classify rice diseases. Other studies have also used the physical properties of the spikelets and grains to classify different types of rice.

Therefore, a good yield prediction and quality measurement system must take into account all factors that directly and/or indirectly influence rice quality.

3. PROPOSED APPROACH

Based on our literature, we observed that not all parameters describing rice quality are used in the same study, and that there is also a lack of heterogeneity in data acquisition sources. Consequently, there is no system that monitors the rice fields in real time to act if necessary. Our approach is therefore to create a system that monitors the condition of the plants, soil and atmosphere in real time, from the sowing of the grain to harvesting. Farmers will be able to access this data remotely. In addition, the output of our monitoring system is the input to another system that predict the yield and quality of rice produced without having to hull the rice spikelets. The forecasting system use a wide range of parameters such as spikelets properties, climate, phenological and geographical data. In addition, this system should also allow the difference between a large type of rice. Details of the forecasting systems will be discussed in a future paper.

Figure 1 shows our real-time rice field monitoring system that we detail its components in the next paragraph.

Our monitoring system consists of four layers:

- The sensor layer: includes smart sensors for data collection and monitoring.
- The network layer: includes the communication technologies between the sensors and the gateway. The choice of these technologies depends on the location of the agricultural field (rural or urban area). We chose to work at first with Lora technology because of its low energy consumption and its long range.
- The service layer: responsible for processing and analyzing the collected data.
- The dashboard layer: allows the visualization of the information from the sensor network. This layer is the one that has a direct interaction with the user (the farmer).

A simpler example offered by our system to the farmer is the smart watering system. This system allows the farmer to remotely control and adapt the irrigation with a single touch on the mobile phone. Also, it allows to program the irrigation according to the temperature and/or humidity values of the plant environment.

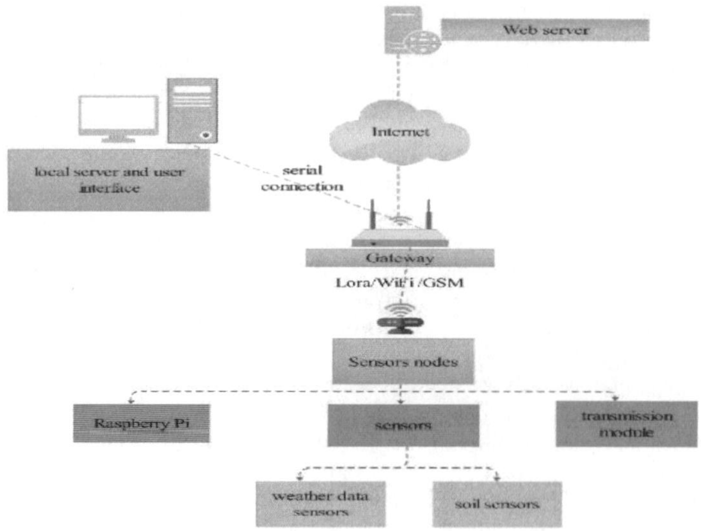

Figure 1. Architecture of the monitoring system

4. CONCLUSION AND PERSPECTIVES

In this paper, we have investigated the measured parameters and machine learning models used in rice quality and yield estimation. In addition, we presented the models that had high accuracy with their results. We then proposed an approach based on the lack of literature, such as the implementation of a real-time rice field monitoring system that will provide farmers with a remote monitoring application for their rice fields. In addition, it will allow them to automate the irrigation of the fields according to the measured values of the field. The data collected from the rice fields will be used as a dataset for prediction systems of rice quality and yield based on machine learning algorithms.

ACKNOWLEDGEMENT

We would like to thank the French Embassy in Mauritania for its financial support for our research.

REFERENCES

Ahmed, Kawcher, Tasmia Shahidi, Syed Irfanul Alam, and Sifat Momen. 2019. "Rice Leaf Disease Detection Using Machine Learning Techniques." Pp. 1–5 in *International Conference on Sustainable Technologies for Industry 4.0 (STI)*

Bouman, B. A. M. 2007. Water Management in Irrigated Rice*: Coping with Water Scarcity*. Int. Rice Res. Inst.

Dawn. 2001. "Factors Affecting Rice Grain Quality." *https://www.dawn.com/news/print/8880*, Published 03 Dec 2001, consulted on December 07 2020

Dwivedi, Priya. 2019. "Understanding and Coding a ResNet in Keras." *https://towardsdatascience.com/understanding-and-coding-a-resnet-in-keras-446d7ff84d33*, Published Jan 4 2019, consulted on December 24 2020.

Forson, Eddie. 2017. "Understanding SSD MultiBox — Real-Time Object Detection in Deep Learning." *https://towardsdatascience.com/understanding-ssd-multibox-real-time-object-detectionin-deep-learning-495ef744fab,* Published November 18 2017, consulted on December 21 2020.

Guo, Yahui, Yongshuo Fu, Fanghua Hao, Xuan Zhang, Wenxiang Wu, Xiuliang Jin, Christopher Robin Bryant, and J. Senthilnath. n.d. "Integrated Phenology and Climate in Rice Yields Prediction Using Machine Learning Methods." *Ecological Indicators* 120:106935.

He, Kaiming, Xiangyu Zhang, Shaoqing Ren, and Jian Sun. 2016. "Deep Residual Learning for Image Recognition." pp.770–78 in *Proceedings of the IEEE conference on computer vision and pattern recognition.*

Huang, Chenglong, Wanneng Yang, Lingfeng Duan, Ni Jiang, Guoxing Chen, Lizhong Xiong, and Qian Liu. 2013. "Rice Panicle Length Measuring System Based on Dual-Camera Imaging." *Computers and Electronics in Agriculture* 98:158–65.

Islam, Taohidul, Manish Sah, Sudipto Baral, and Rudra RoyChoudhury. 2018. "A Faster Technique on Rice Disease Detectionusing Image Processing of Affected Area in Agro-Field." Pp. 62–66 in *2018 Second International Conference on Inventive Communication and Computational Technologies (ICICCT).*

Joshi, Amrita A., and B. D. Jadhav. 2016. "Monitoring and Controlling Rice Diseases Using Image Processing Techniques." pp. 471–76 in *2016 International Conference on Computing, Analytics and Security Trends (CAST).*

Khush, Gurdev S. 2005. "What It Will Take to Feed 5.0 Billion Rice Consumers in 2030." *Plant Molecular Biology,* 59(1):1–6.

Kumar, Ajay, Mahesh Taparia, Amarlingam Madapu, P. Rajalakshmi, Balram Marathi, and Uday B. Desai. 2020. "Discrimination of Filled and Unfilled Grains of Rice Panicles Using Thermal and RGB Images." *Journal ofCereal Science* 95:103037.

Mansaray, Lamin R., Kangyu Zhang, and Adam Sheka Kanu. 2020. "Dry Biomass Estimation of Paddy Rice withSentinel-1A Satellite Data Using Machine Learning Regression Algorithms." *Computers and Electronics in Agriculture* 176:105674.

Pheakdey, Dek Vimean, Tran Dang Xuan, and Tran Dang Khanh. 2017. "Influence of Climate Factors on Rice Yields in Cambodia." *AIMS Geosciences* 3(4):561–75.

Prajapati, Harshadkumar B., Jitesh P. Shah, and Vipul K. Dabhi. 2017. "Detection and Classification of Rice Plant Diseases." *Intelligent Decision Technologies* 11(3):357–73.

Rice knowledge bank. 2020. "Diseases of Rice." *http://www.knowledgebank.irri.org/step-by-stepproduction/growth/pests-and-diseases/diseases,* consulted on 05 December 2020.

Shrivastava, Vimal K., Monoj K. Pradhan, Sonajharia Minz, and Mahesh P. Thakur. 2019. "Rice Plant Disease Classification Using Transfer Learning of Deep Convolution Neural Network."*International Archives of the Photogrammetry, Remote Sensing \& Spatial Information*

Wang, Chenzhi, Zhao Zhang, Jing Zhang, Fulu Tao, Yi Chen, and Hu Ding. 2019. "The Effect of Terrain Factors on Rice Production: A Case Study in Hunan Province." *Journal of Geographical Sciences* 29(2):287–305.

Weng, Lilian. 2020. "Object Detection Part 4: Fast Detection Models."*https://lilianweng.github.io/lillog/2018/12/27/object-detection-part-4.html*, Published December 27 2018, consulted on December 21 2020.

Yang, Qi, Liangsheng Shi, Jinye Han, Yuanyuan Zha, and Penghui Zhu. 2019. "Deep Convolutional Neural Networks for Rice Grain Yield Estimation at the Ripening Stage Using UAV-Based Remotely Sensed Images." *Field Crops Research* 235:142–53.

Yao, Qing, Zexin Guan, Yingfeng Zhou, Jian Tang, Yang Hu, and Baojun Yang. 2009. "Application of Support Vector Machine for Detecting Rice Diseases Using Shape and Color Texture Features." Pp. 79–83 in *2009 international conference on engineering computation.*

Yu, Lejun, Jiawei Shi, Chenglong Huang, Lingfeng Duan, Di Wu, Debao Fu, Changyin Wu, Lizhong Xiong, Wanneng Yang, and Qian Liu. 2020. "An Integrated Rice Panicle Phenotyping Method Based on X-Ray and RGB Scanningand Deep Learning." *The Crop Journal.*

AUTHOR INDEX

Abbasi, Preeta 76
Aretoulaki, Eleni 156
Aromaa, Susanna 69
Bhati, Neetesh 95
Bozkurt, Yusuf 85
Braun, Reiner 85
Bryer, Evan 103
Carvalho, Ana 140
Cheng, Irene 121, 130
Chiranjeevi, Sadu 43
Da Silva, Celmar Guimarães 1
De Pace, Francesco 35
Diallo, Mamadou Tourad 161
Ding, Yueming 19
Elberzhager, Frank 114, 135
Elmashhara, Maher Georges 140
Fauser, Jan 85
Fedotov, Andrey 116
Fukumoto, Junichi 151
Goceri, Evgin 27, 51
Goriachev, Vladimir 69
Hertweck, Dieter 85
Ito, Kazuki 151
Khatraty, Yahjeb Bouha 161
Kjærvik, Joachim Coetzee 145
Koskinen, Hanna 69
Kristensen, Terje Solsvik 145
Liu, Guohua 9
Manuri, Federico 35
Maroutas, Theodoros Nikolaos 156
Meiller, Dieter 126
Mennig, Patrick 135
Mok, P.Y. 19
Nanne, Mohamedade Farouk 161
Nauwynck, Nedra Mellouli 161
Nyabuga, Douglas Omwenga 9
Ordoñez, Alexandra Cortez 59
Oriti, Damiano 35
Patsko, Valerii 116
Pei, Shuonan 121
Pessoa, Ricardo 140
Plakas, George 156
Ponis, Stavros T. 156
Prehofer, Christian 76
Raj, Aparna 95
Rezazadeh, Arash 140
Rhujittawiwat, Theppatorn 103
Ronzino, Fabrizio 35
Rose, John R. 103
Rossmann, Alexander 85
Sanna, Andrea 35
Scharnagl, Tassilo 126
Shetty, Sujala D. 95
Silva, Joaquim 140
Singh, Krishna Kumar 43
Sivalal, Kethavath 43
Späth, Kathleen 114
Storck, Sven 114
Stüpfert, Phil 135
Sun, Xinyao 130
Sá, Elisabete 140
Tamburello, Francesco 35
Vasev, Pavel 116
Vázquez, Pere-Pau 59
Wilder, Colin F. 103
Yang, Fei 121, 130
Zhu, Mingzhi 130
Zhu, Ningbo 121, 130